The Ancestry of Theodore Timothy Judge and Ellen Sheehy Judge

Including the Families of Boland, Roussel, Harman, McMurphy, Kelley, Bohane, Chapin, Freiermuth, Taylor, Moore and Farneman

Compiled and edited by
members of the California Genealogical Society

Oakland, California
2010

Library of Congress Control Number: 2010929198
ISBN 978-0-9785694-9-5

Printed in the United States of America

Published by the **California Genealogical Society & Library**
2201 Broadway LL2
Oakland, CA 94612-3031
Telephone: 510.663.1358
Website : www.CaliforniaAncestors.org
Email: contact@CaliforniaAncestors.org

Dedicated to Ted and Ellen Sheehy

Ted had the vision to provide his extended family with a genealogy—a legacy to be enjoyed now and for generations to come.

❧ Contents

Illustrations

Introduction

Theodore Timothy "Ted" Judge died in Cupertino, California, June 11, 2008. Although neither he nor his late wife Ellen Sheehy Judge left descendants, they shared a mutual interest in family history which they had enthusiastically pursued over the years. In his will, Ted left legacies to numerous charities and institutions, including the Bancroft Library at the University of California at Berkeley, where he had spent many hours as a student. Among his bequests was the requirement that the Bancroft Library, in conjunction with the administrators of his estate, arrange for the publication of a book of Judge and Sheehy genealogy to be distributed to Ted and Ellen's cousins.

Pat Fell, a part-time librarian at the Bancroft Library, who also worked in cataloging at the California Genealogical Society, suggested in May 2009 that the society might handle the project. A meeting to discuss the possibilities was arranged with Patrick Sheehy, executor and a trustee of the estate; a representative of the University; society president Jane Knowles Lindsey; and member Judy Bodycote. After several months of negotiation, an agreement was signed in September 2009. Society members Judy Bodycote, Lavinia Schwarz, and Patricia Smith began the research for the project, assisted by Richard Rees and Laura Spurrier.

Ted's will stated that he wished to provide a genealogy of both his and Ellen's families back to their immigrant ancestors. In the early stages a decision was made to include the ancestors of Ted Judge's stepfather, Albert Sylvan Taylor, who raised Ted and for whom he cared deeply. As research progressed, many lines were discovered that extended back into 17th and 18th century Pennsylvania and New England. After several meetings with Trustee Patrick Sheehy, it was agreed that research would stop at five generations back and would then include descendants from that point.

As a result of the decision to limit coverage to five generations, research already completed on earlier families and their descendants was omitted from the final publication. Some of this research is extensive and covers in particular the families of Moore, Farneman, Kuns, Vannoy, McMurphy, Boland, Dikeman, Coleman and Hail. Omitted research has been archived at the society and is available to interested historians and genealogists.

With less than six months to complete the project Judy Zelver, Lorna Wallace and Barbara Dyer joined the team to provide additional research assistance. Nancy Peterson assumed final writing responsibilities. Bill O'Neil drew helpful maps, and Judy Bodycote not only created attractive pedigree and descendancy charts but also scanned and enhanced most of the photographs included in the book. Carol Glesser, Ted Judge's personal assistant, arranged meetings with Ted's cousin, Bette (Webb) Baughman and her daughter Mary J. Baughman Drake.

Researchers traveled to Gold Country towns and to the Pajaro Valley near Watsonville to research and obtain records. They scoured the internet for clues and contacted a number of researchers who appeared to hold needed information. Society member Matthew Berry offered to do the final layout, moving the material from Microsoft Word to Adobe InDesign. Barbara Dyer did most of the indexing, and Laura Spurrier much of the proofreading. Patrick Sheehy offered his remarkable genealogical study of the Sheehy family compiled over many years, providing us with countless photos and information.

The California Genealogical Society is proud to present to Ted and Ellen Sheehy Judge's cousins and relatives this book that we think would have made Ted and Ellen very happy.

Jane Knowles Lindsey, President
California Genealogical Society, 2004-2010

Acknowledgments

This book could not have been completed without the assistance of many people, generous with both their time and information. First, we are grateful to Pat Fell, who contacted the California Genealogical Society when she heard that the Bancroft Library and representatives of the University of California at Berkeley were looking for someone to complete a genealogical research project. Without that contact, this project would never have materialized.

Special thanks go to Patrick Sheehy, trustee of the Judge estate and genealogist, who not only shared his extensive personal research on the Sheehy family but understood the time and effort required to accomplish a project of this nature. Additionally, this project could not have been accomplished without the enormous collection of Mary J. (Baughman) Drake, who has been researching Judge family lines for many years and generously shared her original documents, newspaper clippings and wonderful photographs. Mary Jane's mother, Betty Jean (Webb) Baughman, provided many stories about the family, complementing her daughter's research.

Carol Levison Glesser, Ted Judge's personal assistant for many years, was instrumental in obtaining photos and information about Ted and and his wife Ellen. She took the time to sort through boxes of memorabilia in order to reconstruct Ted's life and the life he shared with Ellen.

The Rev. Harry D. Freiermuth of Watsonville, great-grandson of Peter J. Freiermuth, generously shared unpublished family stories, photographs, historical documents and data about the Chapin and Freiermuth families in the Pajaro Valley, and allowed us to access his private copy of Jeffrey and Marie Charnley's history of the Michigan Chapin family, with the Charnley's permission.

When it was discovered that an Indian depredation claim was involved, Holly Cutting Baker of Alexandria, Virginia, stepped in and obtained a researcher's card at the National Archives in Washington, D.C., to see if she could find copies. This colorful information, which also provided insight into the travails of many-husbanded Mary Moore Dikeman Farneman Baker, could not have been included without her help.

Julia Sjöberg, a Freiermuth descendant and librarian in Minnesota, answered questions about the comprehensive genealogy of the Freiermuth family she has posted on the Internet. Her thorough and well-documented research saved countless hours of research time. Members of the Paradise Genealogical Society in Butte County, California, provided enthusiastic assistance in obtaining information on the Moore, Boland, Judge, and Taylor Families. We would especially like to thank members Betty Chambers, Kathleen Corrigan, Bev Colgin and Frank Pangburn. Articles in their society's publication, *Genealogical Goldmine,* provided the basis for the story of the murder of Nancy Hatchett Moore and the previous history of the Moore family.

Researchers across the country, located through Internet postings, also provided assistance. Our gratitude goes to Coleman family researchers, Shirley Bates, of Beaverton, Oregon, and Patrick Burke of Brea, California, who led us to Coleman researcher Richard Worthy of Westfield, Indiana. Thanks also go to Moore family researchers Marilyn Moore and Barbara Thomas, who directed us to Joe Logan of Pittsburgh, Pennsylvania. Brenda Clark of Chesapeake, Virginia, posted information on the Internet from her research in the state archives at Richmond that connected the California Bolands to her relatives in Virginia and revealed that the Boland probate settlement had an impact there as well. Lee Adams, historian and coroner of Downieville, provided much of the death and burial information on the Boland and Judge families of Sierra County, California. Jack Armstrong of Longmont, Colorado, author of *Wagons to Californey, 1864,* gave us permission to use information on crossing the plains from his biography of Adam Ludy, a member of the McMurphy party.

Staff members at local historical societies, libraries and other repositories have been particularly helpful. Tom Carey at the San Francisco History Center, San Francisco Public Library, took an interest in our project and helped locate San Francisco material on early immigrants Jacob and Eleanora Harman and the Harman land claim. Files of the Pajaro Valley Historical Association offered information on the early history of Watsonville and burial information on members of the Freiermuth, Sheehy and Chapin families of the Pajaro Valley. Loretta Field at the Santa Clara Mission Cemetery provided historical information on the cemetery and helped our volunteers weed through cemetery records and tombstone locations.

Less local institutions also responded to our plea for help. Employees at the Storey County Recorder's office in Virginia City, Nevada, assisted in the location of land records left by Peter and Mary Ann Harman Roussel. Kent Stoddard, President of the Mono County Historical Society in Bridgeport, California, provided scanned copies of Baker and Farneman photographs, and the museum staff in Bridgeport shared their ledger collection. The Mono Basin Historical Society in Lee Vining, California, gave permission to use the Mono Lake School House picture. Archivist Karen Nitz at the Claire McGill Luce Western History Room of the Harney County Library in Burns, Oregon, provided scanned images of the Fry and Harman family files from their collection.

The contributions of those above, along with the countless hours put in by the California Genealogical Society's large research and production team have created a family genealogy we hope will be appreciated by cousins across the country.

❧ Abbreviations

abt.	about
acc.	according to
aft.	after
b.	born
bef.	before
bk.	book
bp.	baptized; occ. birthplace
bur.	buried
CDA	California Death Abstracts[1]
CDI	California Death Index
cem.	cemetery
CGS	California Genealogical Society
ch.	children
Co.	County
d.	died
Distr.	District
div.	divorced
d.y.	died young
E.D.	Enumeration District (in a census)
FHL	Family History Library, Salt Lake City
I.T.	Idaho Territory
m.	married
n.f.i.	no further information
ODI	Oregon Death Index
p.	page
Pct.	Precinct (in a census or election)
poss.	possibly
prev.	previously
recs.	records
sh.	sheet (pagination reference within a census Enumeration District)
SSDI	Social Security Death Index, a free database on many websites
Twp.	Township
unm.	unmarried, i.e., never married
v. or vol.	volume, of a set of books or a periodical
WMI	Western States Marriages, a collection at Brigham Young University

1. Indexes covering 1905-1939 are on FHL films #1,686,044-1,686,050. Those covering 1940-1995 are on microfiche issued by the Dept. of Health, State of California, but provide less information than two databases that were used here: one at www.vitalsearch-CA.com, covering 1940-2000, and one at Ancestry.com, covering 1940-1997. There are differences among these sources.

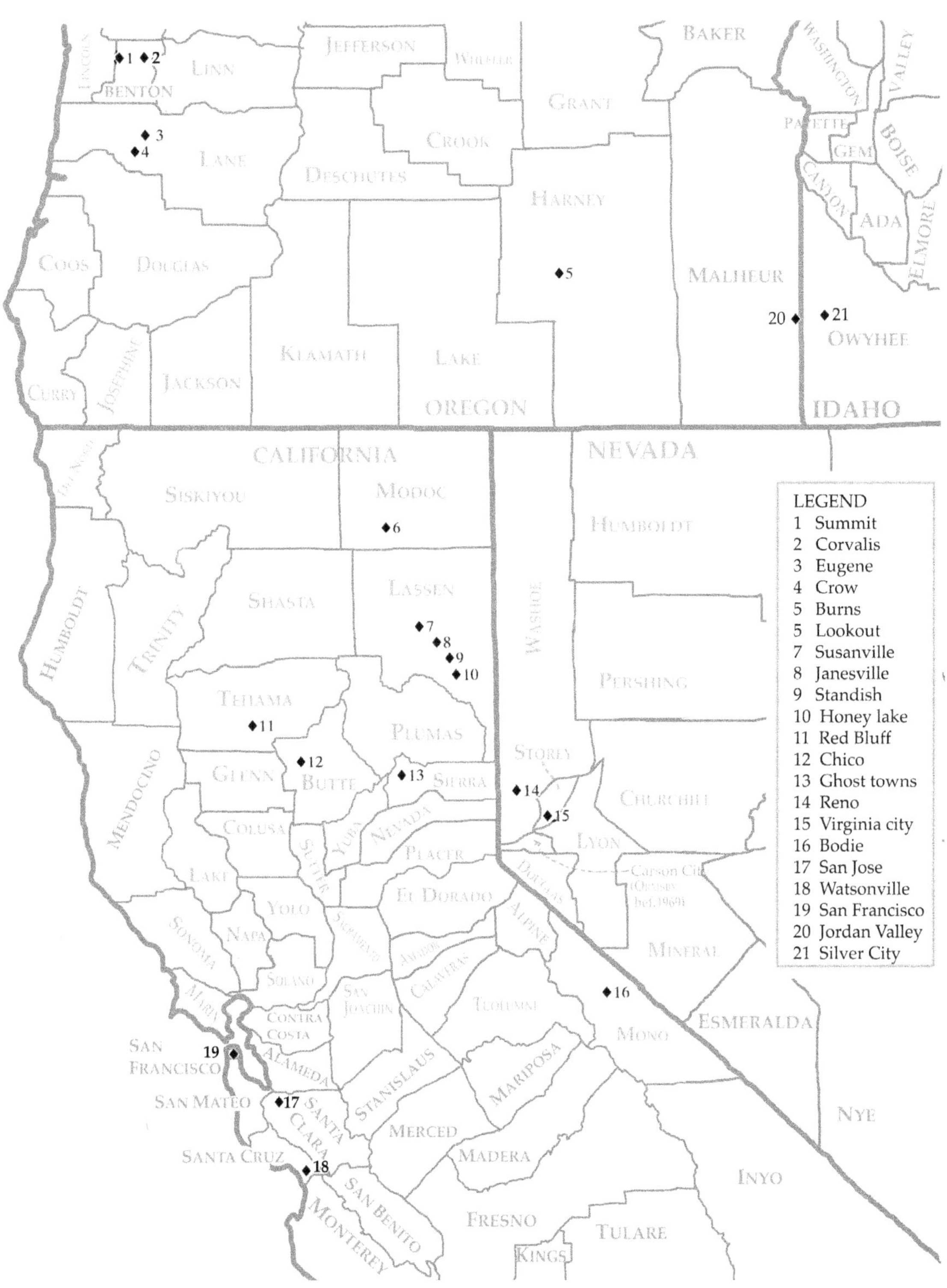

Locations covered in text

❧ Theodore Timothy Judge and Ellen Sheehy Judge

Theodore Timothy Judge was born April 1, 1921, in the small town of Westwood, east of Lake Almanor in Lassen County, California, the only child of Timothy Aloysius Judge and Hazel Agnes Roussel. Shortly afterward, the family moved to Gibsonville, Sierra County, his father's hometown. When Ted was three, his parents divorced, and Ted and his mother moved to Alameda. On May 11, 1929, Agnes married Albert Sylvan Taylor, at the time a grocery store owner and later an employee of the East Bay Transit Company. Ted quickly grew very fond of his stepfather, whom he always referred to as Dad.

Ted as a toddler by the barn holding his hat, c. 1925
From Ted Judge archives

When Ted was about ten, the family moved to the Merriewood section of the Montclair district of Oakland. After a brief move to an apartment nearer Albert's work, they returned to Merriewood, where Ted developed a lifelong friendship with his neighbor, Daryl Boomer. Daryl recalled that Ted, as an only child, enjoyed Daryl's large family and many dogs, while Daryl, on the other hand, enjoyed getting away from the constant mayhem of siblings and pets. Daryl wrote of their different temperaments:

> *I was always interested in how things were made, while Ted was interested in what they could accomplish for him. He was always much more interested in the results, rather than the details of how things were accomplished.*

After graduating from Oakland Technical High School, Ted attended the University of California at Berkeley. He served in the Reserve Officers Training Corps for three years and graduated with a Bachelor of Science degree in Economics with the class of 1942. Ted worked part time throughout high school and during his college years, which did not leave much time for involvement in many college and social activities. Under "activities," the Cal yearbook simply lists Stiles Hall (then a YMCA facility) and the Bancroft Library.

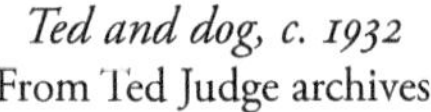

Ted and dog, c. 1932
From Ted Judge archives

Ted on porch, c. 1931
From Ted Judge archives

As a result of a mild case of polio in childhood, Ted was exempted from the draft. Nevertheless, shortly after graduation in October 1942, he enlisted in the Army. After a month of basic training in artillery, he was transferred to the Allied Military Government Program. His education and background qualified him for a year-long training program in Far Eastern studies and language taught at Stanford University in Palo Alto. Ted specialized in the Malay and Dutch languages and Far Eastern history, economics and customs. He fully expected to become a "forward observer," a dangerous assignment on the Malay Peninsula. In spite of this training, when the 70th Division was assembled for service in Europe in 1943-44, Ted was sent to Camp Adair, Oregon, where he trained as a rifleman with the 275th Regiment of the 70th Infantry Division. He then spent the next fifteen months in France and Germany as a private first class rifleman.

His regiment landed in Marseille December 16, 1944, marched north through France into the Alsace, and then into the southern front of the Battle of the Bulge in the Ardennes Forest. From there, in the dead of winter, they pushed on into Germany, near Bischweiler on the west bank of the Rhine River. In poor conditions, with minimal survival training and without proper clothing or boots, the 70th Division spearheaded the Seventh Army's drive into Germany, south of Saarbrücken.

December '44 and January '45 were among the coldest months on record, and many allied troops were ill equipped for the frigid conditions. One of the few stories that Ted later related about his participation in the Battle of the Bulge described men with frozen toes and fingers and the misery of sleeping in a wet or frozen foxhole. He never forgot the intensity of fighting in this last German offensive of the war. Of the more than two hundred sixty soldiers in his unit, Ted was one of fewer than seventy who survived.

For his service he was awarded several medals, including the Combat Infantryman Badge for action under hostile fire, European, African, Middle Eastern and American Campaign medals, and, eventually, the Bronze Star for heroic achievement. Perhaps typical of his generation, Ted rarely spoke about his war experience and awards. He often remarked that only luck allowed him to survive.

When the war in Europe ended in 1945, because he was a single enlisted man with only eighty-six days of combat, Ted was required to remain in Germany and complete his tour of duty. According to his Army pal, Lou Holger, Ted successfully talked his way into a choice assignment with Special Services in Heidelberg, the position of Chief Clerk of the post. He managed five large theaters and four movie houses, supervising military and civilian personnel in their operation and maintenance and directing entertainment content. His administrative skills in this position earned him the trust and respect of both military and civilian employees.

Ted graduates from University of California, Berkeley, 1942
From Ted Judge archives

On completion of his tour of duty, Ted returned stateside and was discharged in March 1946. With his military experiences behind him, he joined the staff of the Pillsbury Company at their main office in Minneapolis, Minnesota. The company, founded in 1872, was at that time one of the oldest and most recognized firms in American food retailing. He quickly rose to Vice President and Investment Manager in charge of sales and acquisitions in the U.S. and Europe, a position that involved extensive travel.

Ted was a quiet, intelligent man with a quick wit and dry sense of humor. Both patient and honest, he seldom, if ever, complained. He was not without opinions, however, and when asked for his views he would offer them readily, not hesitating to express his convictions.

PFC Ted Judge, Rifleman (far right)
From Ted Judge archives

Ted Judge as an adult
From Ted Judge archives

Ted enjoying fishing, undated
From Ted Judge archives

❧

Ellen Margaret Sheehy was born on December 29, 1906 in Watsonville, California, the oldest of five children born to Phillip and Loretta (Freiermuth) Sheehy. She was a beautiful, petite woman of sharp intelligence and a soft manner.

When she was young, her family moved to San Jose, where her father became a prominent attorney. Ellen attended grade school in San Jose and Notre Dame High School, and then enrolled in the State Teachers College of San Jose, where she earned her teaching certificate for kindergarten and primary grades in 1929.

On July 5, 1932 Ellen married Dudley P. Sanford, M.D., at St. James Cathedral in Seattle, Washington. They divorced in 1944, after which she returned to San Jose to continue her education. She earned her Bachelor of Education from San Jose State in 1955 and taught in the Watsonville School District and at Harbor Hill School in San Francisco. She next went to work for the Pillsbury Company and later worked as an accountant.

Ted met Ellen Sheehy by happenstance on one of his many trips to California. Ellen and a good friend and roommate were having a ladies' night out in San Francisco. Ted saw an opportunity to assert his gentlemanly traits and offered to buy them a drink and share a quiet conversation. Ellen and Ted were smitten with one another and agreed to keep in contact. Eventually Ted asked Ellen to marry him.

Ellen, however, was a devout Catholic and did not feel she could marry again without an annulment authorized by the Church or the death of her former spouse. Thus began a long

Ellen in an outdoor chair, undated, c. 1950
From Ted Judge archives

term, long distance relationship that would last for thirty plus years. Ellen finally succeeded in obtaining a church annulment in 1976, at which time Ted was fifty-five and Ellen, sixty-nine. On December 18, 1976, in the chapel of St. Christopher's Convent, San Jose, they married in a quiet ceremony attended by close family and friends.

❧

For two years they lived in Minnesota until Ted retired in 1978. From there they returned to California and made their home in Saratoga for almost two decades. During this period Ted continued to use the financial acumen that had carried him so far at Pillsbury to build his estate and to develop the stock portfolio of the John Sheehy Company, a family-owned business with extensive holdings in the Watsonville area, established by Ellen's grandparents.

Together they shared a love of history and traveled widely both in this country and abroad. Ted particularly loved Ireland, England and Scotland, where he searched for the names and places of his ancestral lines.

In 1996 Ted and Ellen sold their home in Saratoga and purchased a condominium at The Forum, a senior community in nearby Cupertino. Their plan was to live a maintenance-free life, with unlimited time in which to travel and visit friends and family, but, unfortunately, Ellen became ill with leukemia and died May 25, 2000.

Ted and Ellen made many friends over the years they were together and nurtured those relationships: old childhood friends, neighbors, traveling acquaintances and family. It was this strong connection with people and his own fortitude that supported Ted through his loss of Ellen. He spoke often of his gratitude to his friends, his Army buddies and others across the United States for their ongoing connection with him and Ellen.

Following Ellen's death, Ted continued to advise the Sheehy Company and work on his own investments. It was his passion to keep up with what was happening in the business world and the stock market, and he did so meticulously. He liked a good sharp picture on his TV, not so much for shows or movies but to better view stock prices as they scrolled by. In later years when his health declined and his activities became limited, Ted still remained informed on current events, the economy and the stock market, and could carry on a conversation on almost any subject brought his way.

He enjoyed popcorn and a drink as a "cocktail hour special" before dinner. A premium wine was never turned down when offered, and mints or candy were never far out of reach. He enjoyed a good cup of hot coffee, a sweet roll and any chocolate delight. Most of all, however, he loved ice cream—any flavor, any time, day or night! He was a food critic and a decent amateur cook. He made the best chocolate chip cookies, a good cake and a breakfast fit for a king.

Ted was very conscientious about his personal affairs and was endearingly generous in planning his estate. He provided legacies to his family and to numerous charities and institutions, including Stiles Hall and the Bancroft Library of the University of California, Berkeley, places he had known as a college student. He believed strongly in the value of a higher education and generously provided funding for members of his and Ellen's families. This legacy will live on through these children through many generations.

Ted and Ellen's mutual interest in their heritage is reflected in his instructions that a book of family genealogy and stories should be produced for his and Ellen's kin—this book. It was his hope that others would find joy in the discovery process.

As he entered his eighties, Ted suffered a series of setbacks that left him physically weak. He was fortunate to remain mentally sharp until the end and seldom complained about his declining condition. He was loved and cherished by those who knew him well and was admired and respected from a distance by those who didn't. He was a wonderful provider, husband and friend. Mostly quiet, always cordial and polite, he completed his life with honor, pride and dignity. Ted Judge died comfortably in his sleep at age eighty-seven, June 11, 2008.

Book One

The Ancestry of Theodore Timothy Judge

Ancestors of Theodore Timothy Judge

Theodore Timothy Judge
b. 1 Apr. 1921, Westwood, Lassen Co., Calif.
d. 11 Jun. 2008, The Forum, Cupertino, Calif.

Timothy Aloysius Judge
b. 15 Oct. 1894, Gibsonville, Sierra Co., Calif.
d. 6 Apr. 1961, Oakland, Alameda, Calif.
m. 1 Dec. 1919, Susanville, Lassen Co., Calif.

Timothy Thaddeus Judge
b. abt. 1830, Ireland
d. 1922, Quincy, Plumas Co., Calif.
m. abt. 1892

Catherine Margaret F. Boland
b. Sep. 1855, Poker Flat, Sierra Co., Calif.
d. 20 Feb. 1933, Reno, Washoe Co., Nev.

Daniel Boland
b. 1828, Ireland
d. 1922, San Francisco; bur. Marysville, Calif.
m. bef. 1853

Margaret -?-
b. 1828, Ireland
d. bef. 1876

Hazel Agnes Russell
b. 5 Jan. 1900, Karlo, Lassen Co., Calif.
d. 12 Dec. 1988, Santa Clara Co., Calif.

James Peter Roussel
b. 17 Feb. 1866, Calif.
bpt. 4 Mar. 1866, San Francisco, Calif.
d. 22 Nov. 1934, Lassen Co., Calif.
m. 16 Aug. 1889, Harney Co., Ore.

Peter Roussel
b. abt 1831, France
d. aft. 1890 Nev.?
m. 18 Jan. 1859 Santa Clara, Calif.
div. Jan. 1876. Reno, Nev.

Mary Ann Harman
b. 1 Apr. 1841, Madison Co., Ill.
d. 1 Jul. 1909, Santa Clara Co., Calif.

Jacob Harman
bp. France
d. 3 Nov. 1850, San Francisco, Calif.
m. 7 Mar. 1841, Madison Co., Ill.
div. 24 Oct. 1849, San Francisco, Calif.

Eleanora Bush
b. abt. 1821, Germany
d. 17 Nov. 1859, Santa Clara Co., Calif.

Sarah Ellen McMurphy
b. 17 Nov. 1868, California
d. 5 Sep. 1919, Lassen Co., Calif

Silas Wright McMurphy
b. July 1836, St. Lawrence Co., N. Y.
d. 20 Feb. 1908, Benton Co., Ore.
m. 21 Feb. 1861, Henry Co., Iowa

Abner McMurphy
b. 22 July 1798, Orange Co., Ver.
d. 1 Oct. 1886, Lassen Co., Calif.

Eunice Hastings
b. abt. 1799, Massachusetts
d. 15 June 1883, Lassen Co., Calif.

Elizabeth Kelley
b. 3 May 1841, Washington Co., Ohio
d. 4 Sep. 1909, Benton Co., Ore.

John Kelley
b. abt. 1814, Penn.
d. 21 April 1867, Henry Co., Iowa
m. 31 Dec. 1837, Washington Co., Ohio

Sarah Palmer
b. 11 Feb. 1811, New Hampshire
d. 15 Jan. 1901 Frontier Co., Neb.

Overview

Timothy Thaddeus Judge, Ted Judge's grandfather, was an Irish immigrant who, in his early twenties, arrived in California about 1852. Settling in Sierra County, he and his first wife had three children, only one of whom survived. Following his wife's death he mined for many years and in his sixties married a much younger widow, Kate Boland, who had seven children. With Kate he fathered a second family of three, the oldest of whom was named Timothy Aloysius. Timothy Aloysius Judge married Hazel Agnes Russell (Roussel). That short-lived marriage lasted only long enough to produce one child, Theodore Timothy "Ted" Judge.

The Boland saga begins with Kate (Boland) Judge's Irish immigrant father, Daniel. Daniel, with at least one brother, reached California in 1849. He settled in the legendary town of Poker Flat, mined, ran a hotel and operated a store. In the early 70s, Daniel went east to Virginia, where he purchased land on which his brother continued to live. Following his return to California and death a few years later, his widow was forced to sell their mining interests, which spawned lawsuits that continue to be cited in cases and codes today. Their daughter Kate, the first child born in Poker Flat, married as her second husband, Timothy Thaddeus Judge, grandfather of Ted.

Of all Ted Judge's ancestral lines, the one that starts with Jacob Harman and Eleanora Bush, and runs through their daughter Mary Ann and husband Peter Roussel, on to the Roussels' son, James Peter and wife Sarah McMurphy, and then to their daughter, Hazel Agnes (Roussel) Judge, is perhaps the most interesting of all. The Bush-Harman chapter follows this lineage through California, Nevada, Oregon and back to California. Jacob Harman and his much younger wife, Eleanora, were among the earliest American settlers in Yerba Buena, the nascent village that became San Francisco. They left Missouri in the massive first exodus in 1846, not in search of gold, but to populate California and fulfill President Polk's "Manifest Destiny." Many of their travelling companions, including members of the Donner party, never completed the trip. The Harmans claimed land near Mission Dolores, several years after which Eleanora filed for divorce and Jacob died. These two events formed the basis of lawsuits that kept the courts busy for years. After Jacob's death, Eleanora raced through three more husbands, and upon her death left two daughters and much valuable real estate. Her oldest daughter Mary Ann endured a trying marriage with Peter Roussel that moved from the California foothills to Nevada mining country. From there with another husband she moved to southeastern Oregon and finally to Lassen County, California. Mary Ann's son James Peter, "Juniper Jim," was a stagecoach driver in Oregon and later a colorful gunslinger in Lassen County, California.

The classic westward migration of the McMurphys provided the only California Trail diary among the ancestors of Ted Judge. Having married in New England, Abner and Eunice McMurphy migrated first to New York, where their children were born, then to Illinois, then to Iowa. In 1864, both in their sixties, Abner and Eunice, accompanied by almost all of their children and grandchildren, completed the trek west, settling in Lassen County. Their son Silas had already married in Iowa, Elizabeth Kelley, of New England stock but raised in Ohio. They made the trip with a newborn daughter, settled in Lassen County then later moved to Oregon. Sarah, the third daughter of Silas and Elizabeth, married "Juniper Jim" Roussel.

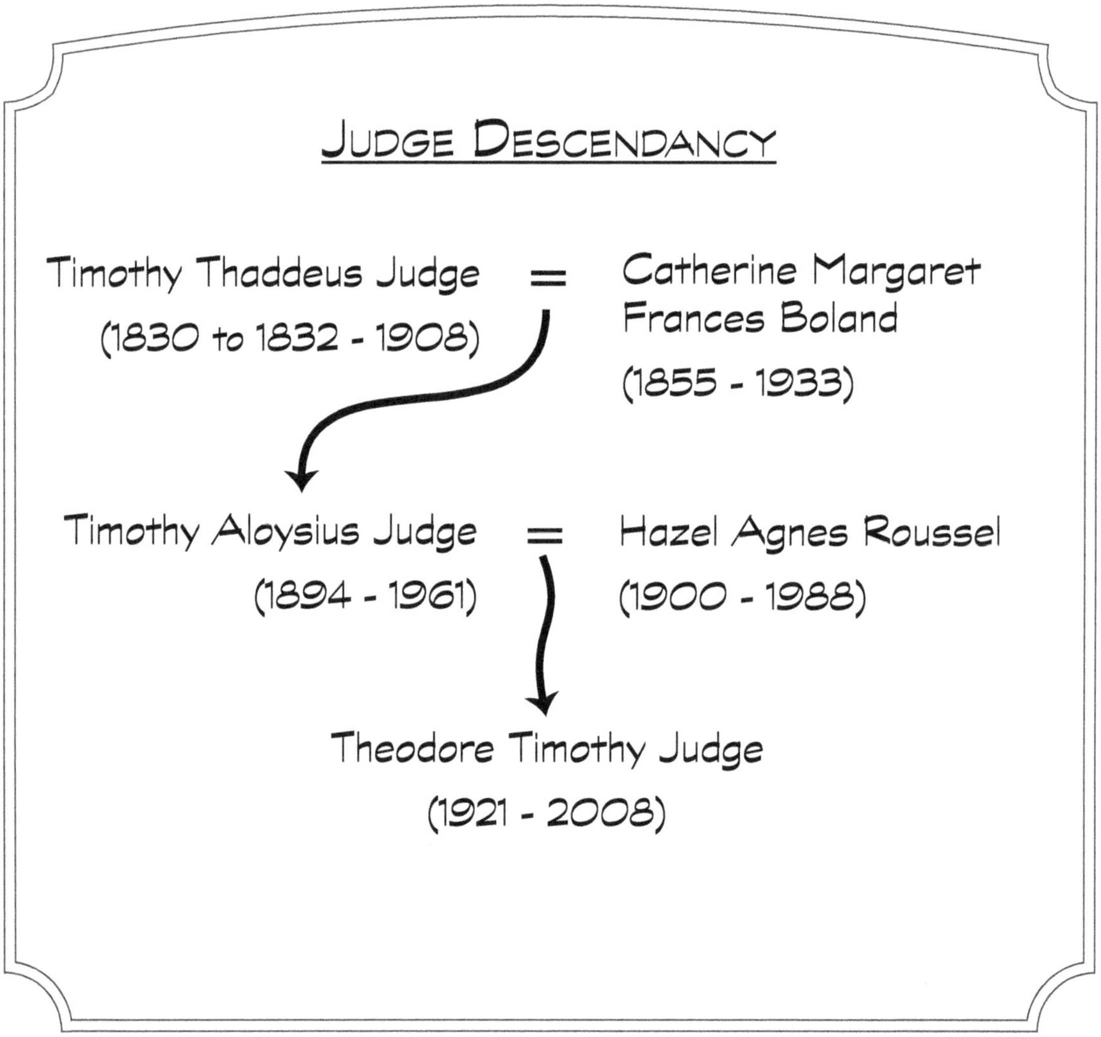

Judge Descendancy

Timothy Thaddeus Judge = Catherine Margaret Frances Boland
(1830 to 1832 - 1908) (1855 - 1933)

Timothy Aloysius Judge = Hazel Agnes Roussel
(1894 - 1961) (1900 - 1988)

Theodore Timothy Judge
(1921 - 2008)

Descendancy of Judge family

❧ Descendants of Timothy Thaddeus Judge

In 1846, a potato blight in Ireland drove 1.8 million refugees to America. Most immigrants initially clustered on the east coast, but after gold was discovered in California in 1848, large numbers came west. Many of Ted Judge's immigrant ancestors were among these emigrants, including his grandfather, Timothy Thaddeus Judge. Timothy Judge came to California during the middle years of the Gold Rush, reportedly in 1852.[1]

Timothy appears to have been very closely related to two other Irish immigrants named Judge who also came to the Sierra foothills: John and Michael Judge, who applied together for naturalization, 2 October 1866, in Sacramento.[2] John, along with Thomas McHugh, attested to Michael Judge's moral character and length of time in the United States. Samuel Deal and Richard Breen supported John's application the same day. John, as learned from his wife Winifred's biography, was born about 1822, immigrated in 1848 and came from North Carolina to California in 1852.[3] Michael Judge, born according to various sources from 1822 to 1831, was said by his daughter to have settled on the Sacramento River in 1852.[4] Several months after John and Michael were naturalized, Timothy filed. On 25 January 1867, in Sacramento, John Judge and William G. Collicott attested to Timothy Judge's character and qualifications.[5] Further research may sort out the relationship among these men.

Both of Timothy's wives were Irish. His first wife, Margaret, came from County Leitrim. His second wife, Catherine "Kate" Boland, the grandmother of Ted Judge, was the daughter of Irish immigrants. Timothy and Kate each brought into their union a number of children from previous marriages, his two and her eight. To this blended family of ten children, they added three of their own. Timothy and both his wives are buried in Gibsonville Cemetery, Plumas County, California. The cemetery exists today, although Gibsonville no longer does.

1. The year of immigration given on both the 1900 and 1910 census enumerations is 1852; Timothy Judge household, 1900 census, California, Sierra Co., Gibson Twp, E.D. 122, sh. 4, dwelling 105, family 105, p. 234; Timothy Judge household, 1910 census, California, Sierra Co, Table Rock Twp., E.D. 104, sh. 4A, dwelling 29, family 19, p. 143.
2. The naturalization records of both John and Michael are from California District Court Records, vols. A-C, 1861-1868, Family History Library (hereafter, FHL) film #980,418.
3. *History of Sacramento County, California with Illustrations (Oakland: Thompson & West, 1880), 245.* John Judge died 31 Dec. 1876 at age 56 and is buried in St. Joseph's Cemetery (Register of Interments, St. Joseph's Cemetery, Sacramento, FHL film #1,065,020).
4. Account of Mary Judge in G. Walter Reed, *History of Sacramento County, California, with Biographical Sketches* (Los Angeles: Historic Record Co., 1923), 663. Michael Judge and his wife Celia (Kane) named children Timothy and Winifred, strongly suggesting these three men were brothers. Michael died at 78, 13 March 1909 in Sacramento Co.
5. Naturalization Records, 6th Judicial District, vols. A-C, 1861-1868 (FHL film #980,418).

CERTIFICATE OF CITIZENSHIP.

United States of America,
STATE OF CALIFORNIA, } SS.
COUNTY OF SIERRA.

NUMBER.

Be it Remembered, That on the Sixth day of July in the year of our Lord One Thousand Eight Hundred and Sixty-eight Timothy Judge formerly of Ireland in the .... at present of the State of California, aforesaid, appeared in the County Court of the State of California in and for the County of Sierra, the said Court being a Court of Record, having Common Law jurisdiction, and a Clerk and Seal, and applied to the said Court to be admitted to become a CITIZEN OF THE UNITED STATES OF AMERICA, pursuant to the directions and requisitions of the Act of Congress of the United States of America, entitled "An Act to establish a Uniform Rule of Naturalization, and to repeal the Acts heretofore passed on that subject;" and of the several Acts in relation thereto.

And the said Timothy Judge having thereupon produced to the Court such evidence, made such Declaration and Renunciation, and taken such Oaths, as are by the said Acts required: thereupon it was ordered by the said County Court that the said Timothy Judge be admitted, and he was accordingly admitted by said Court to be a CITIZEN OF THE UNITED STATES OF AMERICA.

Attest: .... [illegible] Strange Clerk.

Signature: .... Deputy Clerk.

Timothy Judge Certificate of Citizenship, 6 July 1868
From Ted Judge archives

Timothy Thaddeus Judge, 1890
From Ted Judge archives

It is located south of Quincy, about twenty-two miles along and just off the road leading to LaPorte. Driving is at times treacherous; the road is often narrow and winding with no guardrail and may be closed in inclement weather.

Timothy's grandson, Ted Judge, and Ted's nephew, Pat Sheehy, visited this cemetery in the 1990s. It was overgrown. Many towns that Kate and Timothy lived in are gone: Poker Flat, Whiskey Diggings, Gibsonville, Table Rock, and Mt. Pleasant. But there was a time when the mining towns of the Sierra were burgeoning, when gold fever was rampant. There were mines, hotels, dance halls, assay offices, and noise everywhere. Today nature has reclaimed the area. People visit for skiing, hiking and quiet.

The descendancy from Timothy Thaddeus Judge to Ted Judge is very short: Timothy and his second wife Catherine (Boland) Boland had three children, the second of whom was Timothy Aloysius Judge. The brief marriage of Timothy Aloysius Judge to Hazel Agnes Russell produced but one child, Theodore Timothy "Ted" Judge. Sadly, Ted never knew much about his father's ancestry, which is enlarged upon only slightly here. He would have loved researching this book.

Genealogical Descendancy

1. **Timothy Thaddeus[1] Judge** was born somewhere in Ireland about 1830.[6] He immigrated in 1852, came to California soon afterwards, and died in Quincy, Plumas County, California in 1922.[7] Timothy married before 1860, **Mary**_?_, born about 1831 in County Leitrim, Ire-

6. His birth is estimated from both census enumerations and voter registrations, which suggest most often 1830 but occasionally range to 1832. See Timothy Judge household, 1900 Census, California, Sierra Co., Gibson Twp, E.D. 122, sh. 4, dwelling 105, family 105, p. 234; Timothy Judge household, 1910 Census, Sierra Co, Calif., Table Rock Twp., E.D. 104, sh. 4A, dwelling 29, family 19, p. 143. The 1872 California List of Foreign-born Voters indicates his birth was abt. 1830.
7. Burial information for Gibsonville Cemetery is from Lee Adams, comp., *Sierra County Pioneer Cemetery Historic Survey* (Downieville, Calif.: privately publ., 1997); Adams contributed this unpaginated material to U.S. GenWeb Archives, where it is available at http://files.usgwarchives.net/ca/sierra/cemeteries/sier-h-l.txt . Timothy's death was not recorded in the California Death Index (hereafter, CDI). He may have died in Nevada, or possibly his death was not (or not correctly) recorded.

Engraving of Gibsonville during mining days, 1856

land. Mary died 16 December 1876 in Gibsonville, Sierra County, California, and was buried there with her daughter Caly in Gibsonville Cemetery.[8]

In the 1880 census Timothy, a widower, was mining gold and living in Mt. Pleasant, Sierra County, with his two surviving children, Matthew, a miner, and Nellie, who kept house.[9] Timothy married again, around 1892, perhaps in Washington, D.C., **Catherine Margaret Frances "Kate" Boland**, a much younger widow with seven surviving children.[10] Kate had a very interesting history of her own, which is discussed in the Boland chapter.

Timothy Thaddeus Judge continued to mine until he was eighty years old, most of the time in Sierra County. He lived long enough to see his youngest son, Timothy Aloysius Judge, return from duty in World War I, marry Hazel Agnes Roussel, and produce a grandson, Ted Judge, in 1921. He died the following year.

Timothy and his first wife Mary had three children:[11]

8. Vital information from Adams, *Sierra County Pioneer Cemetery Historic Survey*, cited above. Her tombstone in Gibsonville Cemetery reads "Dec 16 1876 45y Born in County Leitrim."
9. Timothy Judge household, 1880 Census, Sierra Co., Calif., Mt. Pleasant Twp., E.D. 101, dwelling 71, family 71, p. 21.
10. Obituaries of Kate Boland Judge: "First Lady of Poker Flat Dies in Her 77th year," *Nevada State Journal* (Reno, Nevada), 21 Feb. 1933, p.3, col. 2 and p. 8, col. 4; "Many Friends Attend Rites for Mrs. Judge," *Nevada State Journal*, 23 Feb. 1933, p. 6, col. 3. The possibility that Timothy Thaddeus Judge and Kate Boland married in Washington, D.C., as stated in one of her obituaries is curious and still being explored.
11. Timothy Judge household 1870 Census, Sierra Co., Calif., Gibson Twp., dwelling 505, family 505, p. 541; burial information for Caly Judge from Lee Adams, comp, *Sierra County Pioneer Cemetery Historic Survey*.

Mt. Pleasant, Sierra County, Judge Family home in 1880

2 i. MATTHEW[2] JUDGE, b. about 1862, m. MARY WHERITY.

ii. MARY ELLEN "Nellie" JUDGE, b. in Gibsonville, Sierra Co., Calif., about 1864, d. at her father's home in Mt. Pleasant, Sierra Co. 30 Aug. 1895. "Nellie" was a teacher in the Island School District and never married. She is interred in Gibsonville Cemetery.[12]

iii. CATHERINE "CALY" JUDGE, b. Gibsonville, Sierra Co., 25 April 1867, d., probably in the same place, 20 Sept. 1870, bur. in Gibsonville Cem.[13]

Following his second marriage, Timothy and his new wife "Kate" had the following children:

3 iv. TIMOTHY ALOYSIUS JUDGE, b. 15 Oct. 1894, m. HAZEL AGNES ROUSSEL.

v. CATHERINE "Katie" JUDGE, b. in Calif., probably in Sierra Co., in June 1897 or 1898, d. of pneumonia following the Spanish flu in Los Angeles, Calif., 24 Jan. 1919. Less than two years earlier, on 29 Nov. 1917, she had married WILLIAM BERG in San Francisco.[14] There were no children.

12. Obituary, *Plumas National Bulletin*, 5 Sep. 1895, p. 3.
13. Adams, *Sierra County Historical Cemetery Survey.*
14. Birth from Tim Judge household, 1900 Census, Sierra Co., Calif., Gibson Twp., E.D. 122, sh. 4, dwelling 105, family 105; marriage from *Plumas National Bulletin* (Quincy, California), 7 Dec. 1917; death from *Plumas National Bulletin*, 30 Jan. 1919, p. 1, col. 4.

vi. MARGARET "Peg" JUDGE, b. in Calif., 11 July 1899, d. in Nevada Co., Calif., 22 June 1977, bur. in Gibsonville Cem.[15] Sometime after the 1930 census, she married STEPHANO "Steve" VARENNA, b. 24 Jan. 1879 in Grosio, Provincia di Sondrio, Regione Lombardia, Italy, died in Butte Co., Calif., 2 May 1949.[16] There were no children.

Combining Timothy's surviving children from his earlier marriage, her surviving children from her earlier marriage, and their own three, Timothy and Kate together raised twelve children. She was known for her healing skills and traveled Sierra County to help the sick.[17] The flu epidemic of 1918 hit them hard, however. Kate lost her son Patrick Boland in December 1918; Timothy and Kate's daughter Catherine died the following month. His daughter Margaret and her daughter Sadie Boland Wilson were seriously ill but survived.[18]

After Timothy's death in 1922, Kate went to Reno to live with her daughter Sadie.[19] She died there in February 1933 and was buried next to Timothy in the Gibsonville Cemetery.[20]

Generation 2

2. MATTHEW[2] JUDGE (*Timothy Thaddeus*[1]) was born in Gibsonville, Sierra County, about 1862.[21] He died 20 January 1909 in Napa County, possibly at the state hospital there, of "disease of the brain," believed related to his work in coal mines. He was buried in St. Mary's Cemetery, Oakland.[22] About 1890, he married **MARY CATHERINE WHERITY**, born in California, 6 July 1865, died 2 March 1951.[23]

Matthew was mining gold in the Sierra in 1880, then is lost track of until after 1900 when his family moved to Berkeley, Alameda County.[24] Mary headed the household in Gibsonville, Sierra County, in 1900.[25]

---

15. Abstracts of California Deaths, 1940-2000, at www.vitalsearch-ca.com (hereafter CDA); Social Security Death Index (hereafter, SSDI).
16. Steve Varenna was in the John E. Wilson household, 1930 Census, Washoe Co., Nevada, city of Reno, Ward 2, E.D. 16-28, sh. 3B, dwelling 82, family 88. Birth and death from SSDI; World War I and II Draft Registration cards for Stefano/Steve Varenna, both on Ancestry.com.
17. Obituary, Kate Judge, *Reno Evening Gazette,* 21 Feb. 1933, p. 10, col. 4.
18. *Plumas National Bulletin* (Quincy, California), 30 Jan. 1919, p. 1, col. 4.
19. In the 1930 Census, Kate, 74 and a widow, was living in Reno in the home of her daughter Sarah (Boland) Wilson, along with Kate's daughter Margaret and future son-in-law, Steve Varenna; John E. Wilson household, 1930 census, prev. cited.
20. Adams, *Sierra County Historical Cemetery Survey;* obituary, Kate Judge, *Nevada State Journal,* 21 Feb. 1933, p. 3, col. 2.
21. Timothy Judge household 1870 and 1880 censuses, Sierra Co., prev. cited.
22. Detailed information from St. Mary's Cemetery at: http://files.usgwarchives.net/ca/alameda/cemeteries/.
23. Mary's information from Mary Judge household, 1900 Census, Sierra Co., Calif., Gibson Twp., E.D. 122, sh.4A, dwelling 91, family 91, p. 234, and CDA.
24. Timothy Judge household, 1880 Census, Sierra Co, Calif., Mt. Pleasant Twp., cited above. The move to Berkeley is based upon a query posted by Paula Wherity on the Judge message board at Ancestry.com reading: "would like any info on Mathew Judge family in Berkeley from abt 1900. Mathew dod abt jan 20, 1909 Alameda County [sic], wife Mary dod mar 02, 1951 had 4 children Leo Mary Irene Loretta...buried at St. Mary's...believe they moved to Berkeley abt 1901. Mary's sister was living in Berkeley in 1900 Elizabeth White...1352 Fleurange per 1920 Census. Mary's maiden name is Wherity." This query is consistent with the following Berkeley city directory listings: 1909—Leo R. Judge, clerk for M.C. Threlkeld, contractor, residing at 1352 Fleurange; 1910—Irene Judge, seamstress, Leo R. Judge, traveling Agent, for M.C. Threlkeld, Mary C. Judge, student at Berkeley Business College, Mrs. M.C. Judge, grocer, all at 1714 Ward; 1911—R. Judge at 1615 [sic] Ward, Mary C. Judge, bookkeeper, and Mary C. Judge (widow of Mathew) at 1715 Ward.
25. Mary Judge household, 1900 Census, Sierra Co., Calif., Gibson Twp., cited above.

Matthew and Mary Judge had four children, the first three, and perhaps all, born in Sierra County:

4 i. LEO RAYMOND[3] JUDGE, b. 25 April 1892, m. ALICE ROSE LACROSSE.

ii. MARY C. JUDGE, b. Oct. 1893, single and working as a stenographer in 1920.[26]

5 iii. IRENE VIRGINIA JUDGE, b. 28 April 1897, m. NESTOR MICHAEL KENNEY.

iv. LORETTA JOSEPHINE JUDGE, b. 11 May 1903, d. unm. 24 July 1987 in Berkeley.[27] At the time of the 1930 census, she was working as a stenographer in a real estate office.[28]

3. **TIMOTHY ALOYSIUS[2] JUDGE** (*Timothy Thaddeus*[1]) was born in the Mt. Pleasant area of Gibsonville, Sierra County, California, 13 October 1894, and died in Oakland, Alameda County, 6 April 1961.[29] He married first **HAZEL AGNES RUSSELL**, daughter of James Peter Roussel and Sarah Ellen McMurphy, 18 November 1919 in Susanville, Lassen County, a marriage that ended in divorce shortly after the birth of their son.[30] In 1930 he married second **MARY FREDERICK**, born in 1902 in Canada.[31] Evidently there were no children from his second marriage.

When Timothy Aloysius was born, Mt. Pleasant had a population of a few hundred people but was home to a hotel, brewery, school, music teacher, shoemaker and many miners. In the 1910 census he lived with his parents and did odd jobs to make money.[32] World War I intervened. He registered for the draft on 5 June 1917 while living in Westwood, Lassen County, at which time he was a machine hand for the Red River Timber Company in Westwood and still receiving some support from his mother.[33] He enlisted in the Army a year later as a member of the 115th Engineers.[34] According to a diary kept either by Timothy or another member of his company, he left Camp Kearney by train on 26 July 1918 for New York. The diary described the trip as "the longest game of poker ever played from California to New York."[35] From there Timothy went to "no man's land," somewhere in France. He was discharged from the Army on 24 July 1919 at the Presidio, San Francisco, California.[36] He was

26. Mary M. Judge household, 1900 Census, Sierra Co., Calif., Gibson Twp., cited above; and M. Judge household, 1920 Census, Alameda Co., city of Berkeley, E.D. 179, sh. 4A, dwelling 66, family 72, 1715 Ward St. She was not found in the 1930 census.
27. SSDI.
28. Mary C. Judge household, 1930 Census, Alameda Co., Calif., city of Berkeley, E.D. 321, sh. 7A, dwelling 126, family 183, p. 215.
29. Delayed certificate of birth, Ted Judge Archives, CGS. Golden Gate National Cemetery record: Judge, Timothy A, b. 10/13/1894, d. 04/06/1961, Pvt. Co. B, 115 Inf. 40th Div., bur. 11 April 1961. His obituary in the *Oakland Tribune*, 9 April 1961, read: "In Oakland, April 6 of 540 E. Cleveland Street, Stockton. Loving father of Theodore Judge of Minneapolis, Minnesota; brother of Mrs. Margaret Judge Varenna of Oroville, and half-brother of Miss Elizabeth Boland of Oroville. A native of Sierra Co., California. Friends are Invited to attend funeral services at the Berkeley Hills Chapel (Page & Oder), 1400 Shattuck Avenue at Cedar, Berkeley, Tuesday, April 11, at 10 o'clock. Interment, Golden Gate National Cemetery. *Stockton Daily Record*, please copy."
30. Marriage certificate #16978, filed 1 Dec. 1919 Lassen Co.; Timothy A Judge of Westwood, 25, sawyer and Hazel Agnes Roussel of Westwood, 19, nurse; first marriage for both; Divorce papers in CGS archives.
31. Timothy A. Judge household, 1930 Census, Alameda Co., Calif., Eden Twp., E.D. 1-256, sh. 23B, dwelling 596, family 606, p. 115; Mary is stated to have married at age 28, her age at that time.
32. Timothy Judge household, 1910 Census, Sierra Co., prev. cited.
33. World War II Draft Card, Timothy Aloysuis Judge, #3249, 3 Dec. 1942, Alameda, Calif., at Ancestry.com.
34. Army enlistment and discharge papers in the Ted Judge files, archived at CGS.
35. This diary was in Ted Judge's effects and is archived at CGS.
36. Military discharge papers, Judge archives, CGS.

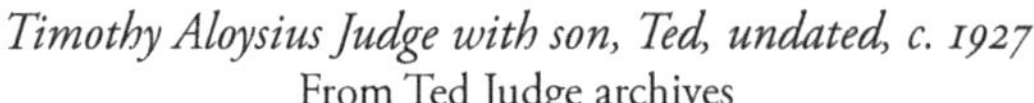

Timothy Aloysius Judge with son, Ted, undated, c. 1927
From Ted Judge archives

Timothy Aloysius Judge, 1950
From Ted Judge archives

interviewed for the local paper about his service, and was offered work in a number of places. He returned to Westwood to work as a carpenter in a box factory.[37]

Timothy and Agnes, then a waitress in a local hospital, married in a Catholic ceremony in Susanville. The marriage floundered amidst accusations of jealousy, lack of support, and his frivolous spending on a very expensive car. Agnes left Timothy 30 November 1923 and filed for divorce on 7 May 1924 in San Francisco. The case was removed to Lassen County and refiled there 4 December 1924, then apparently transferred to Plumas County.[38]

As a consequence of his World War I military service Timothy Aloysius Judge was given a burial with full honors in Golden Gate National Cemetery in San Bruno, 11 April 1961. At the time of his death, although it occurred in Alameda County, he was living in Stockton, where he worked as a milkman.[39]

Timothy and Agnes had one child:

i. Theodore Timothy[3] Judge, b. in Westwood, Lassen Co., Calif., 1 April 1921, d. 11 June 2008 in Cupertino, Santa Clara, California; married 18 Dec. 1976 in San Jose, Calif., Ellen Margaret Sheehy Sanford, b. 29 Dec. 1906, d. 25 May 2000, Cupertino. They are both

37. "Red Cross Given Highest Praise by Quincy Soldier," *Plumas National-Bulletin*, 10 July 1919, p. 1, col. 3.
38. Detailed divorce papers in Ted Judge archives at CGS.
39. Death certificate, Ted Judge archives at CGS.

interred in Mission Cemetery Santa Clara De Asis. Ted and Ellen's lives are described in the biographical chapter at the beginning of the book. Ellen's background and ancestry are covered in Book Two on the Sheehy family.

Hazel Agnes Russell Judge became the wife of Albert S. Taylor in 1929. There were no children from this marriage. Agnes and Albert raised Ted, and he called Albert "Dad." For more information about Agnes's background and ancestry, see the Harman and McMurphy chapters. For Albert's, see Book Three.

Generation 3

4. **Leo Raymond^3 Judge** (*Matthew^2, Timothy Thaddeus^1*) was born in Gibsonville, Sierra County, 25 April 1892. He died in Sacramento, Sacramento County, 18 September 1974.[40] Sometime before 1920 he married **Alice Lacrosse**, who was born in Minnesota, 2 May 1892, and died in Alameda County on 8 June 1995, at the age of 103.[41]

In 1917, when Leo registered for the draft, he described himself as Vice President and Sales Manager, Standard Soap Company, Berkeley, California, and was living in Berkeley.[42] In the 1930 census, Leo, Alice and their one child shared their home in Berkeley with Nestor and Irene (Judge) Kenney and their children.[43]

5. **Irene Virginia^3 Judge** (*Matthew^2, Timothy Thaddeus^1*) was born in California (probably Gibsonville), 28 April 1897; she died in Alameda County, 12 July 1989.[44] In the early 1920s she married **Nestor Michael Kenney**, who was born in California, 26 February 1900, and died in Alameda County, 1 December 1985.[45]

In 1917, when Nestor registered for the draft, he was a clerk at the Sperry Flour Company, San Francisco, California, single, and living in his parents' home in Oakland.[46]

---

40. CDA.
41. *Ibid.*
42. World War I Draft Registration Card, at Ancestry.com.
43. Leo Judge household, 1930 Census, Alameda Co., Calif., city of Berkeley, E.D. 1-316, sh. 3B, dwelling 65, family 87, p. 128B. Nestor Kenney's family is #88.
44. CDA.
45. *Ibid.*
46. World War I Draft Registration Card, at Ancestry.com.

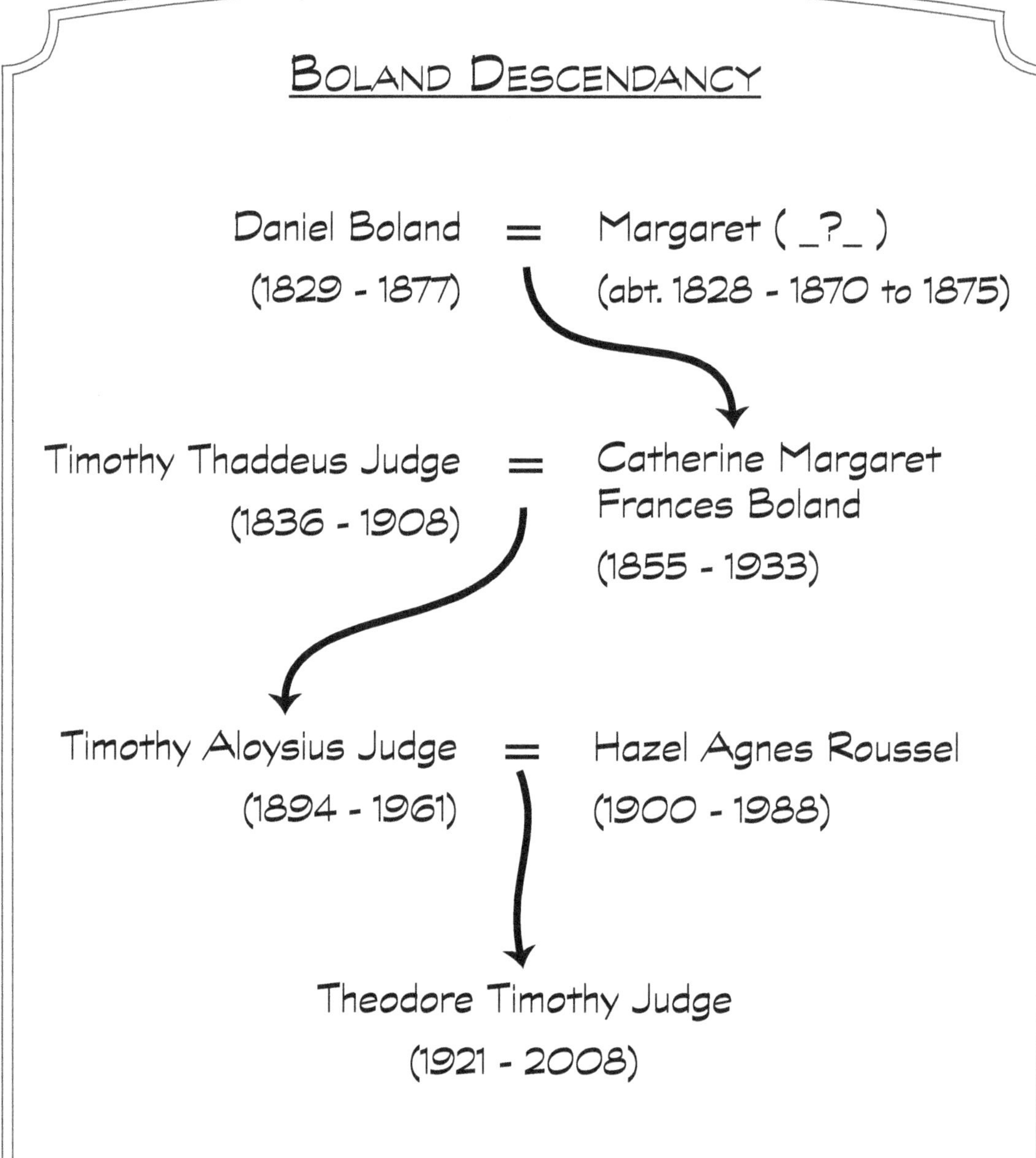

Descendancy of Boland family

❧ Descendants of Daniel and Margaret Boland

The Boland story begins about 1849, when Daniel and perhaps a number of siblings, said by descendants to be from Tipperary, left Ireland for the California Gold Rush. Upon reaching California, they made their way up the steep canyons of the westernmost part of Sierra County. The towns where Daniel Boland and his extended family lived and did business are now only whispers of what they once were, if they exist at all: Poker Flat, Table Rock, Gibsonville, Howland Flat, Whiskey Diggings, Fir Cap Diggings, and La Porte.

Daniel settled in Poker Flat, a hardscrabble mining town reached only by making one's way up the steep trails of Canyon Creek. Made famous by Bret Harte's short story *The Outcasts of Poker Flat,* the town once bustled with saloons, three hotels, a master butcher, a jeweler, a Masonic Hall, a dairy, numerous stores and hundreds of miners, who worked for outfits with names like Last Chance, Lucky Hill and Blue Gravel Mining. Daniel Boland at one time owned or managed one of the hotels. By 1856, the population of the immediate area surrounding Poker Flat had dropped from thousands to about 700, that of Poker Flat itself to under twenty.[1] Following a disastrous fire in 1859, the town was rebuilt, and in 1863 the first school opened. Here Daniel Boland mined and managed a business and as the area declined, somehow scraped by. The story is complicated because in addition to Daniel of Poker Flat and Table Rock, there was a second Daniel Boland, a little over ten years younger, who in 1870 was a merchant in Gibsonville and who married Kate, daughter of the older Daniel.

Whether elder Daniel brought his first wife Margaret with him from Ireland or married her in this country remains to be determined, but the latter seems more likely since their first child was born in California about 1853. The first record found for him was his naturalization record in Downieville, Sierra County, 1 August 1854.[2] The five-year United States residency requirement for naturalization implies that Daniel must have arrived in America before or in 1849. According to descendants, Daniel's brother John mined in the area also, but left California for Virginia, where court evidence suggests he lived on land his brother Daniel purchased. In the 1870 census, a John Boland, age recorded as 29, was enumerated very near to Daniel, the only time he is found in California.[3]

1. James J. Sinnott, *"Over North" in Sierra County* (Fresno, Calif.: Mid-Cal Publishers, 1982), 69.
2. California Tenth District Court, minutes, vol. A, p. 75.
3. Daniel Boland household (dwelling 809) and several doors away, John Boland, age 29 (dwelling 811), 1870 Census, Sierra County, Calif., p. 59. John died, according to descendants, 29 May 1909 in Virginia, at age 73, so would have been 34 in this census, but that discrepancy may not be entirely unusual.

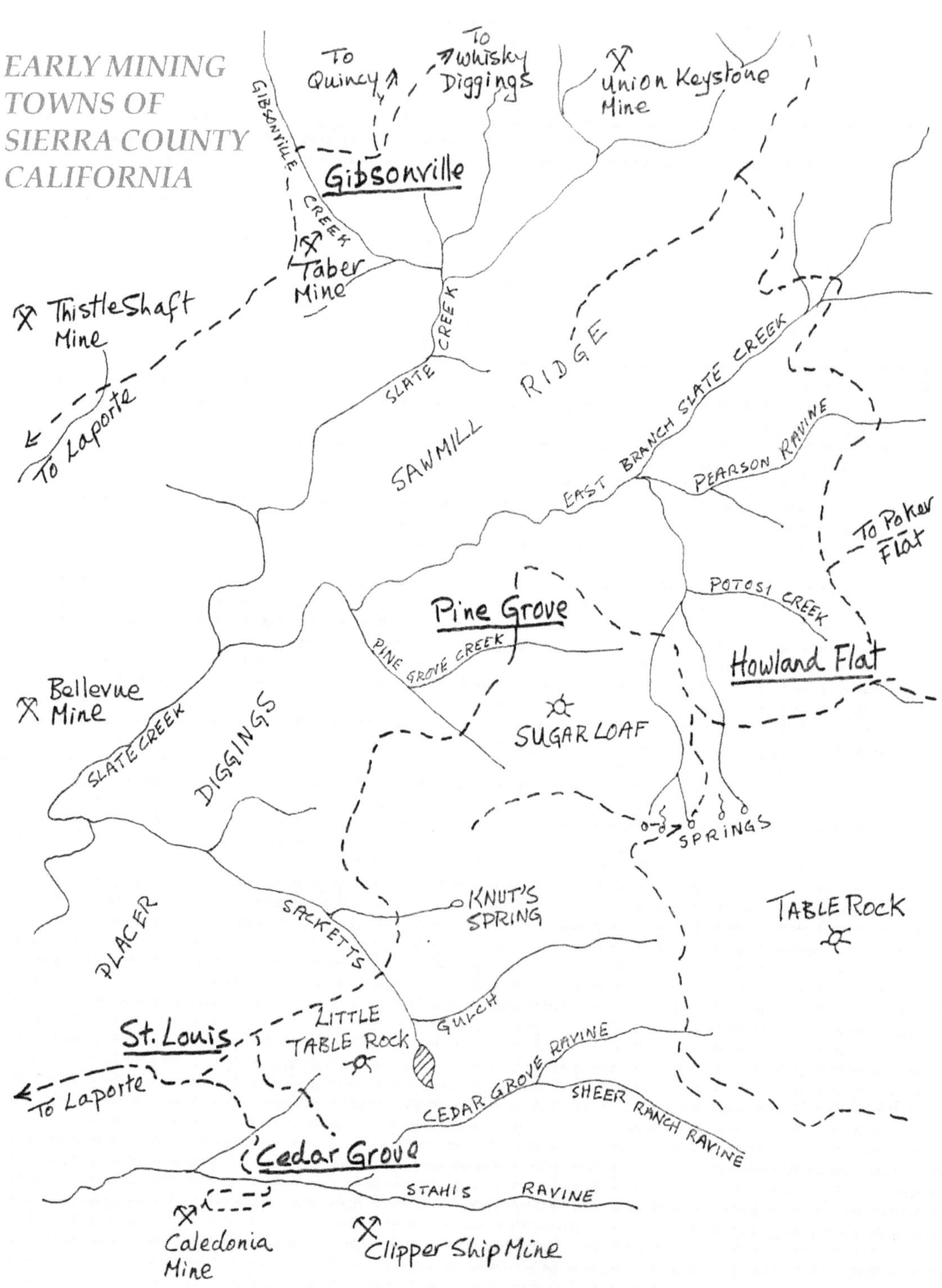

Early Mining Towns of Sierra County, California
Drawn by Bill O'Neil

Daniel Boland the elder died intestate in August of 1877. A descendant of Daniel's brother John provided details of an interesting lawsuit filed in Virginia against Daniel's estate, encompassing the years 1879-1883.[4] It reveals that in 1871, Daniel Boland traveled east and on April 8th purchased 271 acres in Albemarle County, Virginia. His brother John subsequently lived on this property, but the title to this land, according to the lawsuit, was never clear. Daniel meanwhile returned to California and according to the suit, ran a grocery business in Poker Flat, which he stocked with goods purchased from J. M. Pike & Company in San Francisco.

Following Daniel's death, his wife, Ellen, was named administratrix. She filed an inventory and appraisal in Downieville that listed $1,600 in assets and $2,041 in debts.[5] One of the creditors was J. M. Pike, whom Daniel owed $734. Pike went after Daniel's Virginia property to collect on this debt and won. John and his family were evicted, and the Albemarle County land was sold at auction in 1883 to pay this and other debts. From this suit it is also learned, among other things, that Daniel was indeed the brother of John and that Daniel's widow, Ellen, had by then remarried and was called "Ellen Boland McKern" [sic]. In the 1880 census, Daniel McKeever and wife "Helen" were enumerated in Poker Flat with an infant daughter Mary and two Boland daughters, Annie and Helen.[6]

The lawsuit in Virginia was not the end of the Boland estate's woes. Ellen was forced to sell their California property, including several mining claims, to pay the debts. A small procedural omission in the sale of some mining property rendered that sale void at a subsequent transfer. This decision was appealed, and the case ultimately worked its way to the California Supreme Court, where the decision was reversed. "Estate of Boland" has been cited a number of times over the years following, usually in conjunction with unrealized value of mining interests, and has since worked its way into the codes and statutes of California.[7]

Virginia descendants of John Boland knew nothing of a brother Daniel, only of a brother named James. The story passed down in their family was that John, his brother James, and an unrelated third man came from Ireland to dig for gold in California. Later they returned to the East and settled in Albemarle County, Virginia, where John bought land, and John and James started a dairy business. James then returned to Ireland, and John was forced to sell his land in order to provide James with his share of their investment.[8] If true, it seems that

---

4. Information from the state archives in Richmond obtained from Brenda Clark of Chesapeake, Virginia.
5. "In the Matter of the Estate of Daniel Boland deceased," in *The Pacific Coast Law Journal: Containing All the Decisions of the Southern Circuit and Southern District Courts for the District of California, and of the United States Supreme Court and Higher Courts of Other States,* ? vols. (San Francisco: W. T. Baggett & Co., 1880), 5: 708-713 (case no. 6700, filed 21 July 1880).
6. Daniel McKeever household, 1880 Census, Sierra co., Calif., Poker Flat Twp., E.D. 111, p. 22, dwelling and family 77. Daniel's older daughter Catherine ("Kate") by his first wife Margaret was enumerated in nearby Newark Twp. with her husband, also Daniel Boland, a "huckster." The widow Ellen actually married twice more: Daniel McKeever—by whom she had daughters Mary in 1879 and Margaret in 1882—and Malcolm McFarlane in 1884, by whom she had four more children. Daniel McKeever died in 1882 and was buried in the Catholic section of Howland Flat Cemetery. See Records of Howland Flat Catholic Cemetery in Nona Parkin Collection at the FHC in Reno: "Sierra Co., Cemetery, Census & Death Records" (FHL film #1,598,445, item 7); and Sierra County Marriage Records (FHL film #1,293,669, items 5 and 7).
7. See "In the Matter of the Estate of Daniel Boland, Deceased," prev. cited.
8. Information passed down in the family of Brenda Clark of Chesapeake, Virginia, communicated to CGS, June 2009.

in this instance the old genealogical adage held true: there actually were three brothers who came to America from the old country to seek their fortune.

Genealogical Descendancy

1. **Daniel[1] Boland** was born in Ireland about 1829 of unknown parentage. He died of consumption (tuberculosis) in San Francisco, California, 25 August 1877, and was buried in St. Joseph's Catholic Cemetery, Marysville, Yuba County.[9] Daniel married first, about 1852, **Margaret _?_**, born in Ireland about 1828, died in California, 1870-1875.[10] Daniel married second, about 1875, **Ellen/Helen Keating**, born 1854 in New Jersey.[11]

In addition to the census and the Virginia court records, a few tax records were found for Daniel in Sierra County. In 1862 he paid a liquor tax of $4.17, and in 1863, he appeared on the Internal Revenue Service Tax Assessment List: Poker Flat retail dealer $6.67; retail liquor $18.33.[12] The 1870 census records his occupation as miner, but the Virginia court records show he was (perhaps in addition) operating a retail store in Poker Flat.

By his first wife, Margaret, Daniel had two daughters:

i. Mary Ann[2] Boland, b. about 1853 in California, d. probably between July 1870, when she was counted in the census of Poker Flat, and August 1877, when her father died. She was not named in the lawsuits over his estate.

2 ii. Catherine Margaret Frances "Kate" Boland, b. 25 Sep. 1855, m. a widower with the same name as her father, Daniel Boland.

By his second wife, Ellen, Daniel became the father of two more daughters:

3 iii. Anne Boland, b. 1876, m. Francis M. Spencer.

4 iv. Ellen Boland, b. 1877, m. Herbert Felix Hail.

Generation 2

2. Catherine Margaret Frances[2] "Kate" Boland (*Daniel[1]*) was born 25 September 1855 in Poker Flat, Sierra County, California. Kate died in Reno, Washoe County, Nevada, 20 February 1933, and was buried in Gibsonville Cemetery, Sierra County.[13] She married first, 14 November 1875, in Sierra County, **Daniel Boland**, born about 1838 in Ireland, died 13 May 1891, in Whiskey Diggings, Sierra County.[14] He should not be confused with Kate's father,

---

9. Burial records of St. Joseph Catholic Cemetery in Marysville, compiled by Kathy Sedler and posted at the former YubaRoots Genealogy & History website. This has since moved to http://www.yubaroots.com but the cemetery records have not yet been re-posted.
10. Margaret died after 1870, when she appeared in the census, and before about 1875, when Daniel remarried; Daniel Boland household, 1870 census, Sierra Co., prev. cited.
11. Sierra County marriage records do not list this union, but the death record of their first child, Annie Boland Durbin, who died in Sacramento Co., 29 June 1951, establish her parentage. Ellen's relationship to Daniel is also established in the administration of his estate.
12. Tax records viewed at Sierra County courthouse in Downieville, 2009.
13. Kate Boland obituaries: *Nevada State Journal,* 21 Feb. 1933, p. 3, col. 2, and p. 8, col. 4, and 23 Feb., p. 6, col. 3; also, *Reno Evening Gazette,* 21 Feb. 1933, p. 10, col. 4.
14. Original marriage certificate in Ted Judge archives at CGS; Daniel's death was found in a "Days of Old" column (*Plumas National-Bulletin,* 25 May 1916) culled from the *Plumas National* of 16 May 1891.

Catherine Margaret Frances "Kate" Boland, undated
From Ted Judge archives

Stagecoach, typical of those used in this area
Courtesy of Patricia Smith

who bore the same name and was also an immigrant. His relationship to the family has not been determined. Kate married second, in 1892, possibly in Washington, D.C., **Timothy Thaddeus Judge.**[15] For more about Timothy and their children, see the Judge chapter.

Kate was known as the "First Lady of Poker Flat" by virtue of being the first baby born there. According to her obituaries, on the day she was born, all the businesses in town closed to celebrate. One in particular provided insight into her childhood:

> *...A few years after her birth the family moved to San Francisco where she attended St. Francis convent, which was located on the site where the St. Francis Hotel now stands.*[16]

While the 1860 and 1870 census records for Kate's parents suggest they lived in Sierra County continuously, they obviously spent time in San Francisco, at least in the late 1850s when Kate was young.[17] Miners often removed to the city during the winters.

Kate and her first husband, Daniel Boland, had eight identified children:[18]

---

15. That they were married in Washington, D.C. was stated in one of Kate's obituaries. This is curious and is still being explored. It is even more odd since the lawsuit over her father's land in Virginia had been settled more than ten years previously, and the land itself was sold in 1883.
16. *Nevada State Journal*, 21 Feb. 1933, p. 3, col. 2.
17. Daniel Boland household, 1860 Census, Sierra Co., Calif., Poker Flat Twp., post office Table Rock, dwelling 935, family 885, p. 54; Daniel Boland household, 1870 census, Sierra Co., prev. cited.
18. Dates and places of birth of the first seven children listed above were recorded at the same time, followed by birth date of eighth child, Michael, in a ledger of Sierra County births and delayed births at the Sierra County Recorder's Office, Downieville, prev. cited.

i. Daniel^3 Boland, b. 3 Sept. 1876 in Whiskey Diggings, Sierra Co., Calif., d. 2 June 1939 in Reno, Washoe Co., Nevada. This Daniel was a stagecoach driver and a "character." He died as a result of the auto accident which killed his brother-in-law, John Wilson (below).[19] He never married.

ii. Maria Esther Boland, b. on 21 April 1878 in Whiskey Diggings, d. bef. 1900.[20]

iii. Sarah "Sadie" Boland, b. 8 May 1879 in Whiskey Diggings, d. after 1933, when she was mentioned in her mother's obituary. About 1903 she m. John E. Wilson, b. 1873 in Calif.[21] They resided in Quincy, Plumas Co. and later moved to Reno, Washoe Co., Nev. John d. 6 June 1939 of a heart attack while driving near Quartz Point, causing him to lose control of the car.[22] There were no children.

iv. Robert Emmett Boland, b. 29 Nov. 1880 in Whiskey Diggings; d. bef. 1900.

v. William Patrick Boland, b. 24 April 1882 in Whiskey Diggings; mentioned in his mother's obituary, thus d. after 1933.

5 vi. Patrick Joseph Boland, b. 17 Mar. 1884, m. Christina Annie Patterson.

vii. Elizabeth Frances Boland, b. 4 Aug. 1886 in Whiskey Diggings, d. in Oroville, Butte Co., Calif., 1 Jan. 1978.[23] She never married.

viii. Michael Joseph Boland, b. 16 Mar. 1888 in Sierra Co., Calif., d. before 1900.

Kate's children by her second husband, Timothy Judge, appear in the chapter on the Judge family.

3. Anne^2 Boland (*Daniel^1*) was born 22 February 1876 in Poker Flat, Sierra County, and died in Sacramento, 29 June 1951.[24] Anne married first, in Gibsonville, 29 June 1898, **Francis M. Spencer,** born in May 1865 in Canada.[25] Francis died 31 March 1901 and was buried in the Gibsonville Cemetery.[26] Anne next married **William G. Durbin**, born 3 December 1870 in West Virginia, died 31 October 1936 in Sacramento. William was a Forest Service official for thirty years.[27]

Francis and Anne Spencer had one child:

i. Margaret Frances^3 Spencer, b. 4 May 1898 in Calif., d. 25 Nov. 1991 in San Francisco, Calif. She did not marry.

---

19. Death and and cause of death from records and obituary in Parkin, "Sierra Co., Cemetery, Census & Death Records."
20. In the 1900 census, Kate Judge declared she had born eleven children, seven of whom were living. At this point she and her second husband, Tim Judge, had three children, and what appear to be five Boland children can be found in the census, scattered about the Sierra foothills. Despite the fact that she had forgotten to count a child, it is concluded that Maria, Robert and Michael died young.
21. John E. Wilson household, 1920 Census, Plumas Co., Calif., town of Quincy, E.D. 93, sheet 1B, dwelling 27, family 28; John E. Wilson household, 1930 Census, Washoe County, Nevada, Reno Twp., E.D.16-28, dwelling 82, family 88, sh. 3B. The obituary of Daniel names John Wilson as brother-in-law.
22. Death and abstracted obituary in Parkin, "Sierra Co., Cemetery, Census & Death Records."
23. CDA; Obituary, *Oroville Mercury*, 4 Jan. 1978 p. 4, col. 1.
24. Birth and death from CDA.
25. Sierra County Marriage Records, bk. 3, p. 70 (FHL film #1,293,669, item 7).
26. Lee Adams, comp., *Sierra County Pioneer Cemetery Historic Survey*, orig. pub. 1997, prev. cited.
27. Obituary of W. G. Durbin, *Surprise Valley Record* (Cedarville, Modoc County), 5 Nov. 1936; California Death Index, 1930-1939, at www.vitalsearch-ca.com.

4. Ellen[2] Boland (*Daniel*[1]) was born 19 August 1877 in Poker Flat, Sierra County, and died in San Francisco, 26 July 1965.[28] In 1903 she married **Herbert Felix Hail**, born 4 February 1881, in Greenville, Plumas County, died in San Francisco, 11 April 1943.[29]

Herbert's father was editor and publisher of the *Greenville Bulletin* and the *Plumas National Bulletin,* where Herbert trained as a printer and linotype operator. Herbert later worked for the *San Francisco Bulletin* and joined his two brothers-in-law in the import-export business.

Ellen and Herbert had the following children:

i. An unnamed child who died on 9 June 1906 in Plumas Co., Calif., probably at birth.[30]

6 ii. Leonard Keating[3] Hail, b. 6 Sep. 1907, m. Esther Pyrenian and Helen _?_.

iii. Stella Margaret Hail, b. 14 Mar. 1910 in Plumas Co., d. in San Francisco, unmarried, 10 Oct. 1982.[31]

iv. Ruth Leora Hail, b 13 July 1918 in San Francisco, d. June 1978 in Pasadena, Los Angeles Co.[32] Ruth m. bef. 15 April 1943, Sims Hamilton, b. 9 Sep. 1917, d. June 1978, Pasadena.[33]

Generation 3

5. Patrick Joseph[3] Boland (*Catherine*[2], *Daniel*[1]) was born 17 March 1884 in Whiskey Diggings, Sierra County, and died of the Spanish Flu in La Porte, Plumas County, 3 December 1918.[34] On 28 July 1915, Patrick married **Christina Annie Patterson**, born 25 February 1893 in California, died in San Francisco, California, on 18 March 1958.[35]

They had one child, Donald Walter Boland, born 8 October 1916 in Plumas County, died in Santa Clara, Santa Clara County, 12 August 1997.[36]

6. Leonard Keating[3] Hail, Sr. (*Ellen*[2]*Boland, Daniel*[1]) was born 6 September 1907 in San Francisco, and died in Marietta, Cobb County, Georgia, 2 May 2000.[37] Leonard married first**, Esther Pyrenian**, born 26 August 1911 in Ismit, Turkey, died 28 August 1968 in San Francisco.[38] He married second, **Helen _?_**, born 14 November 1906, died 6 May 1995, also in Marietta.[39]

Leonard graduated from Lowell High School in December 1924 and the University of California, Berkeley, in 1929. He worked for forty-three years in San Francisco as a bonding

28. Sierra County Delayed Births 1941-1966, p. 270 (FHL film #1,293,669, item 2); CDA.
29. Birth and death from CDA; obituary, *Feather River Bulletin* (Quincy, Plumas Co.), 15 April 1943, p. 2, col. 2. Information on Hail ancestry is archived at CGS.
30. California Birth Index.
31. Birth from California Birth Index; birth and death from CDA.
32. California Birth Index; birth and death from SSDI.
33. Her married name is mentioned in her father's obituary; his birth and death from SSDI.
34. Sierra County Birth Records, 1857-1905; California Death Index, 1905-1929; *Plumas National* (Quincy, Plumas Co.), 12 Dec. 1919, p. 4.
35. Birth and death from CDA; marriage from *Plumas National*, 29 July 1915, p. 1.
36. Birth from California Birth Index; birth and death from SSDI.
37. Birth and death from SSDI.
38. Birth from passenger list of the *Rialto*, arr. 3 Oct. 1932 in San Francisco from Marseilles, from Ancestry.com online database, "California Passenger and Crew Lists, 1893-1957;" death from CDA.
39. Birth and death from SSDI.

underwriter. He was a Civil War buff and belonged to the Atlanta Civil War Round Table. He spent his later years in Georgia, but is interred at Mt. Tamalpais Cemetery in San Rafael, Marin County, California.[40] [Living children, names withheld]

40. Obituary, *San Francisco Examiner*, 14 May 2000, sec. C, p. 12.

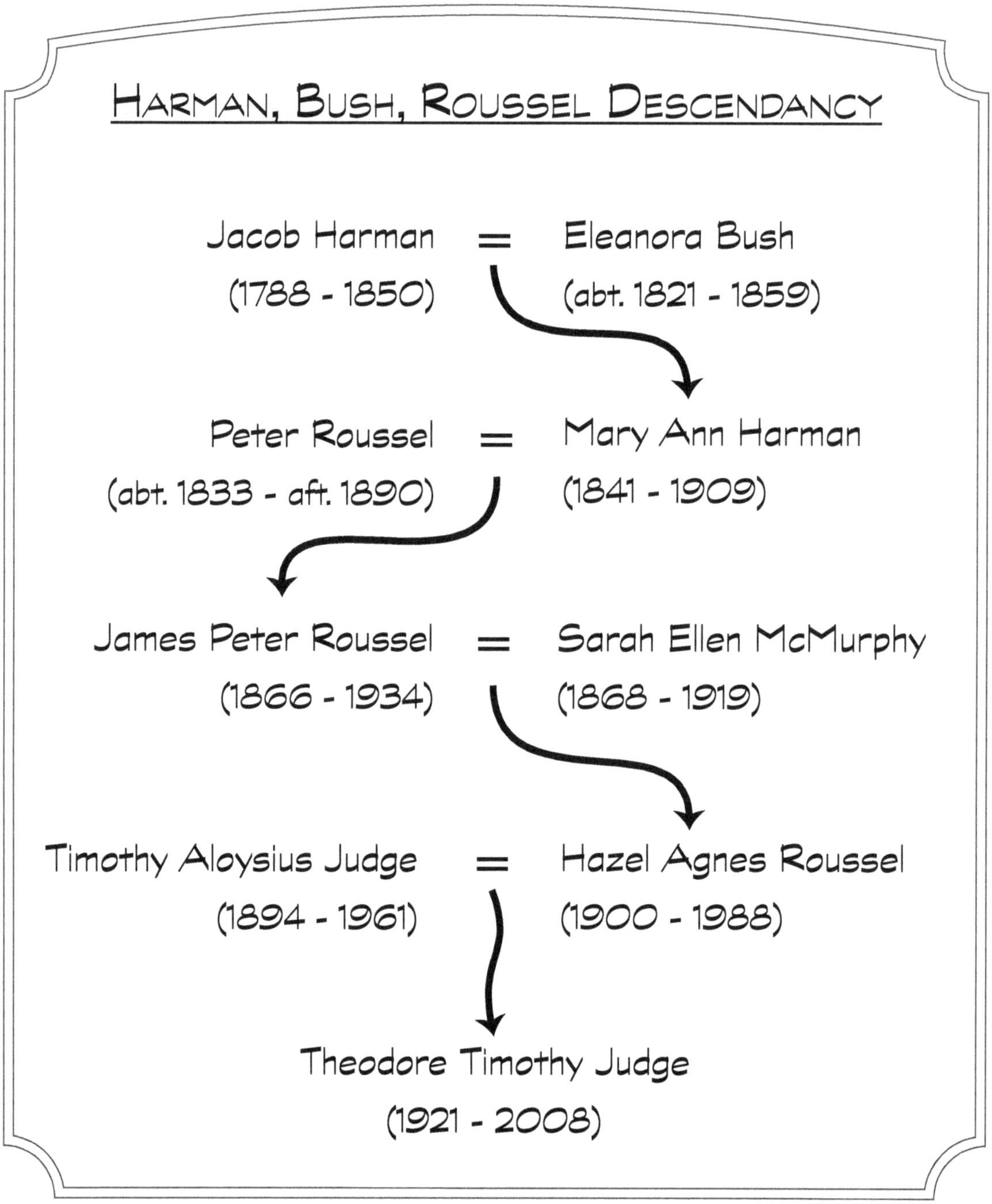

Harman, Bush, Roussel Descendancy

Jacob Harman = Eleanora Bush
(1788 - 1850) (abt. 1821 - 1859)

Peter Roussel = Mary Ann Harman
(abt. 1833 - aft. 1890) (1841 - 1909)

James Peter Roussel = Sarah Ellen McMurphy
(1866 - 1934) (1868 - 1919)

Timothy Aloysius Judge = Hazel Agnes Roussel
(1894 - 1961) (1900 - 1988)

Theodore Timothy Judge
(1921 - 2008)

Descendancy of Jacob Harman to Ted Judge

❧ Descendants of Eleanora (Bush) Harman Foley Woods Holmes

Jacob Harman and Eleanora Bush, the great-great grandparents of Ted Judge, were among the first families to respond to the government's call for Americans willing to settle in California. In 1846, with their young daughter Mary Ann and infant son Jacob, Jr., they made their way west from Missouri, traveling in a massive exodus of more than 500 wagons, over 200 bound for California. With what particular party they traveled has not been determined.[1] After reaching and crossing the Sierra Nevada mountains, they made their way to Yerba Buena (San Francisco), then a sleepy village of at the most 500, less than half of whom were Americans.[2] The trip must have been comparatively uneventful, for had it been otherwise, and had they chosen to join their Donner, Reed and Breen travelling companions who opted to take the Hastings cut-off, someone would have written about the family, and we would know every last detail, including the dinner menu.

In Yerba Buena, Jacob found a piece of land that was to his liking, near the mission and a couple of miles south of town. There he set about building a house and fencing in his forty-plus acres for farming. Even before the *California Star* reported in February 1847 that the Donner party was trapped in the snow on the far side of the Sierra Nevada mountains, Jacob had filed a preemption claim:

> *To the Hon George Hyde, alcalde or Chief Magistrate of San Francisco and Yerba Buena*
>
> *Sir*
>
> *The undersigned, a citizen of the District of San Francisco desiring to settle himself in the country and finding it necessary that he should have some place on which to settle he has taken possession of a lot of land East of the Mission Dolores, which is bounded as follows on the North by Hepp— [likely Hoeppener] Land Ranch or farm, on the South and East by a willow swamp and on the west by Garden Leiderdorff [likely estate of Wm. Alexander Leidesdorff].*

1. For background on the 1846 exodus and Polk's "Manifest Destiny," see Bernard DeVoto, *The Year of Decision 1846* (New York: Truman Talley Books, 2000), reprint of original 1942 publication by Little, Brown & Co. Figures on the number of emigrants are from Dale Lowell Morgan, *Overland in 1846: Diaries and Letters from the California-Oregon Trail,* 2 vols. (Lincoln, Neb.: Univ. of Nebraska Press, 1963), 1: 67, 116. Many diaries and letters have survived from these emigrants, but none that mention Jacob Harman have been found.
2. For historical background on Yerba Buena, see http://www.sfmuseum.org/hist1/early.html and related links.

On the above described tract of land I am improving and still intend to improve claiming all preferences that law may now or hereafter afford to the first occupant of public lands the amount of my claim is one quarter section

Yerba Buena *Jacob Harman*
Jany. 8. 1847.

a true copy of the original claim Recorded Feby 4 A.D. 1850 at 11 am [3]

The Harman Tract, as it came to be called, was located slightly north of Mission Dolores, bounded today by Duboce, Mission, Guerrero and Sixteenth Street, more or less. Jacob built a substantial house and out buildings, cultivated a garden and built up a dairy business consisting of 50-100 head of stock. He left the upper part of his land undeveloped and from it sold his excess wood. Between his farm and San Francisco lay "a barren waste of sand dunes covered with scrub oak." The trail to town was too difficult for wagon travel and had to be negotiated on horseback.[4]

Eleanora was over thirty years younger than Jacob, and their marriage evidently was not made in heaven. She filed for and was awarded a divorce in October of 1849. A division of property was ordered, but before it could be finalized, Jacob appealed the decision to the California Supreme Court on the basis that under Mexican law, then still in place, a Catholic marriage could not be dissolved in civil proceedings. In November of 1850, before the case could be adjudicated, he died. His will provided that of his half of the property, which was becoming increasingly valuable, two-thirds was to go to his son Jacob and one-third to his daughter Mary Ann. Eleanora, in November 1850, almost immediately following Jacob's death, married Michael Foley.[5] The land was ordered to auction, and as the highest bidder, Eleanora bought it back. Eleanora and Michael Foley continued to deal in real estate and finance mortgages, so that by the time Michael died, in November 1853, Eleanora for all intents and purposes was a wealthy woman.[6]

The original Harman claim had taken place during a period when title to land purchased under Mexican law was still being argued in the courts. Clear title to all pre-statehood claims, in fact, did not begin to be affirmed until 1864. In 1853, Eleanora agreed to sell the land at a future date and until then, for $6,000, the Foleys assigned the lease to a tenant and removed to other property. This deed, it turned out, was defective because it lacked the properly notarized certificate of acknowledgment of a married woman with respect to her separate property.[7] The legitimacy of the original claim itself, moreover, was questioned because of

3. San Francisco Miscellaneous Documents, 1847-1851, p. 161 in vol. 2 or 3 vols. archived at San Francisco History Center, San Francisco Public Library (WPA Inventory, group 392). William Leidesdorff sold land "in front of the mission" to Jose Andrada, 6 May 1846, and was granted land by the alcalde "on the south side of Mission Road" in January 1847 (see Alfred Wheeler, *San Francisco Land Titles 1852*, Alta Calif. Steam Printing, 1852). Jacob Harman evidently was of the impression that his claim contained 160 acres of land, while in reality it contained about 48 acres. Its real acreage, the physical description of the land and his development of it are taken from "The Harmon Title," the *San Francisco Bulletin,* 15 April 1874, p. 3, col. 5.
4. "The Harmon Title" *San Francisco Bulletin,* 15 April 1874.
5. Most court cases citing Harman v. Harman, provide a marriage date of 20 November. No other record was found.
6. Foley to Dennison and Wells and Foley to Wells, 28 March 1851 in San Francisco deeds, 5:103-104 and 73-74, Family History Library (FHL) film #974869; Foley to Schell (mortgage), 28 April 1851, San Francisco deeds, 2:537 (FHL film #966,131).
7. See in particular, Ewald v. Corbett, July 1867, in Charles A. Tuttle, *Report of Cases Determined in the Supreme Court of the State of California* (San Francisco: Bancroft-Whitney Co., 1906), v. 32, pp. 493, and McLeran v. Benton, April 1872,

161

Preemption Claim
of
Jacob Harman } To the Hon George Hyde alcalde or Chief Magistrate of San Francisco and Yerba Buena
Sir

The undersigned a citizen of the District of San Francisco desiring to settle himself in the Country and finding it necessary that he should have some place in which to settle he has taken possession of a lot of land East of the Mission Dolores, which bounded as follows, on the North by Heppings Land Ranch or farm, On the South and East by a Willow Swamp and on the west by Garara Leidsdorff

On the above described tract of land I am improving and still intend to improve, Claiming all preferences that law may now or hereafter afford to the first occupant of public land, the amount of my claim is one quarter section

Yerba Buena Jacob Harman
Jany 8. 1847.

a true Copy of the original claim
Recorded Feby 4 AD 1850 at 11 AM

And Reynolds
Recorder Clk

Preemption Claim of Jacob Harman, San Francisco, 8 January 1847.
It is unclear if this claim was ever granted, or even recorded at the time it was made. It does appear, however, as having been recopied in February 1850, on p. 161 in volume 2 of a three-volume series of miscellaneous documents in storage at the San Francisco Public Library History Center. (W.P.A. 1940 Survey No. 392)

San Francisco, 1847
From Frank Soule, *The Annals of San Francisco,* Appleton & Company, 1855

its nearness to the Mission, which subjected it to a restrictive ordinance. Possibly unaware that the title was clouded, Eleanora sold the property, which sale initiated a string of lawsuits that continued for decades. The legal summaries of these lawsuits, along with accompanying newspaper coverage, provide the only clear record of the twisted history of this small family of four.[8]

Michael Foley died, most likely in San Francisco, in November 1853, and Eleanora again married, in August 1854, Thomas Wood(s) , whom she divorced in 1857. Several years later, in October 1859, Eleanora's unmarried son Jacob died, leaving his mother as heir. Less than a month later, Eleanora married yet again, James Holmes, a marriage that was to last only two weeks until Eleanora herself died. That left daughter Mary Ann (by then Mary Ann Harman Harris Roussel) the sole remaining original owner of Harman property. Her story, which is recounted in the following pages, is equally compelling.

Genealogical Descendancy

1. **Eleanora[1] Bush** was born in Germany about 1821.[9] She died in Santa Clara, California, 17 November 1859, and was buried in Mission Santa Clara de Assís cemetery, 19 November

v. 43, pp. 467.

8. In addition to the above citations, a concise summary appeared in *The Pacific Reporter,* vol. 14, pp. 879-881. McLeran v. Benton was ultimately appealed all the way to the U.S. Supreme Court but there was dismissed and certiorari denied.
9. Eleanora's birth is calculated from her age at marriage and at death, and from her recorded age in the 1852 California state census: Family of "Michl Foler," 1852 California Census, San Francisco, p. 499 (FHL film #909,232).

Mission Dolores, San Francisco, c. 1847
From Frank Soule, *The Annals of San Francisco,* Appleton & Company, 1855

1859.[10] As "Laura Busch," Eleanora married in Madison County, Illinois, 7 March 1841, a very much older man, **Jacob Harman**, born in France or Germany about 1788.[11] Jacob died in San Francisco in a cholera epidemic, 3 November 1850, and was buried on his farm near Mission Dolores.[12]

On 20 November 1850, shortly after Jacob's death, Eleanora married **Michael Foley**.[13] Born in Limerick, Ireland, about 1821, he died 9 November 1853, and was buried in the cemetery at Mission Dolores in San Francisco.[14] Following Michael's death, Eleanora married again, 16 May 1854 in Santa Clara, **Thomas Wood(s)**, born in Pennsylvania, son of William Woods and Margaret McLaughlin.[15] There were no children. Eleanora sued for divorce in 1857, and won—once they tracked Thomas down.[16] Eleanora's fourth and last marriage was

10. Burial record of Elenora Woods Holmes in Mission Santa Clara records at Santa Clara University Archives.
11. Date and place of marriage from Illinois Statewide Marriage Index, 1763-1900, database at the Illinois State Archives website, www.ilsos.gov. Jacob's country of birth varies among records. The article reporting his death states France, as does the 1900 census enumeration of his daughter Mary Ann. In the 1880 census, Mary Ann reported Germany. Jacob's year of birth is estimated from his age at death, 62. Eleanora at her marriage was 19 and judging from the birthdate of daughter Mary Ann, eight months pregnant. Except for some newspaper articles, Jacob's surname usually was spelled "Harman" and has been standardized here as such.
12. "Jacob Harmann, 62, Cholera..." *Daily Alta Californian,* San Francisco, 4 Nov. 1850, p. 2, col. 3.
13. Details of Eleanora's many marriages are perhaps best recounted in McLeran v. Benton, cited above. If, as believed, he was the Michael Foley buried at Mission Dolores, his parents were Thomas Foley and Katherine Ryan, as indicated in the burial register.
14. Tombstone Mission Dolores San Francisco California; and burial record no. 5191 in Mission Dolores burial register.
15. Santa Clara County Marriage Records, Book A, p.51, Family History Library (FHL) film #1,302,022; also marriage # 3103 in marriage records of Mission Santa Clara de Assis, Archives of Santa Clara University.
16. Eleanora Woods v. Thomas Woods, 13 July 1857, Santa Clara County Superior Court, case no. 1037 (legibility poor), copies from files of Mary J. Drake of Cupertino, Calif. (CGS Archives).

to **James Holmes**, also in Santa Clara, 4 November 1859.[17] Again, there were no children. Eleanora died two weeks later, intestate.

Following Eleanora's death, James Holmes inherited one third of her estate.[18] Several lawsuits were subsequently filed involving her heirs, who were James and her two daughters, Mary Ann (Harman) Roussel and Kitty Foley.[19]

Jacob and Eleanora Harman had two children:

2 i. Mary Ann² Harman, b. 1 Apr. 1841, m. George Harris, Peter Roussel, and George Fry.

ii. Jacob Harman, b. abt. 1846, perhaps along the California Trail, but more likely in Illinois.[20] Jacob died in San Jose, 15 Oct. 1859, "in his thirteenth year" and was buried in Mission Santa Clara cemetery, 16 Oct. 1859.[21] In 1852, at age six, he was enumerated in the California State Census in the San Francisco household of his mother and stepfather, Michael Foley.

Jacob's untimely death has been the subject of many family stories and speculation: (1) that he was subject to kidnapping to persuade his mother to grant clear title to the Harman property in San Francisco; (2) that he was buried up to his neck and left to die; and (3) that he was murdered and stuffed down the well of his neighbor, James Lick. However, his Mission Santa Clara burial record does not mention a violent death, and the local papers do not mention his death at all.

Eleanora, by her second husband, Michael Foley, had two more children:

iii. Ellen Foley, born abt. 1850, assumed to have d. bef. her mother (bef. Nov. 1859).[22]

3 iv. Catherine Foley, b. 6 July 1851, m. Earl Jordan and Isaac Winters.

Generation 2

2. Mary Ann² Harman (*Eleanora¹ Bush*) was born in Illinois, likely in Madison County, 1 April 1841.[23] She died in Santa Clara, 30 June 1909, and was buried at Mission Santa Clara, 3 July 1909.[24] Mary Ann married in a civil ceremony in Santa Clara, 13 December 1857, **George Harris**, born about 1829 and died before 20 January 1859.[25] Mary Ann next married at Mission Santa Clara, 20 January 1859, **Peter Roussel**, born in Guitre, Gironde, France, 17 July 1833, son of Gervais and Maria Roussel.[26] In 1878 in Nevada, Mary Ann,

17. Marriage records of Santa Clara County, Book C, p. 296 (FHL film #1,302,023).
18. Photocopies of original actions made at Santa Clara County Courthouse by descendant Mary J. Drake of Cupertino, Calif., from files archived at CGS.
19. Cited above.
20. The 1852 California State Census, previously cited, records that he was born in and previously lived in Illinois.
21. Burial records of Mission Santa Clara, Jacobus Harman, entry no. 9023, original ledgers in Archives of Santa Clara University.
22. She was not mentioned in her mother's probate, but appeared in the 1852 state census, previously cited.
23. Date and place of birth come from her marriage record to Peter Roussel, Mission Santa Clara records, Santa Clara University Archives. A number of sources, however, record that she was born in Rock Island, Ill. Land records show that the Harmans owned land in Rock Island Co. between Dec. 1841 and Oct. 1845, dates that follow Mary Ann's birth. Rock Island Co. is likely where Mary Ann spent her early childhood.
24. California state death certificate, Mary Ann Fry; Santa Clara Catholic Cemetery burial permit and tombstone.
25. Marriage Recs. of Santa Clara Co., Bk. 1, p. 18 (FHL film #1,302,022). A Catholic marriage was recorded at Mission Santa Clara, 31 Jan. 1858 (see following). George's year of birth is from his age at marriage.
26. Marriage records from Mission Santa Clara, Santa Clara University Archives.

Mary Ann Harman with George Fry, Sr., undated
Courtesy of Mary J. Drake

following her divorce from Peter, married **George Fry, Sr.**, born in England about 1831 and died in Janesville, Lassen County, California, 25 February 1899.[27]

As a child, Mary Ann was one of the first students to attend Notre Dame School for Girls in San Jose, where as Mary Foley, or Harman, or under several other aliases, she boarded starting in 1851.[28] She was only seventeen at her marriage to George Harris, which evidently ended in less than a year with the death of her husband. There were no children.

27. Marriage: George H. Fry household, 1880 U.S. Census; Nevada, Washoe Co., Washoe Twp., E.D. 63, p. 16D, dwelling 120, family 122. George Fry's death was reported in the Burns Times Herald, 4 March 1899 (Fry file in Clair Luce History Room of Harney County, Ore., Public Library).
28. Mary Dominica McNamee, *Light in the Valley; The Story of California's College of Notre Dame* (Berkeley, Calif.: Howell-North Books, 1968), 8. At the time there was much publicity about the value placed on the Harman Tract and it seems her mother may have been afraid of kidnapping.

Two years later, Mary Ann married Peter Roussel. Following their marriage, they lived for a number of years in San Jose and then moved to American Flat, Storey County, Nevada, south of Virginia City on the Comstock Lode. In November 1867, on 7½ acres that Peter had purchased in 1865, Mary Ann filed a declaration of homestead for herself, her children and her orphaned half sister (Kitty Foley), perhaps to protect herself and her family from debtors. She listed a "dwelling house, two outhouses, one hot or glass house and fences."[29] Two years after that, Mary Ann and Peter sold the American Flat property and moved to a farm on nearby Steamboat Creek in Washoe County, east of Virginia City.[30] Soon, however, the completion of the Virginia & Truckee Railroad through Carson City reduced traffic through Steamboat and Washoe City. This led to a loss of population, which in turn caused the relocation of the county seat to Reno. For the Roussels, this created the need to move again if they were to operate any kind of business. They retained the Steamboat property but moved once again, opening what appears to have been a hostelry or tavern called 5 Mile House, located on Geiger grade (Nevada route 341), north of Virginia City.[31]

The off-again-on-again, stormy marriage of the Roussels eventually ended when Mary Ann left Peter and moved to Virginia City in 1873. She filed for divorce in Reno, 23 August 1875, citing extreme cruelty, physical abuse and failure to provide.[32] Mary Ann and her surviving children moved back to the Steamboat property, and Peter appears to have gone to Bodie in Mono County to mine. He did not die in Santa Barbara, as the children were told, but continued to carry on investments in the mining arena for several years.[33]

In 1878 in Nevada, Mary Ann married George Fry Sr., also on his third marriage. Their combined families totaled twelve children, and they had two of their own. In 1882, the Steamboat property was foreclosed upon; the Frys later sold their belongings at auction and left Nevada for southeastern Oregon and the newly surveyed town of Burns.[34] There they were able to purchase several city lots.[35]

Mary Ann appears to have been a fairly active businesswoman in Burns. She constructed and operated a livery stable and restaurant and worked as a nurse and midwife.[36] In 1893, the Frys purchased land in southwest Lassen County, California, where Mary Ann's daughter Anna and her husband, William Allen, had settled.[37] George and Mary Ann sold their remaining property in Burns and moved to Lassen County in 1895, taking with them their

29. Roux to Roussel, 15 May 1865, property in American Flat, Storey Co., Nev. (Storey Co. deeds, bk. Z, pp. 119-121. It was this land that Mary Ann Roussel declared a homestead on 20 Nov. 1867 (Storey Co. miscellaneous records series, "P of A" bk. D, pp. 171-172). The property was sold, 6 Oct. 1869 (bk. 29, p. 666-67).
30. Peter Roussel household, 1870 Census Washoe Co., Nevada, city of Washoe, dwelling 80, family 75, p. 498.
31. Storey Co. deeds, Roussel to Noce, 29 Feb 1872, unsourced deed in files of Mary J. Drake. The property description includes kitchen furniture, bar and bar fixtures.
32. Copies of Washoe County court records from files of Mary J. Drake.
33. Peter Roussel, 1880 Census Mono Co., Calif., Bodie Twp., dwelling 120, family 122, E.D. 47, p. 28D. Six deeds in Mono Co. Calif., Mining Claims bk. B: 28, 28, 30, 32, 42, and bk. Q: 436-37, filed Oct. – Dec. 1879, show Peter Roussel turning a $20 investment into $3000. In 1890 Peter was listed as a member of the Virginia City Pioneer Assn. in Charles W. Haskins, *The Argonauts of California* (New York: Fords, Howard and Hulbert, 1890), 373. His date or place of death is not known.
34. *Reno Evening Gazette,* 17 Oct 1882, p. 2, col. 6 (Martin v. Fry foreclosure); notice in same paper 24 Oct. 1882, p. 4, announcement of Sheriff's sale of 157+ acres including all tenements and appurtenances. *Reno Gazette,* 25 April 1884, p. 4, col. 4: "Auction!... 5 room house, furniture, wagon, cows, horses, etc."
35. Harney Co. deeds in files of Mary J. Drake: Crookshanks to Fry (1884 and 1890); Cahn/Kahn to Fry (1890 and 1893).
36. Business ads from *East Oregon Herald* (files of Mary J. Drake); Fry files at Harney Co. Public Library.
37. Dennings to Fry, Lassen Co. deeds (1893), bk. J, p. 493.

younger children, Earl and Pearl.[38] The Burns newspaper society columns continued to note their annual migration to visit family, now reversed.[39] George Fry died in Lassen County in 1899.[40]

In 1900, Mary Ann was enumerated as a nurse while living with her son Earl and daughter Pearl.[41] Eight years later, she sold her remaining real estate and moved to Santa Clara County to live with her daughter Anna. She died there, 30 June 1909.[42]

Mary Ann (Harman) and Peter Roussel had seven children

4 i. ANNA LOUISE[3] ROUSSEL, b. 28 May 1860, m. WILLIAM HENRY ALLEN.

5 ii. CHARLES LESLEY ROUSSEL, b. 24 Dec. 1862, m. ELMYRA _?_.

iii. LOUIS ROUSSEL, b. in Calif. (likely San Jose), 22 Dec. 1863, d.y. in Virginia City, Nev., Jan. 1869.[43] He was bur. in the Catholic Cemetery at Gold Hill, Nev.[44]

6 iv. JAMES PETER ROUSSEL, b. 17 Feb. 1866, m. SARAH ELLEN MCMURPHY.

7 v. HENRIETTA "Etta" ROUSSEL, b. 27 May 1867, m. TOM DODSON and WILLIAM CUMMINS.

vi. ANGUS HAYES ROUSSEL, b. in 1868 in Virginia City, d. in Sep. 1870.[45]

8 vii. ELINOR "Ella" HAYES ROUSSEL, b. in Apr. 1871, m. JOHN MORRELL and GEORGE FRY JR.

Mary Ann and George Fry had two children:

9 viii. PEARL GERTRUDE FRY, b. 11 Apr. 1879, m. FREDRICK H. FISK and WILLIAM HENRY KEELER.

10 ix. EARL LEROY FRY, b. 14 Apr. 1881, m. TRESSIE ANN HANKLER.

3. **CATHERINE[2] "Kitty" FOLEY** (*Eleanora[1] Bush*), second child of her mother's (second) marriage to Michael Foley, was born in San Francisco, 6 July 1851.[46] She died in Burns, Harney County, Oregon, 23 January 1915 and was buried there in Burns Cemetery.[47] Catherine married first, in 1877, **EARL JORDAN**, born abt. 1848 in Pennsylvania, died 1 July 1880 in Virginia City, Nevada .[48] Following Earl's death, she married **ISAAC WINTERS**, born about 1864 in California, died before 1910 and probably before 1906.[49]

38. Deed, M. A. and G. H. Fry to G. H. Fry Jr. (1896), Harney Co., from files of Mary J. Drake.
39. Files of Mary J. Drake.
40. George Fry death, prev. cited.
41. Mary A. Fry household, 1900 Census, Lassen Co., Calif., Twp. 2., E.D. 49, sh. 3B, dwelling 68, family 68.
42. Calif. death certificate, Mary Ann Fry, from files of Mary J. Drake. Numerous obituaries appeared in San Jose papers, including the *San Jose News,* 2 July 1909.
43. Birth calculated from his age at death shown in Storey County burial records, p. 9, Storey Co. Recorder's office, Virginia City, Nevada: Roussel, Charles L. [sic.], died 25 Jan. 1869; age 5 yr 1m 3d. (Charles Lesley Roussel actually died in 1910; this entry is clearly a mistake, yet has been copied many times).
44. The 1870 census mortality schedule, Storey Co., Nevada, at Ancestry.com.
45. Birth year estimated from 1870 Census, double enumeration: P. Rosell household, Storey Co., Nev., Gold Hill, dwelling 4, family 4, p. 78, and Peter Russell household, Washoe Co., city of Washoe, dwelling 80, family 75, p. 498. His death is from a 1926 DAR interview of Anna Allen of Tuolumne Co., copy on file at Santa Clara Co. Historical and Genealogical Soc. Library.
46. State of Oregon death certificate, Catherine Winters.
47. Birth and death from record of Katy J. Winters, Burns Cemetery records at www.findagrave.com; obituary, *Harney County News,* 30 Jan 1915 from files of Mary J. Drake.
48. Earl Gordon household, 1880 Census, Storey Co., Nev., Virginia City, E.D. 47, p. 207A, dwelling 37, family 38; death from Storey Co. coroner's records, 1879-1887, at Ancestry.com.
49. Isaac Winters household, 1900 Census, Harney Co., Ore., Burns, E.D. 161 p. 131A; Katie J. Winters household, 1910 Census, Harney Co., Ore., city of Burns, E.D 77, p. 9B, dwelling 222, family 224. Her daughter Vera's marriage in

Kitty, like her half-sister Mary Ann, attended Notre Dame School in San Jose, which likely was her home following her mother's death when Kitty was nine.[50] She was provided with a guardian to administer her inheritance until she reached the age of choice; five years later, her half sister Mary Ann Harman Roussel assumed the guardianship, and Kitty joined the Roussels in Nevada.[51]

On 24 December 1877, in Reno, Washoe County, Catherine married Earl Jordan.[52] Perhaps about 1886, Catherine married again, Isaac Winters, who appears to have died shortly after 1900. To support herself and her children, Catherine ran the Oregon Hotel in Burns and in 1910 was working as a school janitor.[53]

Catherine and her first husband, Earl Jordan, had one child, Minnie, who was born about 1879, and is thought to have died of diptheria as a young child in Washoe County, Nevada.[54]

Catherine and Isaac Winters had six children:[55]

i. Vera[3] Winters, b. in Calif., May 1887, d. in Milwaukee, Multnomah Co., Ore., 3 May 1960.[56] Vera m. first, in Harney Co., Ore., 28 May 1906, Carl Von Welker, b. Penn. abt. 1878.[57] She m. second, 9 Dec.1915, Dalton Gibbs, b. Texas, 10 Nov. 1882, d. Idaho, Jan. 1963.[58] Evidently divorced from Dalton, she married third, _?_ Jacobs.[59]

ii. Otie L. Winters, b. Burns, Ore., 1 Dec. 1889, appears to have d. bef. 1918.[60] Otie m. 10 June 1909, Harney Co., Ore., Charles Scribner, b. Ore. 5 Sep. 1885, d. aft. 1918.[61]

1906 was "at the home of her mother," suggesting her father was no longer around.

50. Entries in her mother's probate file include payments to Notre Dame School for Kitty.

51. She was doubly enumerated in 1870 Census in Virginia City, Storey Co.: once in dwelling 1, family 1, stamped p. 417; and again in dwelling 19, family 19, script p. 170.

52. "Western States Marriages" collection at Brigham Young Univ., available at http://abish.byui.edu/specialCollections/index.cfm, hereafter WMI. In the 1880 census of Virginia City he is listed as Earl Gordon, with Katy and one year old daughter Minnie, who was not found in 1900; Earl was recorded as suffering from cancer (1880 Census Storey Co., E.D. 81, p. 5, dwelling 37, family 38, p. 207A) and died shortly afterward.

53. Marcus Whitman, *An Illustrated History of Baker Grant Malheur and Harney Counties* (Chicago: Western Historical Publishing Co., 1902), 654. In the 1910 Census, Kitty (as Catherine) headed a household consisting of daughters Mamie and Isa (Harney Co., Ore., city of Burns, E.D. 77, sh. 9B, dwelling 222, family 224).

54. Earl Gordon household, 1880 Census, Storey Co., Nev., Virginia City, E.D. 17, p. 207A, dwelling 37, family 38; files of Mary J. Drake.

55. The 1900 census states 8 children 5 living, Only seven are accounted for. Catherine's obituary in the *Harney County News,* 30 Jan 1915, lists as survivors Mrs. Dalton Gibbs, Miss Mamie Winters, Mrs. Orville Stoy, all of Burns, and Mrs. Charles Scribner of Idaho (files of Mary J. Drake). Because a number of the Winters' grandchildren are still living, this line was not followed into the next generation.

56. Birth from Isaac Winters household, 1900 census, Harney Co., prev. cited; death from *Portland Oregonian*, 5 May 1960, p. 5, col. 3.

57. Vera's first marriage from WMI; Carl's information from Carl Von Welker household, 1910 Census, Harney Co., Ore., city of Burns, E.D. 77, sh. 9A, dwelling 219, family 221. Carl was recorded as a piano musician.

58. Vera's second marr. to Dalton Gibbs from Harney Co. Library, Western History Room marriage database (under "Welker"); Dalton Gibbs's birth from World War I draft registration card at Ancestry.com., death from SSDI. Dalton was noted as "single" in the 1930 Census (Washington Co., Idaho, Cambridge pct., E.D. 44-18, sh. 2A, p. 260). Their son Gerald, born in 1919 (also from Harney Co. Library), appears from the SSDI to have died in 1989 at an unidentified location. Vera, in 1960, also left Mrs. Catherine Howry of California, daughter from her first marriage.

59. The surname Jacobs is from the files of Mary J. Drake and is consistent with Vera's obituary.

60. Harney County Newspaper Birth Announcements, database available at Harney Co. Library website; her death before 1918 is implied on Charles's WWI draft reg. card on which his closest relative listed is daughter Isabelle Eleanora, who in 1920 was living in the household of her uncle, Jesse Scribner in Twin Falls Co., Idaho.

61. Harney County Newspaper Marriage Announcements, database at Harney Co. Library website; Chas. Scribner's birth from WWI draft reg. card (1918) and 1910 Census, Charlie H. Scribner household, Malheur Co., Idaho, Crowley pct.,

iii. Otis Winters, (twin of Otie) b. 1 Dec. 1889, died of a heart problem in Harney Co., Oregon, 26 Mar. 1905.[62]

iv. Mary "Mamie" Winters, b. in Harney Co., Ore, Jan. 1892, d. Multnomah Co., Ore., 27 July 1976.[63] She m. 11 Aug. 1918, William Gould, b. 11 March 1886, Kansas, d. Harney Co., 6 Feb. 1942.[64]

v. Isa/Isola Winters, b. in Harney Co., Ore., Apr. 1894.[65] Isa m. 1 Feb. 1912, Orville Stoy, b. in Chehalis, Wash., 1 Oct. 1892, d. Jan. 1971 in New Mexico. "Orval" and a son Harold were bur. in Janesville Cem., Lassen Co., Calif.[66]

vi. Unnamed infant, d. 24 May 1893.[67]

Generation 3

4. **Anna Louise[3] Roussel** (*Mary Ann[2] Harman, Eleanora[1] Bush*) was born in Santa Clara California, 28 May 1860, and died in Oakland, California, 19 November 1939.[68] She married, 15 June 1879 in Reno, Washoe County, Nevada, **William Henry Allen,** born in Illinois about 1855, and died in San Jose, California, on 21 Aug. 1920.[69]

Although born in Santa Clara County, Anna was raised for the most part in Nevada mining camps. In 1880 William and Anna were farming in Mason Valley, Nevada.[70] In 1890 and 1894, the Allens purchased government land in Lassen County, California.[71] Later they moved to Columbia, Tuolumne County, and then to San Jose.[72]

William and Anna Allen had the following children:

i. George Thomas[4] Allen, b. in Nev., 7 June 1880. He d. in Columbia, Calif., 20 Nov. 1897, several weeks after being kicked by a horse.[73]

ii. Mary Rachel Allen, b. in Nev., 20 Sep. 1881, d. in Nev., 21 Dec. 1881.

E.D. 95, sh. 3A, dwelling and family 36.

62. Otis's birth and death from death certificate and obituary in *Burns Times Herald*, both in the files of Mary J. Drake.
63. Birth and death from Oregon Death Index at Ancestry.com (hereafter, ODI).
64. Marriage from Oregon Marriage Index at Ancestry.com; William's birth from WW1 draft reg. card and death from ODI.
65. Isa's birth from Isaac Winters household, 1900 census, prev. cited; her birth and death from SSDI. Isa may have been Helen Isola Rhodes, b. 17 Apr. 1894 as Helen Isola Winters in Idaho, d. San Francisco, 4 Aug. 1951 (CDA).
66. Marriage from marriage index at Harney Co. Library; his birth from WWI draft reg. card and death from Janesville Cem. records at www.findagrave.com.
67. *East Oregon Herald*, 24 May 1893 (clipping in files of Mary J. Drake).
68. All information on this family, unless otherwise cited, is from a 1926 DAR interview of Anna Allen of Tuolumne Co., copy on file at Santa Clara Co. Historical and Genealogical Soc. Library; Anna's death confirmed in California Death Index, 1930-1939.
69. Obituary in the *San Jose Evening News*, 25 Aug. 1920, p. 10.
70. William Allen household, 1880 Census, Esmeralda Co., Nev., Mason Valley, E.D. 13, p. 26B, dwelling 214, family 225.
71. Patent database at Bureau of Land Management, General Land Office website, http://www.glorecords.blm.gov/.
72. William Allen households, 1900 Census (Tuolumne Co., Twp. 2, E.D. 125, sh. 8A, p. 33) and 1920 Census (Santa Clara Co., Calif., San Jose Twp., E.D. 168, sh. 4A, dwelling 95, family 100, p. 174.) Over these years, William was a teamster.
73. The *Union Democrat* (Sonora Calif.), quoted at www.findagrave.com.

Anna (Roussel) Allen photo
Courtesy of Mary J. Drake

iii. FLORENCE HENRIETTA ALLEN, b. in Nev., 30 July 1883, d. in Alameda Co., 25 Jan. 1933.[74] Florence m. 28 Oct. 1913, WILLIAM E. HART, a painter, b. Texas abt. 1884.[75] By 1930 they had moved to Ventura, Calif. No known ch.

11 iv. WILLIAM IVY ALLEN, b. 6 Dec. 1885, m. MARY CHEATAM.

v. LESLIE ROUSSEL ALLEN, b. 26 May 1888; m. 2 June 1917, ANNE JEAN LEWARNE, b. abt. 1893.[76] In the 1930 census, Leslie, recorded as married but without Anne Jean, was living in Georgia and working at a cannery.[77]

12 vi. ZELLA PEARL ALLEN, b. 29 Sep. 1890, m. JOHN P. MCGRATH.

vii. ELMER EDMOND ALLEN, b. in Calif., 21 Oct. 1897, d. in Luane Valley, San Bernardino Co., Apr. 1969.[78] He m. 13 Sep. 1913, FLORENCE BASTIN (or BASTAIN), b. in Calif., 12 Nov. 1897, d. as Florence Muhm, 5 Mar. 1984.[79] They were div. bef. 1930, at which time he was a building contractor.[80]

74. California Death Index, 1930-1939.
75. William E. Hart household, 1930 Census, Calif., Ventura Co., city of Ventura, E.D. 56-21, sh. 7A, dwelling 106, family 112, p. 31.
76. In 1918, on his WWI draft registration card, Leslie was married and farming in Highland Springs, Lake Co., Calif; he stated he was born in Susanville, 26 May 1888.
77. Leslie Allen, 1930 Census, Georgia, Jones Co., Militia Distr. 300, E.D. 85-3, sh. 3B, p. 605.
78. Abstracts of California deaths, 1940-2000, database at www.vitalsearch-ca.com (hereafter, CDA).
79. *Ibid.*
80. Anna L. Allen household, 1930 Census, Calif., Santa Clara Co., Redwood Twp., town of Los Gatos, E.D. 43-30, sh.

viii. Eveleen Anna Allen, b. 28 Jan. 1904 in Calif., d. in Punta Gorda, Charlotte Co., Fla., 2 Feb. 1985.[81] Eveleen married, abt. 1929, John B Minshall, b. in Wisc., 19 Apr. 1904, d. Santa Clara, Calif., 27 Apr. 1976.[82]

Eveleen graduated from San Jose State College, earned an M.A. from Columbia University in New York, and took graduate courses at Stanford. She taught at schools in Tuolumne County (California) and served as both teacher and headmistress at Jefferson and College Park schools in San Jose. John operated a sporting goods store in San Jose.[83] John and Eveleen had no children.

5. **Charles Lesley[3] Russell/Roussel** (*Mary Ann[2] Harman, Eleanora[1] Bush*) was born in San Jose, California, 24 Dec. 1862, and died 4 October 1910 in Harney County, Oregon.[84] Charles Lesley married about 1892, **Elmira _?_** , born in Oregon in October 1868.[85] He is listed as the co-owner of the stables in Burns in an ad that appeared in the *East Oregon Herald,* 8 Aug. 1889.[86]

Charles and Elmyra Roussel had one child:

i. Tressie B.[4] Russell, b. in Washington, Mar. 1897.[87]

6. **James Peter[3] Roussel** (*Mary Ann[2] Harman, Eleanora[1] Bush*) was born in California, 17 February 1866, and was baptized at Mission Dolores in San Francisco, 4 March 1866.[88] James died in Lassen County, 23 November 1934, and was buried in Susanville Cemetery.[89] He married in Burns, Harney County, Oregon, 16 August 1889, **Sarah Ellen McMurphy.**[90] Sarah Ellen was born in Lassen County, California, 17 November 1868.[91] She died there, 3 September 1919, and was buried in Susanville Cemetery.[92]

These dry statistics hardly do justice to one of the more colorful figures in Lassen County history. Jim was only nine when his mother, Mary Ann, divorced his father, Peter Roussel. With her third husband, George Fry, and their combined families in tow, including her six still unmarried children, they moved to Burns, Oregon, where Mary Ann pursued a number of business interests.

When James married Sarah McMurphy in 1889, he was already a dashing figure. He had been a stage coach driver between Burns, where he lived, and Pendleton, Umatilla County,

7A, dwelling 214, family 218, p. 239.

81. Florida Death Index, 1887-1998, database at Ancestry.com.
82. Birth and death from abstracts of California deaths, 1940-2000, at www.vitalsearch-ca.com (hereafter CDA).
83. Obituary, *San Jose Mercury News,* 27 Feb. 1985.
84. Death index at Harney Co. Library website.
85. Charles L. Russell household, 1900 Census, Ore., Umatilla Co., E.D. 113, sh. 14A, dwelling 285, family 286, p. 103. Elmyra likely was Almyra/Elmira Dickerson, b. Oct. 1866 in Umatilla Co., Ore., d. 28 Apr. 1918, the dau. of Terisha and Clarissa Dickerson (see 1870 Census, Umatilla Co., Ore., Walla Walla pct., p. 4; and 1880 Census, Milton pct., E.D. 110, p. 11A, family 205). Information posted at Ancestry.com seems to support this, but it has not been pursued.
86. Files of Mary J. Drake.
87. *Ibid*; see also 1900 Census, Umatilla Co., Ore., Valley pct., E.D. 133, sh. 103, dwelling 285, family 286.
88. Baptismal entry, Mission Dolores original ledger, film at Catholic Archives at Menlo Park, Calif.
89. Death certificate, James Rossell [sic] in files of Mary J. Drake; bur. Susanville Cem., Lassen Co. Calif., "James Russell" on headstone.
90. Marriage certificate, Harney Co., Ore., files of Mary J. Drake.
91. Death certificate, Mrs. Sara Ellen Raussel [sic], files of Mary J. Drake.
92. *Ibid.*

Sarah (McMurphy) Roussel and daughters
Courtesy of Mary J. Drake

Oregon.[93] A thin man with a handlebar moustache, he sported a tall felt hat and a red kerchief and carried a pair of pearl-handled pistols.[94] Known as "Juniper Jim," he gave the impression of being a tough gunman, but at the same time was a story teller and musician—accordion, piano, and fiddle—and a talented blacksmith as well.[95] He embellished his own reputation as an impulsive gunslinger with wild tales of adventures in Oregon, but was indeed a quick and accurate shot and an agile horseman.

The Roussels' marriage may have been a mismatch from the beginning, but somehow Sarah endured for seventeen years and five children before filing for divorce in March 1906. During these years, first in Oregon, then after 1890 in Lassen County, California—where they raised

93. Transcription of Mary J. Drake interview with Josie and Hazel Agnes Roussel, her mother and aunt, from files of Mary J. Drake.

94. Much of the background material on the lives of Juniper Jim and Sarah is taken from two sources: Donald T. Garate, *Red Rock to Ravendale* (Ravendale: privately published by author, 1975), 60-64; and their granddaughter, Bette Baughman, interviewed 10 Feb. 2010.

95. Baughman interview, 10 Feb 2010; Garate, *Red Rock to Ravendale,* p. 61.

James Peter Roussel ("Juniper Jim") (far right) and buddies, undated
Courtesy of Mary J. Drake

livestock on ranches around Ravendale and Smoke Creek—Sarah was often left alone and at one point had to bury her own child in the dead of winter. Nonetheless, "Juniper Jim," had his own following and was appreciated by neighbors for his skills as a handyman. Thus, when Sarah ultimately filed for divorce, people in the area where they lived took sides.[96] Her plea was replete with descriptions of Jim's mismanagement and neglect of their livestock. Jim, in turn publicly announced that if she divorced him, he would take the proceeds from the sale of their livestock and she would be left destitute.

Their divorce was never finalized. Sarah moved to Susanville, and Jim found a place where he could surround himself with his collections, everything from teaspoons to trucks. In 1913, Juniper Jim was arrested for cattle rustling, in actuality a pre-arranged "setup" involving the theft of only two cows, for which the jury returned a verdict of "not guilty." His earlier reputation as a gunslinger and self-described stage robber type made excellent fodder for local newspapers, but the support of his friends ultimately saw him through.

James and Sarah Roussel had five identified children, six in all, according to the 1910 census:[97]

i. Elizabeth A.[4] Roussel (twin), b. in Ore., 22 May 1890, d. 6 May 1922.[98] Elizabeth m. 5 Aug. 1908, Joseph Maze, a farmer, b. in Calif. abt. 1865, d. in Lassen Co. Calif., 28 Mar. 1954.[99] They did not have children.

96. Divorce proceedings, Roussel v. Roussel, Superior Court of Lassen County, Calif., 23 Oct. 1905, Case #1459.
97. James P. Roussel household, 1910 Census, Calif., Lassen Co., Twp. 2, E.D. 32, sh. 4B, dwelling 8, family 8, p. 244.
98. The birth of twins was mentioned in the newspaper (Harney Co. Library birth database); birth date from Elizabeth's death certificate in the files of Mary J. Drake.
99. Maze marriage from files of Mary J. Drake; his information from CDA.

Wedding of Lizzie Roussel and Joseph Maze, 1908
Courtesy of Mary J. Drake

ii. Leroy Laurence Roussel (twin), b. 22 May 1890, d. in Burns, Oregon, 11 June 1890.

iii. James Wright "Brother" Roussel, b. in Burns, 28 June 1892, d. in San Leandro, Alameda Co., Calif., 20 Oct. 1938.[100] James m. aft. 1930, Anna _?_.[101] James is the hero of a story told by Juniper Jim's granddaughter Bette Baughman. It seems that when his younger sister Agnes, who had a defective eye from birth, was accidentally hit in that eye when still a toddler, James, not that much older, managed to hitch up the wagon and drive her to the hospital. Sadly, the eye was lost, a defect that embarrassed Agnes throughout life.

13 iv. Hazel Agnes Roussel, b. 5 Jan. 1900, m. Timothy Aloysius Judge.

14 v. Josie Frances Roussel, b. 17 Mar. 1901, m. Francis R. Webb.

7. **Henrietta[3] "Etta" Roussel** (*Mary Ann[2] Harman, Eleanora[1] Bush*) was born in Virginia City, Nevada, 27 May 1867, and died in Malheur County, Oregon, 11 July 1960.[102] Etta mar-

100. Alameda Co., California, death certificate, James Wright Roussel, #058235.

101. *Ibid.*

102. DAR interview of Anna Allen of Tuolumne Co., 1926, copy on file at Santa Clara Co. Historical and Genealogical Soc. Library; death from ODI.

"Brother" (James Wright Roussel), undated
Courtesy of Mary J. Drake

ried in Burns, 10 October 1887, **Tom Dodson**, and second, 20 November 1901, **William Cummins**, born in Oregon about 1873.[103]

Tom and Etta Dodson had one child:

i. Drucilla[4] Dodson, b. in Burns, July 1888. Drucilla m. in Boise, Idaho, 3 Sep. 1919, Louis Spielman, born in Minn. abt. 1890.[104]

8. Elinor Hayes[3] "Ella" Roussel (*Mary Ann[2] Harman, Eleanora[1] Bush*) was born in Nevada in April 1871, and died in Burns, Harney County, Oregon, 25 April 1910.[105] Elinor married in Grant County, 30 June 1887, **John Morrell**. Her mother, Mary Ann, gave permission for the marriage, stating therein that Elinor was of age.[106] John Morrell died tragically in Harney County about 1890.[107] Ella married second, in Burns, 5 December 1892, her step-brother **George Fry, Jr.**, born in Illinois, 15 December 1862, the son of George Henry and

---

103. Etta's marriages from WMI, in which Etta is indexed as "Ronsell" and William Cummins is "G. W. Cummins."
104. Drucilla's birth from Etta Dodson household, 1900 Census, Harney Co., Ore., city of Burns, E.D. 161, sh. 2B; their marriage from WMI.
105. Elinor's birth from George Fry household, 1900 Census, Harney Co., Ore., Poison Creek pct., E.D. 161, sh. 8B, dwelling 178, family 184; her death and obituary from the *Burns Times Herald*, 30 Apr. 1919 (files of Mary J. Drake).
106. Marriage certificate and letter in files of Mary J. Drake.
107. His tragic death was reported in detail two years later, when his widow, Ella, had his body disinterred and reinterred in Burns Cemetery. It seems that he had mental problems, wandered off into the desert where he died of exposure, and was buried there at the time it was discovered (*East Oregon Herald*, 20 July 1892, clipping in files of Mary J. Drake).

Delilah (Slane) Fry.[108] George died in Burns, 24 August 1940 and was buried there in Burns Cemetery.[109]

According to his obituary, George was a successful businessman. Starting with a small retail shoe store, he worked up to a large mercantile business, property development, including the first brick building in Burns, and banking. His will left $14,000 to his descendants.[110]

John and Ella Morrell had two children, both born in Burns:[111]

i. John Leslie[4] Morrell, b. 28 May 1888, d. in Plumas Co., Calif., 9 Jan. 1947.[112] John m. abt. 1922, Fannie _?_, b. in Ore., 29 Mar. 1895, d. in Malheur Co. Ore., 5 Dec 1968, as Fannie Medlin.[113]

ii. Zella Morrell, b. 5 Dec. 1889, d. in Burns, 26 Dec. 1889.[114]

Ella and her second husband, George Fry, had six children, all born in Burns:

iii. Leland Henry Fry, b. 22 Jan. 1893, d. 6 July 1962, Sanpete Co., Utah.[115] Leland m. in Burns, 11 Jan. 1915, Pearl Lauderdale, b. abt. 1892 in Tenn.[116] In the 1920 census, his occupation was electrician and in 1930, "telephone co. manager."[117]

iv. Marietta Catherine "Mary" Fry, b. 14 Nov. 1895, d. in Tulare Co., Calif., 20 July 1985.[118] Mary Catherine m. first, in Burns, 12 May 1914, James M. Wilson, b. abt. 1892. She m. second, 23 Oct. 1926, in Marin Co. Calif., Clarence Henry Malone.[119] [Living descendants, names withheld]

v. Eveleen Elinor Fry, b. 14 Feb. 1898, d. in Portland, 16 Jan. 1936.[120] Eveleen m. in Burns, 9 Nov. 1916, Augustus "Gus" Bardwell, b. Ore., 23 Sep. 1892, d. Deschutes Co., Ore., 17 Oct. 1970.[121] Both were bur. in Burns Cem.[122] In 1920, Gus was a deputy assessor, and in 1930, an "abstractor."[123]

vi. Georgia Gertrude Fry, b. 4 Aug. 1900, d. Harney Co., 24 Feb. 1935.[124] Georgia m. Reginald Gustafson, b. Ore., 28 Sep. 1897, d. Multnomah Co., Ore., 3 May 1985.[125]

---

108. George's birth from Burns Cemetery records at www.findagrave.com; marriage from WMI.
109. Death from ODI; burial at www.findagrave.com.
110. *Burns Times Herald,* undated; also final accounting of probate filed in Harney Co., 29 Jan. 1943, vol. G, p. 122 (both refs. from files of Mary J. Drake).
111. DAR interview of Anna Allen of Tuolumne Co., 1926, prev. cited.
112. Birth and death from CDA.
113. Marriage year approximated from 1930 Census (John L. Morrell household, Lassen Co., Calif., Honey Lake Twp., E.D. 18-4, sh. 26A, dwelling 605, family 642, p. 50); Fannie's birth from SSDI, death from ODI.
114. *East Oregon Herald,* 5 Dec. 1889, and 19 Dec. 1889, provided by Harney Co. Public Library, Western History Room.
115. Birth from WWI draft reg. card, death from files of Mary J. Drake; see also, George Fry household, 1900 Census, Harney Co., Ore., Poison Creek pct., E.D. 161, sh. 8B, dwelling 178, family 184.
116. Marriage reported in *Harney County News,* 16 Jan. 1916; birth from Leland Fry household, 1920 census Harney Co. Ore. Burns, E.D. 70 sh. 2A, dwelling 36, family 38.
117. Fry household, 1920 census, cited above; Leland Fry household, 1930 census, Sanpete Co., Utah, Moroni city, E.D. 20-21, sh. 7B, dwelling 138, family 138.
118. Birth and death from CDA.
119. Wilson marriage reported in *Harney County News,* 16 May 1914 (clipping provided by Harney County Public Library); Malone marriage license from files of Mary J. Drake.
120. Eveleen Elinor's birth and death from ODI and www.findagrave.com.
121. Birth from WWI draft reg. card; marriage from *Harney County News,* 9 Nov. 1916; death from www. findagrave.com.
122. Burns Cem. records at www.findagrave.com; Gus is buried with his second wife, Henrietta.
123. Augustus Bardwell household, 1920 Census, Harney Co., Ore., city of Burns, E.D. 70, sh. 5A; August Bardwell household, 1930 Census, Harney Co., Ore., city of Burns, pct. 2, E.D. 13-18, sh. 3B.
124. *Burns Times Herald,* 25 Feb. 1935 (Harney Co. Library files).
125. Birth and death from ODI and SSDI.

Eleanor "Ella" (Roussel) Fry
Courtesy of Mary J. Drake

George Fry, Jr.
Courtesy of Mary J. Drake

vii. Drucilla Fry, b. 7 Oct. 1902.[126] She d. on 2 Sept. 1954, Multnomah Co., Ore., and was buried in Santa Clara Catholic Cemetery.[127] Drucilla m. abt. 1928, Lionel D. Bowden, b. in Texas abt. 1910.[128]

viii. Anna Earline Fry, b. 7 Apr. 1906, d. 1973; m. William Albert and Jack Campbell.[129]

9. **Pearl Gertrude^3 Fry** (*Mary Ann^2 Harman, Eleanora^1 Bush*) was born in Nevada, 11 April 1879 and died in Los Angeles, Calif., 18 April 1957.[130] On 24 August 1902 in Burns, Pearl married **Fredrick H. Fisk**, born in Canyon City, Grant County, Oregon, 8 March 1876, died in Enterprise, Wallowa County, Oregon, 30 July 1941.[131] After that marriage ended in divorce, Pearl married second, also in Burns, 8 July 1917, **William Henry Keeler/Keiler**, born in Illinois about 1871.[132]

Frederick and Pearl Fisk had two children:

126. Birth from 1926 DAR interview of Anna Allen of Tuolumne Co. prev. cited.
127. Death from ODI; photograph of grave, and receipt for burial and new stone in files of Mary J. Drake.
128. Lionel Bowden household, 1930 Census, Inyo Co., Calif., E.D. 14-2, sh. 3B, dwelling 79, family 81.
129. Birth from George Fry household, 1910 census, Harney Co., Ore., city of Burns, E.D. 91, sh.1B, and Santa Clara Mission Cemetery records, Santa Clara, Calif.; Albert marriage from DAR interview of Anna Allen of Tuolumne Co., prev. cited; Campbell marr. from Fry file at Harney Co. Library.
130. Birth and death from CDI; marriage reported in the *Burns Times Herald,* 30 Aug. 1902 (Harney Co. library website).
131. ODI.
132. Marriage from Oregon Marriage Index at Ancestry.com; copy of marriage certificate in files of Mary J. Drake.

i. Charles W. R.[4] Fisk, b. Ore., 5 June 1903.[133]

ii. Otis Burnard Fisk, b. Ore., 2 Dec. 1905, d. in El Monte, Los Angeles Co., Calif., 4 Mar. 1966.[134] He m. aft. 1930, Joyce A. Ammons, b. Minn., 25 May 1910, d. in Santa Rosa, Calif., 6 Sep. 1997.[135]

Pearl and William Keeler (or Keiler) also had two children:

iii. Gwendolyn Mabelle Keeler, b. in Ore., 28 Apr. 1918.[136]

iv. Pearl Gertrude Keeler, b. 13 Jan. 1920 in Lexington, Morrow Co., Ore., d. in Roseburg, Douglas Co., Ore., 21 Aug. 2001.[137]

10. **Earl Leroy[3] Fry** (*Mary Ann[2] Harman, Eleanora[1] Bush*) was born in Steamboat, Nevada, 14 April 1881, and died in Contra Costa County, California, 16 July 1951.[138] Earl married in Harney County, 26 November 1906, **Tressie Ann Hankler**, born in San Francisco, 17 August 1888, died in Alameda County, 6 October 1968.[139]

Tressie, an orphan, was living in the George Fry household before she married Earl.[140] She apparently divorced Earl after they had three sons and married Fred Davis.[141]

Earl and Tressie Fry had three children:

i. William Ernest[4] Fry, b. Oregon, 20 Nov 1907, d. 17 July 1930.[142]

ii. Elmer Milton Fry, b. in Janesville, Lassen Co., Calif., 23 Nov. 1910, d. in Martinez, Contra Costa Co., Calif., 28 Nov. 1988.[143] Elmer m. in Feb. 1931 in Martinez, Calif., Alberta N. Lakey, b. in McCloud, Siskiyou Co., Calif., 14 June 1912, d. Martinez, 4 Nov. 1977.[144]

iii. Hubert D. Fry, b. Lassen Co., Calif., 22 Oct. 1919, d. in Washington Co., Ore., 1 May 1989.[145]

---

133. Birth reported in *Burns Times Herald,* 6 June 1903. Charles was alive at the time of the 1920 census (Wm. H. Keiler household, 1920 Census, Marion Co., Ore., Lexington pct., E.D. 131, sh. 2B, dwelling 42, family 44) and was likely the C. R. Fisk enumerated with wife Beatrice and dau. Shirley in 1930 in Bernalillo Co., N. Mex., city of Albuquerque, E.D. 152, sh. 17B, dwelling 459, family 766.
134. Birth and death from CDA; funeral notice, *Pasadena* (Calif.) *Star News,* 2 Mar. 1966, p. 20, col. 2.
135. Birth and death from CDA; identity of Joyce Ammons from information posted by granddaughter Kristina Worley in connection with her Coffin line.
136. *Harney County News,* 4 May 1918 (Harney Co. Library files); Wm. H. Keiler household, 1920 census, Morrow Co., Ore., prev. cited.
137. SSDI; see also obituary of Gertrude Pearl Keeler Neal, publ. 14 Sep. 2001 in the *News Review* (Douglas Co. Ore.) which lauds her as a pilot, licensed in Chico, Calif., a fashion model, an executive secretary, wife and mother.
138. Birth and death from CDA, and Lassen Cemetery records (Susanville) at Lahontan Images website, http://www.citlink.net/~lahontan/archivelinks/Lassencemetery.htm.
139. Birth and death from CDA; obituary, *Oakland Tribune,* 8 Oct. 1968, p. 22E.
140. George Fry household, 1900 Census, Harney Co. Ore., prev. cited.
141. Fred Davis household, 1930 Census, Alameda Co., Calif., city of Berkeley, E.D. 1-285, sh. 4A, dwelling 82, family 86, p. 171.
142. Birth and death from Lassen Cemetery records (Susanville) at Lahontan Images website.
143. Copy of Contra Costa Co. Death Certificate in files of Mary J. Drake.
144. CDA; death certificate in files of Mary J. Drake.
145. Death and wife's name from ODI; Lassen Cemetery records (Susanville) at Lahontan Images website.

Hazel Agnes Roussel (far left), a nurse at Providence Hospital
Courtesy of Mary J. Drake

Generation 4

11. **William Ivy[4] Allen** (*Anna Louise Roussel[3], Mary Ann Harman[2], Eleanora[1] Bush*) was born in California, 6 December 1885; he died after 1930.[146] In about 1915, William married **Mary Avilla? Cheatam**, born in Honolulu, Hawaii, about 1884.[147]

William and Mary Allen had three children, one of whom, Alden E. Allen, was born in San Francisco, 24 August 1919, and died in Orange County, California, 16 February 1994.[148]

12. **Zella Pearl[4] Allen** (*Anna Louise[3] Roussel, Mary Ann[2] Harman, Eleanora[1] Bush*) was born in California, 29 September 1890, and died in Cleveland, Cuyahoga County, Ohio, 23 April 1974.[149] On 20 December 1907, Zella married **John Patrick Joseph McGrath**, born in California, 1 March 1882, died after 1944.[150]

146. Birth from WW1 draft reg. card; William Allen household, 1930 census, San Bernardino Co., Calif., city of Cucamonga, E.D. 36-23, sh. 11B, dwelling 254, family 268.
147. Mary M. Avilla, the daughter of Manuel and Christina Avilla of Honolulu (1910 census), evidently was the widow of or divorced from Richard Cheatham by 1920, by which time she had married William Allen and had three small children. In 1907 she had Ginevra Cheatham, of whom no more could be learned. In the 1930 census, cited above, she did not report her first marriage. For birth of Ginevra see "Hawaii Births and Christenings" at Family History Library Pilot website, http://pilot.familysearch.org; see also Manuel Avilla [Pieretto?] household, 1910 census, Honolulu, Hawaii, E.D. 48, sh. 17B, dwelling 167, family 171.
148. Births from California Birth Index; Alden's death from CDA.
149. DAR interview of Anna Allen, 1926; death from Ohio Death abstracts at Ancestry.com.
150. Marriage from 1926 DAR interview of Anna Allen; John McGrath's birth from WW2 draft reg., Alameda Co., Calif.; 1944 voter reg. places them in Oakland, Alameda Co., both databases at Ancestry.com.

John and Zella McGrath had two children, one of whom, GEORGE M. MCGRATH, was born in San Joaquin County, 8 June 1916, and died in Punto Gordo, Charlotte County, Florida, in May 1984.[151]

13. HAZEL AGNES⁴ ROUSSEL (*James Peter³, Mary Ann² Harman, Eleanora¹ Bush*) was born in Karlo, Lassen County, California, 5 January 1900.[152] She died in Santa Clara County, California, 12 December 1988.[153] On 1 December 1919, Agnes married in Susanville, Lassen County, **TIMOTHY ALOYSIUS JUDGE**, born in Gibsonville, Sierra County, 15 October 1894.[154] This marriage ended in divorce in 1924. In Oakland, 11 May 1929, Agnes, who by profession was a nurse, married again, **ALBERT SYLVAN TAYLOR**, born in San Francisco, 16 August 1899. Albert Taylor died in Saratoga, Santa Clara County, 9 September 1995.[155] Timothy Judge also married again, Mary Fredericks, born in British Columbia, Canada about 1902.[156] A resident of Stockton, California, he died in Oakland, 6 April 1961. Based upon his service in World War II, he was buried in Golden Gate National Cemetery in San Bruno. (For more information, see chapters on the Judge and Taylor families.)

They had one child:

i. THEODORE TIMOTHY⁵ "Ted" JUDGE, b. in Westwood, Lassen Co., 1 April 1921, d. 11 June 2008.[157] Ted married 18 Dec. 1976, at St. Christopher's Convent in San Jose, as her second husband, ELLEN MARGARET SHEEHY, born 29 December 1906, died 25 May 2000. Their biographies are covered in the introduction.

14. JOSIE FRANCES⁴ ROUSSEL (*James Peter³, Mary Ann² Harman, Eleanora¹ Bush*) was born 17 March 1901; she died in Santa Clara County, 14 November 1966.[158] Josie married, 24 June 1923, **FRANCIS R. WEBB**, born in Wisconsin, 14 November 1903.[159] Francis Webb, a railroad employee, died in Campbell, Santa Clara County, 4 March 1971.[160] They were divorced.

Francis and Josie Webb had three children:

i. BETTY JEAN⁵ WEBB, b. in Alameda Co., 17 Jan. 1925.[161] Betty changed the spelling of her name to Bette and m. first, GARLAND VAUGHN BAUGHMAN, b. 22 Mar. 1920 in Arkansas, died 13 December 1996 (divorced).[162] She m. second, 28 July 1995 in Las Vegas, ROBERT SARGENT WILSON, b. 26 Mar. 1923, Santa Clara Co., d. 23 Feb. 2002, Santa Clara County.[163] Bette and Garland Baughman had two children: Mary Jane, born 18 December 1946 in Illinois, and James, born 23 April 1953 in California. James died 3 September 2000. Mary Jane

151. Birth from California Birth Index; death from SSDI.
152. Birth and death from CDA; this is consistent with 1900 Census (James Russell household, Lassen Co. Calif., Twp. 5, E.D. 52, sh. 3A, p. 126).
153. CDA.
154. Marriage license, files of Mary J. Drake; birth and death from Golden Gate National Cemetery records.
155. Additional information in Book Three, Taylor family.
156. Timoth (Timothy) A. Judge household, 1930 Census, Alameda Co., Calif., Eden Twp., E.D. 1-256, sh. 23B, dwelling 596, family 606.
157. SSDI.
158. Birth and death from CDA.
159. Files of Mary J. Drake.
160. CDA.
161. California Birth Index; information printed with permission from Bette Baughman Wilson, who has generously provided much information on her ancestry.
162. SSDI.
163. SSDI; information printed with permission from Bette Baughman Wilson.

Bette Jean (Webb) Baughman at the grave of her grandfather, "Juniper Jim" Roussel, Susanville
Courtesy of Mary J. Drake

documented and expanded upon her mother's family research to form a large and impressive collection that has been invaluable in reconstructing the Roussel and Harman families. She is also identified in this book as Mary Jane Drake.

ii. DONNA MAY WEBB, b. 6 May 1927, d. in Stockton Calif., 28 Mar. 2007; m. _?_ SPENCE.

iii. PATRICIA ROSE WEBB, b. 13 Oct. 1930, m. LEON TALESFORE.

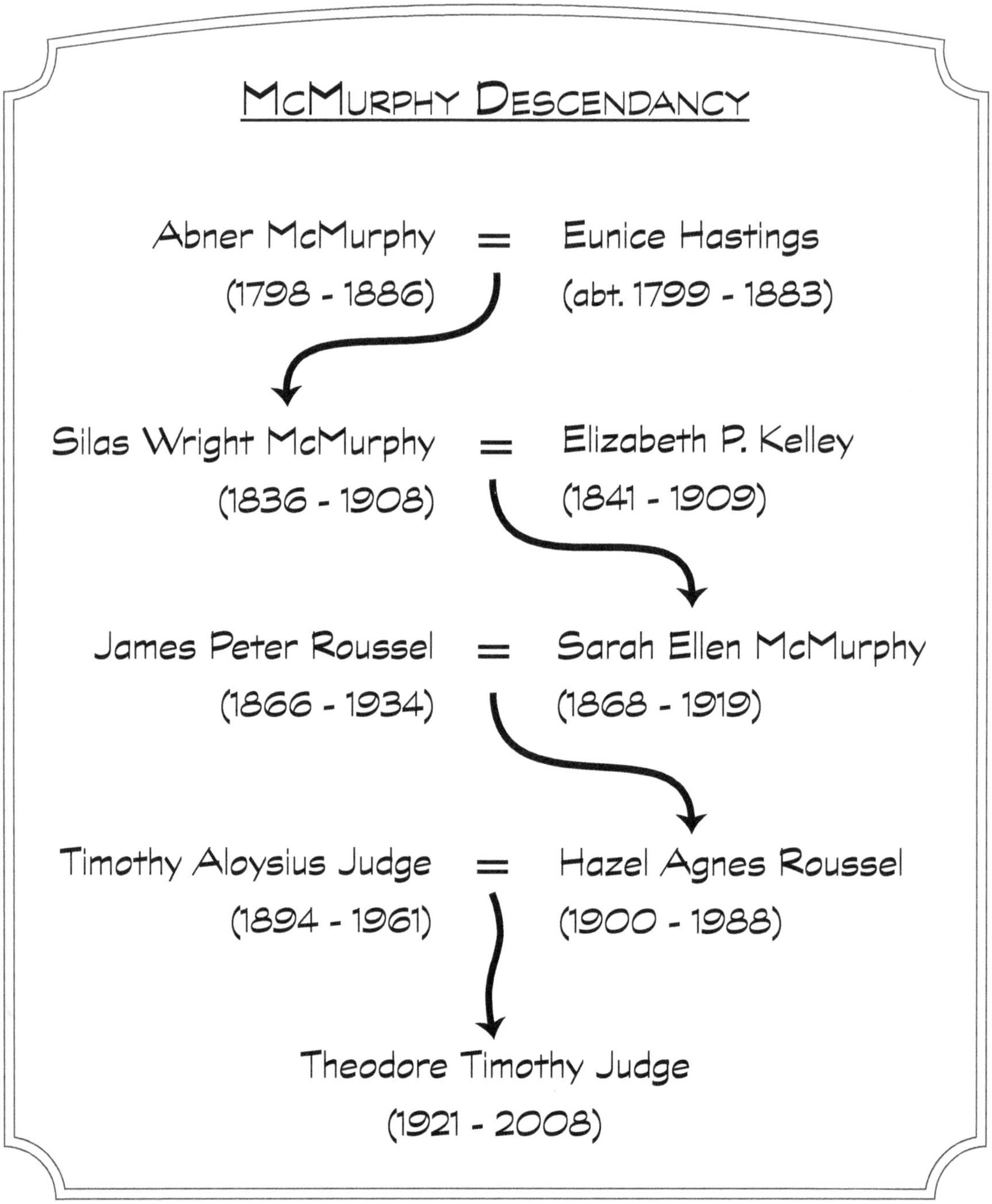

McMurphy Descendancy

Abner McMurphy (1798 - 1886) = Eunice Hastings (abt. 1799 - 1883)

Silas Wright McMurphy (1836 - 1908) = Elizabeth P. Kelley (1841 - 1909)

James Peter Roussel (1866 - 1934) = Sarah Ellen McMurphy (1868 - 1919)

Timothy Aloysius Judge (1894 - 1961) = Hazel Agnes Roussel (1900 - 1988)

Theodore Timothy Judge (1921 - 2008)

Descendancy of McMurphy family to Ted Judge

❧ Descendants of Abner McMurphy and Eunice Hastings

Over the course of his life, Abner McMurphy moved from New England to California along a classic migration trail. His parents, Alexander McMurphy and Lucy Burroughs, came from New Hampshire. Abner was born in Vermont in 1798, perhaps in Randolph, Orange Co.[1][2] By 1830 he had married Eunice Hastings and settled in St. Lawrence County, New York, where his six children were born. In 1841, Abner next moved west to Illinois, where he purchased public domain land in Sangamon County, and where the family was still living in 1850.[3] In 1852, they moved to Iowa, first to Keokuk, Lee County, then to Marion Township in Henry County.[4]

As evidenced in the 1850 and 1860 census enumerations, the family lived in comfortable circumstances.[5] It surely was not because of economic necessity that they decided to uproot again and move west. On the contrary, according to the account given by Abner's grandson, Jacob W. Broadwell, the trip had been planned for many years.[6] By this time, all of their children had married and had families of their own. Their widowed daughter, Cynthia, was living with them, but all of the other children, according to Broadwell's account, had farms that would have needed to be sold. Abner and Eunice's children and their spouses and children, with the exception of daughter Laura Ramsey and her family, prepared to move to California.

---

1. Vermont Sec. of State, *General Index to Vital Records of Vermont, Early to 1870*, Family History Library (hereafter, FHL) film #27,627.
2. Abner's mother deserves her own note. Lucy Burroughs was married earlier to Joseph Kneeland. He died in an Indian attack on their home in Royalton, Vt., on Oct. 16, 1780. In a petition for compensation years later, she described a horrifying episode in which their house and its contents were burnt, their cattle and swine stolen, and Joseph himself murdered. She spent two days and a night in the wilderness with her three month old baby until she was rescued. As Lucy McMurphy, she petitioned for ownership of the property Joseph would have been granted once he settled permanently in Royalton. The bloody memories must have stayed with her for the rest of her life. Source: *State Papers of Vermont, vol. 10, General Petitions, 1793-1796* (Montpelier, Vt., 1958), pp. 110-11.
3. Public Domain Land Tract Sales, database at Illinois State Archives, www.cyberdriveillinois.com; Abner McMurphy household, 1850 census, Sangamon Co., Ill., dwelling 1600, family 1600, p. 232 written / left side of 242.
4. J. M. Guinn, *History of the State of California and Biographical Records of the Sierras,* (Chicago: Chapman Pub. Co., 1906), 623.
5. Abner McMurphy household, 1850 Census, Sangamon Co., Ill., dwelling 1600, family 1600, p. 232; A. M. McMurphy household, 1860 Census, Henry Co., Iowa, Marion Twp., dwelling 2624, family 2314, p. 335. The value of their real estate, $2,000, was next to the highest in the neighborhood.
6. Josephine Gardner, 1933 interview of Jacob W. Broadwell, grandson of Abner; titled "Our Trip across the Plains" in Oregon State Library Archives, Oregon State Library, WPA Records, Benton Co., Part 1, Inventory #7, Publication #9 (hereafter, Broadwell interview).

In April 1864, after supplies had been purchased and other arrangements finalized, the large "McMurphy-Bailey" party, consisting of Abner and Eunice, by then in their sixties, five of their children and grandchildren, and three other families, was ready to depart.[7] Broadwell told of his six-year-old cousin, Abe Ramsey, who wanted so much to go with them and was desolate when told this would not be possible. His sympathetic parents decided to accompany the party in a spring wagon as far as the first encampment, spend the night and return home the next day.

Even though Abner was sixty-five years old at this time, he was made captain of the train. One of the three families that traveled with them was headed by Adam Ludy, who wrote an account of the crossing many years later.[8] Both Ludy and Broadwell recount that in more than one instance it was Abner who effectively led the group and negotiated food purchases and cattle sales along the way.

After the wagon train had crossed the Missouri River into Omaha, they fell in with another train. With the added numbers, they were able to travel fairly safely all the way to and over the Rockies. By the sixties, detailed guide maps had been prepared, with landmarks to look out for, such as Chimney Rock and the Thousand Mile Tree. No doubt the travelers were cheered by the sight of these reassuring guideposts, knowing they were not going astray.

According to Adam Ludy's and J.W. Broadwell's accounts, the main hazards of the crossing, other than dangerous terrain, included the ever-present possibility of attacks, illness (Rocky Mountain fever) and thievery.[9] The Sioux were fighting among themselves, and some were desperate for food or horses. Unscrupulous whites, given the opportunity, would also steal horses and stock, and shots were occasionally exchanged between wagon trains.

Both Broadwell and Ludy reminisced about dogs that accompanied them on the trail. Broadwell had a dog that became so tenderfooted from walking, he asked to take it into the wagon but was denied. Eventually the poor animal became separated from the wagons and was lost. Ludy's dog was so ill-tempered that the men would beat him away from the wagons with a whip. Eventually the dog turned back in the direction from which they had come and by some miracle managed to return to his former home, a journey of about five hundred miles.

The wagon train reached Janesville, Lassen County, 9 September 1864, where Abner traded stock for a ranch and settled his family.[10] Others in the party turned north to Oregon or continued down the Sacramento River valley.

Abner served as Justice of the Peace of Janesville in 1867 and 1868, and in the 1870 census, described himself as a saloon keeper.[11] Whether that meant he owned the saloon or managed

---

7. Broadwell says they left the 10th day of March and Ludy says the 11th day of April. Ludy was probably correct because Broadwell states the youngest child was two weeks old, who he identifies as Iowa. That would be Ida Iowa McMurphy, who was born in April.
8. Jack Armstrong, *Wagons to Californey, 1864: the Story of Adam Edward Ludy, 1831-1910* (Longmont, Colo.: self-published, c. 1996), 21-29.
9. Broadwell interview.
10. Arrival date from the *Lassen Advocate,* 18 September 1914, as found in *Trail Talk*, Newsletter of the California Nevada Chapter, Oregon-California Trails Assn. No. 67, Spring 2005, p. 18. A deed in the files of Mary J. Drake (CGS Archives) states that Abner bought from Robert Cain, in October 1864, half interest in a ranch in the Elysian Valley, for which he paid $3,000.
11. Asa Merrill Fairfield, *Fairfield's Pioneer History of Lassen Co., Calif.,* (San Francisco: H. S. Crocker, 1916), 408 and

Main Street Susanville, 1864
Courtesy of Mary J. Drake

it is impossible to tell; at the time his real estate was reported valued at $3,000, but this likely was the land in Elysian Valley in which he was part owner. Stock raising would have been difficult for a seventy-one year-old man, and he and Eunice may have moved into town. Abner filed two land patents in Lassen County on 1 November 1873 for a total of 311 acres.[12] Family members Harper McMurphy, Jefferson Hart and Justus Bailey also filed on that date, and in the 1880 census, Abner and Eunice are seen surrounded by their extended family.[13]

Genealogical Descendancy

1. **Abner[1] McMurphy** was born on 23 July 1798 in Vermont. He died in Lassen County, California, 1 October 1886 and was buried there in Janesville Cemetery.[14] Sometime around 1821, probably in New York State, Abner married **Eunice Hastings**. Born about 1799 in Massachusetts, Eunice died 15 June 1883 in Lassen County and was buried beside her husband.[15]

Abner and Eunice had six children who survived childhood, all born in New York:

2 i. Cynthia[2] McMurphy, b. 26 Aug. 1825, m. William King Broadwell.

3 ii. Hyman Harper McMurphy, b. 24 July 1828, m. Dolly Ann Bailey.

4 iii. Mary McMurphy, b. 30 June 1832, m. Justus Rich Bailey.

5 iv. Miranda McMurphy, b. 26 May 1834, m. Jefferson Hart.

474.

12. Bureau of Land Management Land Entry Database at www.glorecords.blm.gov.
13. Abner McMurphy household, 1880 Census, Lassen Co., Calif., Janesville Twp., E.D. 54, sh. 12, dwelling 180, family 180. Complete, referenced descendancies of Abner's siblings are available from CGS.
14. Abner McMurphy household, 1850 Census, Sangamon Co., Ill., dwelling 1600, family 1600, p. 232; Lassen Co., Calif. burial database at www.findagrave.com (hereafter, Lassen County burials at www.findagrave.com).
15. Abner McMurphy household, 1850 Sangamon Co., Ill., Census, prev. cited.

6 v. SILAS WRIGHT MCMURPHY, b. July 1836, m. ELIZABETH KELLEY.

7 vi. LAURA JANE MCMURPHY, b. about 1839, m. JOHN T. RAMSEY.

Generation 2

2. CYNTHIA[2] MCMURPHY (*Abner*[1]) was born 26 August 1825 in New York State.[16] She died in Lassen County, California, 31 December 1908 and was buried there in Janesville Cemetery.[17] On 30 April 1846, in Sangamon County, Illinois, Cynthia married **WILLIAM KING BROADWELL.**[18] Born about 1825 in Illinois, William died in Sangamon County between 1856 and 1857 and was buried there in Broadwell Cemetery.[19]

In the 1850 census, Cynthia, William and their two boys were living with William's extended family, along with fifty year-old John Broadwell, likely William's father.[20] Following William's death, Cynthia and her three children moved to her parents' household and, in April 1864, accompanied the rest of the family to California. There, Cynthia lived with one or another of her children until her death.

William and Cynthia Broadwell had three children, all born in Illinois and all buried in Janesville Cemetery in Lassen County:[21]

i. ISAAC[3] BROADWELL, b. about 1847, d. 17 Nov. 1892 in Lassen Co.[22]

ii. JACOB WILLIAM BROADWELL, b. 13 Oct. 1848, d. 10 May 1940 in Lassen Co. Jacob m. first, JULIA FLORENCE COOMBS, b. 14 Oct. 1855, d. 25 Sept. 1898, and second, KATE L. RUNYON, b. 13 July 1861, Indiana, d. 19 Feb. 1941 in Monterey Co., California.[23]

iii. LUCY BROADWELL, b. 28 Nov. 1850, d. 8 Feb. 1889, prob. in Lassen Co.[24] Lucy m. GEORGE ROBINSON LYBARGER, b. 27 Nov. 1830 in Ohio, d. 7 Oct. 1916 in Calif.

3. HYMAN HARPER[2] MCMURPHY (*Abner*[1]) was born on 24 July 1828 in New York State. Harper died in Lassen County, California, 23 February 1894 and was buried in Janesville Cemetery.[25] In Sangamon County, 30 June 1853, Harper married **DOLLY ANN BAILEY.**[26] Born 2 December 1836 in New York State, Dolly died on 4 May 1909 and was buried in Janesville Cemetery.[27]

---

16. Place of birth from A. M. McMurphy household, 1860 Census, Henry Co., Iowa, Marion Twp., dwelling 2624, family 2314, p. 335; exact date from burial record.
17. Lassen County burials at findagrave, Cynthia Broadwell headstone.
18. Illinois Statewide Marriage Index 1763-1900, at www.illinoisstatearchives.org.
19. Sangamon Geneal. Soc., *Estate Record Index, 1821-1907* (1989), 1: 260. Letters of Aministration were issued 5 May 1857. Burial from John Roger Ball, Cemetery Index for Sangamon Co., Ill. (no details; 1978), 48.
20. William Broadwell household, 1850 Census, Sangamon Co., previously cited.
21. Lassen County burials at findagrave. Most information on this family, unless otherwise noted, has been taken from records at this website.
22. C. Broadwell household, 1870 Census, Lassen Co., Calif., Janesville Twp., dwelling 91, family 92, p. 10.
23. Abstracts of California death records, database at www.vitalsearch-ca.com (hereafter, CDA).
24. George Lybarger household, 1880 Census, Lassen Co., Calif., Johnstonville Twp., dwelling 11, family 11, p. 2.
25. Harper McMurphy household, 1860 Census, Henry Co., Iowa, Marion Twp., page 335, dwelling 2625, family 2315; Lassen County burials at findagrave.
26. Illinois Statewide Marriage Index 1763-1900, prev. cited.
27. H. H. McMurphy household, 1880 Census, Lassen Co., Calif., Janesville Twp., E.D. 54, p. 10, dwelling 138, family 138; Cemeteries of Lassen Co. (Archives) at www.lahontanimages.com.

Portrait of Hyman Harper McMurphy
Courtesy of Mary J. Drake

Although married in Illinois in 1853, Hyman was in Iowa by 1854 when his first child was born and probably moved there at the same time as his parents. In 1864, Hyman sold his 800 acre farm in Henry County, Iowa, and with his family, his parents and his siblings, traveled by ox team to California. Once in California, the family settled in Honey Lake Valley, Lassen County. There Hyman purchased land, farmed and raised stock until he died.[28] After Hyman died, his widow, Dolly, continued to live on the farm until 1902, when she moved into Janesville. Her daughter Ina and grandson Kenneth Way lived with her in her home after Ina's divorce, presumably until Dolly's death.[29]

Hyman and Dolly McMurphy had the following children, the first four born in Iowa and the last four born in California:[30]

28. Guinn, *History of the State of California and Biographical Records of the Sierras,* 623; H. McMurphy household, 1870 Census, Lassen Co., Calif., Janesville Twp., dwelling 39, family 40, pg. 4; and H. H. McMurphy household, 1880 Census, prev. cited.
29. Harry McMurphy household, 1900 Census, Lassen Co., Calif., Twp. 2, E.D. 49, sh. 4, dwelling 78, family 78; Guinn, *History of the State of California and Biographical Records of the Sierras,* 623.
30. Unless otherwise referenced, information on births and deaths is from the 1900 Census and burial data at www.findagrave.com and Cemeteries of Lassen Co. (Archives) at www.lahontanimages.com.

i. Harry Fulton[3] McMurphy, b. Jan. 1855, d. 17 Oct. 1927, Lassen Co., bur. in Janesville Cem. Harry m. 26 Nov 1885 in Lassen Co., Carrie Amelia Fetter, b. 31 May 1869 in Calif., d. 15 Nov. 1957 in Butte Co., Calif.[31]

ii. Fannie Eunice McMurphy, b. 18 Apr. 1857, d. 26 Nov. 1924, bur. Janesville Cem. Fannie m. first, 3 Jan. 1876 in Lassen Co., John Oscar Hemler, b. Dec. 1849 in Ohio, d. 10 Apr. 1916 in Calif., bur. in Susanville Cem., Lassen Co.[32] They were divorced about 1900 and she m. second, Thomas Lemuel Barham, b. 28 Dec. 1856 in Missouri, d. 8 Mar. 1922, bur. in Janesville Cemetery.[33]

iii. Laura P. McMurphy, b. Mar. 1859, d. 11 Aug. 1924 in Lassen Co.[34] Laura m. in Lassen Co., 25 Nov. 1880, John L. Fisher.[35] John was b. 16 Nov. 1854 in Ohio and d. 12 June 1907. Both were bur. in Janesville Cem.[36]

iv. Molly McMurphy, b. Jan. 1861, d. 8 May 1950 in Sequim, Clallam Co., Wash.[37] Molly m. Thomas W. McPherson, b. 1850 in Maine and d. bef. 1910, prob. in Seattle, Wash.[38] Molly m. second, Hiram E. Ricketson, b. Ill., d. Clallam Co., Wash., 1933.[39]

v. Viola McMurphy.[40]

vi. Mattie E. McMurphy, b. 2 Apr. 1866, d. 14 Oct. 1924 in Lassen Co., bur. in Janesville Cem.[41] Mattie m. first, in Lassen Co., 24 Sep. 1884, James A. Wood.[42] James was b. 10 Oct. 1851 in Canada, d. 25 Sep. 1921, and was bur. in Janesville Cem.[43] Mattie m. second, Walter B. DeWitt, b. 1863, d. 1948, bur. Janesville Cem.

vii. George Bailey McMurphy, b. 16 July 1868, d. 4 Apr. 1913, bur. Janesville Cem.[44] George m. 31 Dec. 1891 in Lassen Co., Rosa Bagin, b. abt. 1869 in Calif.[45]

viii. Lola Belle McMurphy, b. May 1870, d. 1910-1920 in Iowa.[46] Lola Belle m. Joseph Sherman Spillers, b. Feb. 1868 in Missouri, d. 1923 in Dallas Co., Iowa, bur. in Wiscotta Cem.,

---

31. Lassen County *Marriage Records,* 1864-1926, Index to Certificates, Bk. B, p. 149 (FHL film #1,851,397); death from CDA.
32. Lassen Co. *Marriage Records,* 1864-1926, Index to Certificates, Bk. B, p. 30; John's birth from Lassen County Burials.
33. Thomas L. Barham household, 1910 Census, Lassen Co., Calif., Twp. 2, E.D. 32, sh. 3A, no dwelling # listed, family 6.
34. John L. Fisher household, 1900 Census, Lassen Co., Calif., Twp. 3, E.D. 50, sh. 11, dwelling 237, family 241; California Death Index, 1905-1929.
35. Lassen County *Marriage Records,* 1864-1926, Index to Certificates, Bk. B, p. 83.
36. John L. Fisher household, 1900 Census, prev. cited.
37. T. W. McPherson household, 1900 Census, Seattle, King Co., Wash., pct. 5, E.D. 102, sh. 12, dwelling 149, family 191; Washington State death certificate index 1907-1960, at www.washingtonstatedigitalarchives.com.
38. T. W. McPherson household, 1900 census, prev. cited.
39. Washington State death index and 1930 census, Clallam Co., Wash., Sequim twp., E.D. 533, sh. 1A, family 4.
40. The only mention of this child is in Guinn, *History of the State of California and Biographical Records of the Sierras,* 623. However, since there is no mention of her in Janesville Cemetery records, she is presumed to have been born in Iowa.
41. Cemeteries of Lassen Co. (Archives) at www.lahontanimages.com (Mattie Wood DeWitt listing).
42. Lassen Co., Index to Marriage Certificates, Lassen Co. Recorder, Book B, 136.
43. James A. Wood household, 1900 Census, Lassen Co., Calif., cited above; Lassen Co. burials at www.findagrave.
44. H. H. McMurphy household, 1880 Census, Lassen Co., Calif., Janesville Twp., E.D. 54, dwelling 138, family 138; Lassen County Burials.
45. Lassen County *Marriage Records,* 1864-1926, Index to Certificates, Bk. B, 230. While no death record was found for Rosa McMurphy, a guardianship was established for their daughter, Echo McMurphy, on 17 July 1913 in the Probate Court of Lassen Co., Calif., shortly after the death of her father George (Lassen Co., Superior Court Index (Archives) at www.lahontanimages.com).
46. J. S. Spillers household, 1900 Census, San Francisco, San Francisco Co., Calif., E.D. 16, sh. 10, dwelling 174, family 215; Joseph S. Spillers household, 1910 Census, Guthrie Co., Iowa, Jackson Twp., E.D. 57, sh. 1B, dwelling 15, family

Dallas Co.[47] In 1900 the Spillers had been married six years and were living in San Francisco, where he was a "dealer in notions." They then evidently moved to Iowa, where in 1910, he was a farm laborer and in 1920, when widowed, a meat cutter.

ix. JENNIE PEARL MCMURPHY, b. 2 May 1876, d. 26 Aug. 1896, prob. in Lassen Co., bur. in Janesville Cem.

x. INA LUELLA MCMURPHY, b. 5 Oct. 1879, d. 11 Apr. 1963 in San Mateo Co., Calif.[48] Ina m. in Susanville, Lassen Co., 1 Aug. 1906, ARAD WAY, b. 31 Jan. 1881 in Calif., d. 9 June 1962 in Lassen Co.[49] They were divorced.[50]

4. **MARY² MCMURPHY** (*Abner*¹) was born 30 June 1832 in New York State; she died 7 June 1909.[51] On 4 November 1852, in Sangamon County, Illinois, she married **JUSTUS RICH BAILEY**, son of Moody and Fannie Bailey. Born on 16 December 1829 in St. Lawrence County, New York, Justus died 23 April 1917.[52] Both Justus and Mary were buried in Janesville Cemetery.[53]

The Baileys traveled with her family from Illinois to California in 1864.[54] Mary became ill on the trip west, and they arrived in Chico with only $10.00. They lived in Chico for a year on a rented farm and then moved to Lassen County, where they evidently purchased one hundred and sixty acres north of Janesville and homesteaded another quarter section nearby. In 1871 they sold the land and purchased the hotel in Janesville, which they operated for nine years before trading it for a ranch, where they established a feed lot for stock. After retirement, Justus served as a school trustee for many years.

The Baileys had five children, the first three born in Iowa, the last two in California:

i. SILAS W.³ BAILEY. b. abt. 1856.[55]

ii. IRA EUGENE BAILEY, b. 13 Sep. 1859, d. 2 Feb. 1943, Oakland, Alameda Co., Calif., interred along with his wife Sofia in Chapel of the Chimes Mausoleum, Oakland.[56] Ira m. SOFIA A. WAGNER, b. 16 Jan. 1873 in Oroville, Butte Co., Calif., d. 20 Aug. 1958, Oakland, Alameda Co.[57]

15; Mahalia Painter household, 1920 Census, Dallas Co., Iowa, Redfield Twp., E.D. 18, sh. 4A, dwelling 80, family 123, p. 211 (Joseph recorded as a widower).

47. J. S. Spillers household, 1900 Census, above; Iowa Gravestone Project at www.iowagravestones.org ("Joseph S. Spillers 1868-1923").
48. CDA.
49. Marriage from *The Saturday Bee,* (Sacramento, Calif.) 9 Aug. 1906, p. 7; CDA.
50. L. F. Barham household, 1920 Census, Lassen Co., Calif., Honey Lake Twp., E.D. 32, sh. 3A, dwelling 55, family 63; Ina L. Way is listed in the household as a sister-in-law and is divorced.
51. Cemeteries of Lassen Co. (Archives) at www.lahontanimages.com, Mary Bailey listing.
52. California Death Index, 1905-1929, at www.vitalsearch-ca.com; "Some Iowans who Went to California" in *Hawkeye Heritage* (Iowa Geneal. Soc.), vol. 7(2): 85 (April 1972).
53. Where exact birthdates are shown in this family, the information if not otherwise cited was taken from Lassen County burials at findagrave or from CDA.
54. This and the following biographical information from Guinn, *History of the State of California and Biographical Record of the Sierras,* 537.
55. Justus R. Bailey household, 1856 Iowa State census, Henry Co., Center Twp., dwelling 239, family 286, p. 510.
56. Birth and death from CDA; interment confirmed at Chapel of the Chimes, Oakland, California—Consistancy Room, Tier E2, #3.
57. Obituary, *Oakland Tribune,* 24 Aug. 1958, p. 54, col.6.

iii. George Benton Bailey, b. 10 Sep. 1863, d. 29 Jan. 1957 in Lassen Co., bur. in Janesville Cem.[58] George m. 26 Nov. 1890, Annie Kate Theodore, b. 16 Jan. 1872 in Calif., d. in Lassen Co., 30 Mar. 1969, bur. in Janesville Cem.[59]

iv. Walter Leroy Bailey, b. 11 Sep. 1866, d. 7 June 1927 in Lassen Co., bur. in Janesville Cem., Lassen Co.[60]

v. Lola J. Bailey, b. June 1868, d. 13 Jan. 1936, Alameda Co.[61] Lola m. George O. DeWitt, b. Dec. 1867 in Calif., d. 29 Oct. 1932 in Monterey Co., Calif.[62]

5. **Miranda² McMurphy** (*Abner*¹) was born 26 May 1834 in New York State; she died 22 March 1914 in Standish, Lassen County, and was buried in Janesville Cemetery.[63] Miranda married in Henry County, Iowa, 27 December 1855, **Jefferson Hart**.[64] He was born about 1829 in Illinois and died in Lassen County, California, on 17 March 1886.[65]

Miranda and Jefferson began their married life in Henry County, where they had a farm.[66] On 9 October 1861, Jefferson enlisted in the Fourth Iowa Cavalry, Company K, and served as a second corporal. He was discharged 31 March 1863 at Keokuk, Iowa, for a disabling disease of the hips.[67]

When they crossed the country in the McMurphy wagon train, they had three children under five. It is not surprising that Adam Ludy wrote that the women, upon reaching the end of the journey, "had become insane."[68] In 1870, the Harts declared little in real estate, but in 1873, Jefferson Hart, along with several members of the family, received a land entry patent for eighty acres in Lassen County.[69] Following Jefferson's death in 1886, his sons continued to farm the land for several years. Miranda continued living on the farm until she moved in with her daughter's family, where she lived until she died.[70]

Jefferson and Miranda Hart had seven children:[71]

58. CDA; Lassen County burials at findagrave.
59. Guinn, *History of the State of California and Biographical Records of the Sierras,* 669; Lassen County Burials, Annie K. Bailey headstone.
60. California Death Index, 1905-1929; Lassen County Burials.
61. Geo. O. DeWitt household, 1900 Census, Lassen Co., Calif., Twp. 3, E.D. 54, sh. 2, dwelling 73, family 73; California Death Index, 1930-1939, at www.vitalsearch-ca.com.
62. Geo. O. DeWitt household, 1900 Census, Lassen Co., Calif., cited above; California Death Index, 1930-1939.
63. Miranda Hart death certificate (1914), Calif. State Board of Health, Bureau of Vital Statistics. Miranda's death certificate states that her mother's maiden name was Eunice Hastings.
64. Henry Co., Iowa, *Marriage Records,* 1836-1931 (FHL film #965,926).
65. J. Hart household, 1870 Census, Lassen Co., Calif., Janesville Twp., dwelling 43, family 44, p. 5; Cemeteries of Lassen Co. (Archives) at www.lahontanimages.com.
66. Jeff Hart household, 1860 Census, Henry Co., Iowa, Marion Twp., dwelling 2551, family 2271, p. 329.
67. William Forse Scott, *Roster of the Fourth Iowa Cavalry Veteran Volunteers 1861-1865,* (New York: J. J. Little & Co., 1902), 170.
68. Jack Armstrong, *Wagons to Californey, 1864: the story of Adam Edward Ludy, 1831-1910,* prev. cited, 29.
69. J. Hart household, 1870 Census, Lassen Co., Calif., Janesville Twp., dwelling 43, family 44, p. 5; Bureau of Land Management, Land Entry Database at www.glorecords.blm.gov.
70. James B. Leavett household, 1910 Census Lassen Co., Calif. , Twp., #3, Standish pct., E.D. 33, sh. 5A, dwelling 90, family 92. Miranda is living with the family and listed as mother-in-law, her death certificate in 1914 says she had been a resident there for six years and four months.
71. Births are taken from census enumerations as indicated; births and deaths from Cemeteries of Lassen Co. (Archives) at www.lahontanimages.com unless otherwise referenced.

i. CLARENCE L.[3] HART, b. abt. 1859 in Iowa, d. 2 Feb. 1879 in Lassen Co., Calif., bur. Janesville Cem., Lassen Co.[72]

ii. CHARLES FRANCIS HART, b. Jan. 1861 in Iowa, d. 16 Jan.1938 in Susanville, Lassen Co., Calif.[73] Charles was only three when he crossed the plains with his parents. With the exception of two years spent at the Stockton Business College, he spent the rest of his life in Lassen County, teaching there in public schools for thirty years. He outlived all his siblings except for May, the youngest, and like them all, was buried in Janesville Cemetery.[74]

iii. ALFRED ED HART, b. Feb. 1864 in Iowa, d. 10 Oct. 1924 in Napa Co., California , bur. in Janesville Cem.[75]

iv. WILLIAM RALPH HART, b. about 1866 in Calif., d. 11 Aug. 1933, in Lassen Co., bur. in Janesville Cem.[76] William m. ADA LORETTA _?_ .[77]

v. ELBERT H. HART, b. May 1869 in Calif., d. 1 Apr. 1921 in Napa Co., Calif., bur. Janesville Cem., Lassen Co.[78]

vi. RICHARD HART, b. abt. 1871 in Calif., d. Dec. 1887 in Calif.[79]

vii. MAY LILLIAN HART, b. 16 Feb. 1874 in Calif., d. 10 Oct. 1943 in Lassen Co., bur. in Janesville Cem.[80] May m. 11 Oct. 1899 in Clinton, Lassen Co., JAMES BYERS LEAVITT.[81] James was b. 26 Feb. 1878 in Calif., d. 1 Sep. 1942 in Lassen Co., and was bur. in Janesville Cem.[82]

6. SILAS WRIGHT[2] MCMURPHY (*Abner*[1]) was born about July 1836, probably in New York State, and died in Benton County, Oregon, 20 February 1908.[83] He married, 21 February 1861 in Henry County, Iowa, **ELIZABETH P. KELLEY,** daughter of John Kelley and Sarah Palmer.[84] Born on 3 May 1841 in Ohio, Elizabeth died 4 September 1909 in Benton County, Oregon.[85] Both Silas and Elizabeth were buried in Summit Cemetery in Benton County.[86]

Silas, although probably born in St. Lawrence County, New York, occasionally listed his birthplace as Canada. St. Lawrence County is close to the border, so that may have been possible, but his siblings consistently stated they were born in New York. When he was a boy, his family moved to Sangamon County, Illinois, and in 1856, on to Henry County, Iowa, where

72. Jeff Hart household, 1860 Census, Henry Co., Iowa, Marion Twp., dwelling 2551, family 2271, p. 329.
73. Edward A. Hart household, 1900 Census, Lassen Co., Calif., Twp. 2, E.D. 49, sh. 1, dwelling 10, family 10.
74. Obituary, *Lassen Advocate,* (Susanville, Calif.), 17 Jan. 1938, p. 1 col. 7.
75. Edward A. Hart household, 1900 Census, prev. cited; California Death Index, 1905-1929. Edward A. Hart appears as Alfred Ed. Hart in many documents.
76. Birth estimated from J. Hart household, 1870 Census, Lassen Co., Calif., Janesville Twp., dwelling 43, family 44, p.5; California Death Index, 1930-1939; Cemeteries of Lassen Co. (Archives) at www.lahontanimages.com.
77. William Ralph Hart household, 1910 Census, Lassen Co., Calif., Twp. 1, E.D. 31, sh. 1, dwelling 5, family 5.
78. Charles N. Hall household, 1900 Census, Kern Co., Calif., Judicial Twp., E.D. 25, sh. 7, dwelling 130, family 130; California Death Index, 1930-1939; Cemeteries of Lassen Co. (Archives) at www.lahontanimages.com.
79. J. Hart household, 1870 Census, Lassen Co., Calif., Janesville Twp., dwelling 43, family 44, p. 5; Lassen Co. Obituary index at www.lahontanimages.com.
80. CDA; Lassen County burials at findagrave, May L. and James B. Leavitt on same headstone.
81. "The Leavitt-Hart Wedding," clipping of wedding in Clinton dated Oct. 17, 1899, in records of Mary J. Drake, likely from the *Lassen Advocate.*
82. California Death Index, 1905-1929; Lassen County burials at findagrave.
83. S.W. McMurphy household, 1900 Census, Harney Co., Ore., Burns pct., E.D. 161, sh. 6, dwelling 132, famly 138; Oregon Cemetery transcriptions, Benton Co., at www.orgenweb.org.
84. Henry County, Iowa, Clerk of the District Court, *Iowa Marriage Records, 1836-1931* (FHL Film #965,926).
85. State of Oregon, Certificate of Death No. 2368, (1909), Elizabeth McMurphy, Benton Co., Oregon State Archives.
86. Oregon Cemetery transcriptions, Benton Co., prev. cited.

he married. There is no record of his having served in the Civil War, although he was of an age to have done so. There is no way to know if he received an exemption as the only son still at home with aging parents.

Silas and Elizabeth, along with a two-week-old baby, left Iowa for California in April 1864 with the McMurphy-Bailey wagon train. Upon reaching California, they settled in Lassen County, where he farmed and where three more children were born. By 1870, Silas and Elizabeth acquired land in Lassen County valued at $1,000.[87] In October 1875, Silas and Elizabeth, with her sister and brother-in-law, filed a quitclaim deed to Elizabeth's brothers, Alonzo and Harrison Kelley, for their share of the 164 acres in Henry County, Iowa, they had inherited from her father, John Kelley. In 1879, they added 540 acres to their Lassen County holdings.[88]

Three years later, the family pulled up stakes again and moved to Harney County, Oregon. As Silas's daughter Isabel later recounted:

> *I was born in 1866 and in 1882 my parents moved to eastern Oregon and settled about twelve miles from Burns toward Silver Creek, at a place we called "Sage Hen Valley." I got all my schooling in California. After we came to Oregon we were twelve miles from school. That was too far for me to go even though we had saddle horses. Our nearest neighbors were four miles away. That was great cattle country, but father raised horses. On a visit to Idaho I met [my future husband] ... and later I went back and married him.*[89]

Silas and Elizabeth were still in Harney County when the 1900 census was taken.[90] After their daughter Ida died in Harney County in 1907, they moved to Summit, Benton County, Oregon, where daughter Isabel and her husband lived. Silas died there the following year. A short time later, Elizabeth, evidently despondent, committed suicide with strychnine. Her body was found in the empty house where she once lived with Silas.[91]

Silas and Elizabeth McMurphy had five children:

i. John Abner[3] McMurphy. b. 25 Jan. 1862, d. 24 Sep. 1863.[92]

8 ii. Ida Iowa McMurphy, b. abt. 1864, m. James G. Shelton.

9 iii. Isabel McMurphy, b. 1866, m. William E. Bedell and William M. Clark.

10 iv. Sarah Ellen McMurphy, b. 1868, m. James Peter Roussel.

11 v. Mary Calista McMurphy, b. 1872, m. William Henry Canaday.

7. Laura Jane[2] McMurphy (*Abner*[1]) was born about 1839 in New York State and died in April 1870 in Marion Twp., Henry County, Iowa, of typhoid.[93] She was buried in Hickory

87. S. McMurphy household, 1870 Census Lassen Co., Calif., Janesville Twp., dwelling 99, family 100, pg. 11.
88. Copy of Lassen Co. deed (bk. _?_, p. 699), Harry F. McMurphy to Silas and Elizabeth McMurphy, in the files of Mary J. Drake.
89. Interview of Mrs. William Clark, Benton Co. Interviews, Oregon State Library Archives, WPA Records, part 1, inventory #7, publication #9.
90. S. W. McMurphy household, 1900 Census, Harney Co., Ore., Burns pct., E.D. 161, sh. 6, dwelling 132, family 138.
91. "Aged Summit Lady Suicides" in *The Weekly Gazette-Times* (Corvallis, Oregon), 10 Sep. 1909, p. 2, col. 6.
92. Handwritten "family Bible," small red book among Ted Judge manuscript items at CGS.
93. Abner McMurphy household, 1850 Census, Sangamon Co., Ill., prev. cited; Laura Ramsey, 1870 Mortality Schedule, Iowa, Henry Co., Marion Twp., file p. 8, line 3, family 100.

Portrait of Silas and Elizabeth (Kelley) McMurphy
Courtesy of Mary J. Drake

Grove Cemetery in Henry County.[94] On 4 October 1855, in Henry County, she married **John T. Ramsey**, son of Thomas Ramsey, also of Mt. Pleasant.[95] Born 13 January 1824 in Kentucky, John died on 10 June 1890 in Lassen County and was buried in Janesville Cemetery.[96]

Laura was the only one of Abner's children who did not move to California. She was only thirty-one years old when she died and left, in addition to her husband, a twelve-year-old son and nine-year-old daughter. John Ramsey married a second time in Iowa, probably around 1874, Eliza L. _?_ and had six more children.[97] In 1877, Laura's two children, without their father, moved to Lassen County, where in 1880, Mattie at nineteen was working as a governess and "Abbie," twenty-one, was a farm laborer.[98] In 1887, John and his second family also moved to Lassen County, where he died three years later.

John and Laura Ramsey had the following children:

---

94. *Henry Co., Iowa, Cemetery Records* (FHL film #965,942, item 5, p. 53).
95. Ruth L. Colby, comp., *Henry County, Iowa, Marriages, 1836-1857* (Hartford, Ky.: McDowell Pub., 1977), 81. Abner gave his consent to his daughter's marriage 4 Oct. 1855.
96. John T. Ramsey household, 1870 Census, Henry Co., Iowa., Marion Twp., p. 18, dwelling 103, family 100; Lassen County burials at findagrave.
97. John T. Ramsey household, 1880 Census, Mt. Pleasant, Henry Co., Iowa, Ward 3, E.D. 95, page 14, dwelling 129, family 150.
98. Hiram Gates household, 1880 Census, Lassen Co., Calif., Milford Twp., E.D. 54, dwelling 113, p. 8D.

i. THOMAS ABNER[3] "Abbie" RAMSEY, b. 12 Feb. 1858 in Mt. Pleasant, Henry Co., Iowa, d. 28 Sep. 1939, in Susanville, Lassen Co., bur. Susanville Cemetery.[99] Thomas m. MINNIE L. MASTEN, b. 16 Nov. 1867 in Knights Landing, Yolo Co., Calif; Minnie d. 27 Mar. 1942 in Susanville and was bur. next to her husband.[100]

ii. MARTHA ELLEN "Mattie" RAMSEY, b. 10 Feb. 1861 in Iowa, d. 19 Oct. 1950 in Lassen Co., bur. Janesville Cem.[101] Mattie m. first, FABIUS MAXIMUS WINCHELL, a teacher and hotel landlord, b. 17 Aug. 1843 in Mason Co., Mich. He d. 16 Feb. 1892 in Lookout, Modoc Co., and was bur. there in Adin Cem.[102] Mattie m. second, H. PERRIN READ, b. Mar. 1849 in Missouri,[103] d. 25 Oct. 1906 in Petaluma, Sonoma Co., Calif.[104]

Generation 3

8. IDA IOWA[3] MCMURPHY (*Silas*[2], *Abner*[1]) was born in April 1864 in Iowa and died 5 December 1907 in Harney County, Oregon.[105] Ida married in Grant County, Oregon, 17 November 1886, **JAMES G. SHELTON.**[106] James was born about 1863 in Oregon and died before 1900, when Ida was enumerated as a widow.[107]

James and Ida Shelton had one child

i. SILAS[4] SHELTON, born in Nov. 1887 in Idaho.[108]

9. ISABEL[3] MCMURPHY (*Silas*[2], *Abner*[1]) was born in May 1866 in California, probably Lassen County.[109] She died 1 December 1938, in Lane County, Oregon, and was buried in Summit Cemetery, Benton County.[110] On 17 November 1886 in Grant County, Oregon, Isabel married **WILLIAM E. BEDELL.**[111] Isabel had one child from this marriage, Silas Alfred. She and William probably divorced before 1890, although no record was found. Two William Bedells were enumerated in Idaho in 1900, one aged thirty-three with a wife and family and married thirteen years, the other a prisoner.

They had one child:

---

99. "Some Iowans who Went to California," in *Hawkeye Heritage*, p. 87, prev. cited; California Death Index, 1930-1939; Lassen County burials at findagrave.
100. "Minnie L. Ramsey Dies in Lassen," *Nevada State Journal* (Reno, Nev.), 29 Mar. 1942 (unpaginated obituary posted at www.cagenweb by Mary Taylor, 9 Nov. 2008; Lassen County burials at findagrave, Minnie L. Ramsey headstone.
101. CDA; Cemeteries of Lassen Co. (Archives) at www.lahontanimages.com.
102. Alexander Winchell, *Family of Winchell in America* (Ann Arbor, Mich.: Chase's Steam Printing House, 1869), 104; also "Death of F. M. Winchell" transcribed in "Excerpts from Modoc Exchange" (1892) at www.cagenweb.org; also, Modoc County cemetery database, at www.cagenweb.org.
103. H. P. Read household, 1900 Census, Modoc Co., Calif., Lookout Twp., E.D. 81, sh. 7, dwelling 142, family 145.
104. *Petaluma Courier*, p. 1, col. 3, abstracted in the *Big Valley Gazette*, 25 Oct. 1906 at Newspaper Archives website.
105. S. W. McMurphy household, 1900 Census, Harney Co., Ore., Burns pct., E.D. 161, sh. 6, dwelling 152, family 138; State of Ore., Certificate of Death 5602, Harney Co. 1907, Oregon State Archives.
106. Grant County Marriages, bk. B, p. 6. Until 1889, Harney Co. was a part of Grant Co.
107. Hawkins Shelton household, 1880 Census, Ada Co., Idaho, Dist. 2, E.D. 2 , p. 27, dwelling 294, family 294; in 1900 Ida was living in her father's household, S. W. McMurphy household, prev. cited.
108. S. W. McMurphy household, 1900 Census, prev. cited.
109. William M. Clark household, 1900 Census, Benton Co., Ore., Blodgett Twp., E.D. 6, sh. 3, dwelling 50, family 50.
110. State of Oregon, Certificate of Death 548, Benton Co., Oregon State Archives; Summit Cemetery, Benton Co., Ore., Row 3, #45, from www.rootsweb.ancestry.com/~orbenton/Cemeteries/.
111. State of Oregon, Clerk of the Court, Grant County Marriages, bk. B, p. 6. Isabelle and her sister Ida were married in a double ceremony.

Portrait of Ida (McMurphy) Shelton and son Silas
Courtesy of Mary J. Drake

i. Silas Alfred[4] Bedell Clark, b. 22 Nov. 1887 in Nampa, Canyon Co., Idaho.[112] He d. 29 Jan. 1979 in Benton Co., Ore., and was bur. in Mt. Union Cem., Philomath, Benton Co.[113] Silas took his stepfather's surname, Clark. He m. first, 8 June 1921, in Nashville, Lincoln Co., Ore., Theresa Brody, b. 14 Nov. 1875 in Oregon City, Clackamas Co., d. 23 Nov. 1940 in Philomath.[114] He m. second, Mae _?_, b. 1913, d. 1985.[115] Both wives are buried in Mt. Union Cemetery, Philomath.[116]

Isabel married a second time, 28 November 1890 in Nampa, Canyon County, Idaho, **William M. Clark.**[117] William was born in 1858 in Illinois; he died in Benton County, 3 September

---

112. U.S. Selective Service System, Benton, Co., Ore., World War I Draft Registration Cards, 1917-1918 (FHL film #1,851,980).
113. State of Oregon, Certificate of Death 79-01888, Benton Co., Oregon State Archives; Oregon Tombstone Transcription Project, Benton Co., at www.orgenweb.org.
114. Ben H. Swett, "John Swett of Newbury Descendants," Rootsweb World Connect program at www.rootsweb.com.
115. Oregon Tombstone Transcription Project, Benton Co., Mae Clark listing.
116. Ben H. Swett, "John Swett of Newbury Descendants."
117. "Western States Marriages" database at http://abish.byui.edu/specialCollections/westernStates (hereafter, WMI); Ada County, vol. A, p. 239. Although the event took place in Canyon Co., the records were interfiled with Ada Co. records.

Portrait of Mary McMurphy (L) and Ida McMurphy (R)
Courtesy of Mary J. Drake

1942, and was buried beside his wife.[118] Prior to this marriage William had been married, also in Canyon County, to Frances Shelton, sister of James Shelton, the husband of Isabel's sister Ida. William and his first wife had a son, George, who in 1900 was living with Frances' parents. Frances is presumed to have died since she wasn't found on the 1900 census.

Both Isabel and William, her second husband, were interviewed for the WPA Historical Records survey. He said he opened a store in DeVitt, Oregon, a small town close by Summit, where he became the first postmaster. After selling the store, they moved to the Cascade Mountains, above Eugene on the Mackenzie River, where they bought a store and he served as Leaburg postmaster. They sold that store, repurchased their previous store in DeVitt, and Isabel became the postmistress.[119] This is consistent with the 1930 census of Benton County, where William was enumerated as the proprietor of a general store.[120]

118. William M. Clark household, 1900 Census, Benton Co., Ore., prev. cited. Birth and death from State of Oregon, death records, Oregon State Archives; burial from www.rootsweb.ancestry.com/~orbenton/Cemeteries/.
119. Mrs. William Clark interview, Oregon State Library Archives, WPA Records, part 1, inventory #7, publication #9, Benton Co. interviews.
120. William M. Clark household, 1930 Census, Benton Co., Ore., Blodgett Twp., E.D. 2-4, sh. 1B, dwelling 20, family 20.

William and Isabel had the following children, some born in Idaho, at least five in Oregon:

ii. Robert Clark, b. 10 Oct. 1891, d. 29 Nov. 1902, and was bur. in Summit Cemetery, Benton Co., Ore.[121]

12 iii. Ida Belle Clark, b. 1893, m. Sherman W. Cadwalader.

iv. Marvin Bryan Clark, b. 23 Mar. 1896, d. May 1984 in Benton Co.[122] Marvin was a dairy farmer in Benton Co.; he m. 16 June 1920, Thelma Marks, b. 5 June 1899, d. 4 June 1984.[123] Both were bur. in Summit Cem.[124]

v. Sarah Elizabeth Clark, b. Feb. 1898 in Oregon, m. 6 Sep. 1916 in Benton Co., William Dallas Stevens.[125] William was b. abt. 1891 in Montana, and d. in Nov. 1984 in Washington Co., Ore.[126]

vi. Wright V. Clark, b. 6 Oct. 1902 in Devitt, Benton Co., Ore., d. 24 Mar. 1985 in Benton Co., and bur. in Oaklawn Cem.[127] He was a dairy farmer like his brother Marvin and lived next to him for many years.

vii. Charles W. Clark, b. 20 Oct. 1904 in Ore. He d. 27 January 1951 in Benton Co., and was bur. in Corvallis in Oaklawn Cem.[128] Charles m. Minnie_?_.[129]

viii. Virgil G. Clark, b. 27 Apr.1907 in Benton Co.[130] He d. there 28 Mar. 1974 and was bur. in Summit Cem.[131] Virgil m., in Benton County, 13 July 1929, Lois L. Spence.[132]

ix . Grover A. Clark, b. 23 Apr. 1908 in Benton Co.[133] He d. 18 May 1983 in Philomath and was bur. in Oaklawn Memorial Park in nearby Corvallis.[134] Grover m. 19 Aug. 1931, Nada Johnson, b. 2 Aug. 1910.[135]

---

121. William M. Clark household, 1900 Census, Benton Co., Ore., prev. cited; Summit Cemetery records from www.rootsweb.ancestry.com/~orbenton/Cemeteries/.
122. Marvin E. Clark household, 1930 Census, Benton Co., Ore., Summit Twp., E.D. 2-31, sh. 3A, dwelling 62, family 62; date of birth from SSDI; death from SSDI.
123. Benton Co. Marriages at www.orgenweb.org.
124. Her birth, death and burial from www.rootsweb.ancestry.com/~orbenton/Cemeteries/.
125. Birth from William Clark household, 1900 Census, Benton Co., Ore., prev. cited; marriage from Benton Co. Marriages at www.orgenweb.org.
126. Place of birth from William D. Stevens household, 1920 Census, Multnomah Co., pct. 303, South Kelly Butte, E.D. 195, sh. 7B, dwelling 172, family 172; dates of birth and death from State of Oregon, Certificate of Death 84-20800, Washington Co., Oregon State Archives. William's death certificate states his spouse's name was Alma. Sarah's death certificate was not found. They were either divorced or Sarah died and he married a second time.
127. Benton County Pioneers at www.orgenweb.org; Benton Co. Cemeteries at www.orgenweb.org. Wright is buried in Sec. 4, Row 149, grave 3; next to him in Sec. 4, Row 149, grave 2 is Jessie Mae Patterson Clark b. 1909, d. 1970, whose headstone says, "Wife-Mother."
128. Date of birth from files of Mary J. Drake. Death and burial: State of Oregon, death certificate no. 22, 1951, Benton Co., Oregon State Archives; and Oaklawn Cemetery records at www.rootsweb.ancestry.com/~orbenton.
129. State of Oregon Death certificate of Charles W. Clark, listing wife as Minnie Clark, Benton Co., 1951 #22.
130. Birthplace from William Clark household, 1910 census, Benton Co., Oregon, Summit pct. 8, E.D. 58, sh. 5B, dwelling 121, family 121; date of birth from SSDI.
131. Summit Cemetery records at www.rootsweb.ancestry.com/~orbenton/Cemeteries/.
132. Benton Co. Marriages at www.orgenweb.org.
133. Virgil Clark household, 1930 Census, Linn Co., Ore., Crawfordsville pct., E.D. 22-14, sh. 1A, dwelling 13, family 13; date of birth from SSDI.
134. SSDI; Oaklawn Cemetery database at http://www.rootsweb.ancestry.com/~orbenton.
135. Information from records of Mary J. Drake; their marriage date is in burial information posted at the Oaklawn Cemetery database at http://www.rootsweb.ancestry.com/~orbenton.

10. Sarah Ellen[3] McMurphy (*Silas*[2], *Abner*[1]) was born on 17 February 1868 in Lassen County, California, and died on 3 September 1919. She was buried in Susanville Cemetery, Lassen County, California. Sarah married on 16 August 1889 in Harney County, Oregon **James Peter Roussel**. For details and sources, see Harman Chapter.

11. Mary Calista[3] McMurphy (*Silas*[2], *Abner*[1]) was born 26 January 1872 in Janesville, Lassen County, California, and died in Eugene, Lane County, Oregon, 20 April 1954. Mary was buried in Gates Cemetery, Crow, Lane County.[136] She married in Multnomah County, 22 December 1897, **William Henry Canaday**, born 26 May 1863 in Eugene, Lane County.[137] William died 14 March 1948 in Springfield, Lane County.[138] He was a photographer and an early gallery proprietor; he opened the first gallery in Burns, Harney County.

They had the following children:

13 i. Ambrose Wright[4] Canaday, b. 1899, m. Edna May Waldron.

14 ii. Sylvester Madison Canaday, b. 1901, m. Aleta Mae Wooley.

15 iii. Marion Leroy Canaday, b. 1904, m. Opal Wooley.

iv. Lois Henrietta Canaday, b. 3 Aug. 1908 in Ore., d. Sep. 1967 in Lane County, Ore., bur. Sunset Hills Cem., Eugene.[139] Lois m. first, Riley Gosnell, second, Edward C. Wilson, and third, Charley Nelson.[140]

v. John Robert Canaday, b. 11 Mar. 1911 in Ore. and d. 17 Feb. 2001 in Cottage Grove, Lane Co.[141] John m. first, Arda June Lambert, b. 13 June 1922, d. 29 April 1943, and following Arda's death, her sister, Zaida Madge Lambert, b. 1921, d. 1961.[142] All were bur. in Mulkey Cem. in Eugene.

Generation 4

12. Ida Belle[4] Clark (*Isabel*[3]*McMurphy, Silas*[2], *Abner*[1]) was born in December 1893 in Idaho, and died on 16 June 1931 in Yamhill County, Oregon.[143] Ida married in Benton County,

136. Birth, marriage and death from transcribed obituary and headstone of Mary C. Canaday at www.findagrave.

137. Marriage records, Multnomah County, 1897, vol. 12, p. 42, at Genealogical Forum of Oregon website, www.gfo.org.; unknown comp., *An Illustrated History of Baker, Grant, Malheur and Harney Counties with a Brief Outline of the Early History of the State of Oregon* (Spokane: Western Historical Publishing Co., 1902), 666-7.

138. Lane Co., Oregon, cemetery records at www.findagrave.com.

139. William Canaday household, 1930 Census, Lane Co., Ore., Goshen Election pct., E.D. 20-71, sh. 1A, dwelling 6, family 6. Birth and death from SSDI and obituary in files of Mary J. Drake.

140. In the William H. Canaday household, 1930 Census of Lane Co., Ore. (Goshen Election pct., E.D.. 20-71, sh 1A, dwelling 6, family 6), Lois was listed as Lois Gosnell, married. Her husband's first name Riley is from information from records in files of Mary J. Drake. An unidentified newspaper obituary for Lois Nelson in the files of Mary J. Drake states that "her husband Ed. Wilson passed away six years ago. She married Charlie Nelson in Reno, Nev., October 1966."

141. William Canaday household, 1930 Census, Lane Co., Ore., Goshen Election pct., E.D. 20-71, sh. 1A, dwelling 6, family 6; dates of birth and death from SSDI.

142. Birth and death dates of both sisters from www.findagrave.com.

143. William Clark household, 1900 Census, Benton Co., Ore., prev. cited; State of Oregon, death certificate 125, Yamhill Co., Oregon State Archives, under "Eda" Cadwalader.

14 February 1910, **Sherman W. Cadwalader**, born in Indiana, June 1883.[144] Sherman died 18 October 1938 in Marion County, Oregon.[145]

Sherman and Ida (Clark) Cadwalader had three known children:

i. Sherman Wilbur[5] Cadwalader, b. 10 July 1910, Gold Hill, Jackson Co., Ore., d. 23 July 1910 in Jackson Co., bur. at Rock Point, Jackson Co.[146]

ii. Leroy Cadwalader, b. in Ore., 29 Oct. 1911, d. 14 Oct. 1988 in Beaverton, Washington Co., bur. Willamette National Cem., Happy Valley, Clackamas Co.[147][148]

iii. Daughter, b. about 1913, n.f.i.

13. Ambrose Wright[4] Canaday (*Mary[3]McMurphy, Silas[2], Abner[1]*) was born in Oregon, 4 July 1899, and died 14 August 1980 in Crow, Lane County.[149] Ambrose married in Eugene, 3 August 1927, **Edna May Waldron.**[150] Edna was born 11 December 1899 in Nebraska, and died in Lane County in April 1976.[151] Both were buried in Gates Cemetery, Crow.[152]

Ambrose was in the sawmill and logging business in Spencer, Lane County, with his brother Marion.[153] He later opened a building supply store in Crow, which he operated for many years. Ambrose was very active in the civic affairs of Crow, serving on both the school board and the museum board. He died when his car accidentally veered off the road into a pond.

Ambrose and Edna had four children, including Marjorie Canaday, born 16 Jan. 1929, who married 3 July 1948, Thomas C. McCulloch.[154] Marjorie died 20 April 2003, Thomas two years later, 22 June 2005.[155]

14. Sylvester Madison[4] Canaday (*Mary[3]McMurphy, Silas[2], Abner[1]*) was born 3 June 1901 in Oregon; he died 26 October 1995, and was buried in Gates Cemetery in Crow.[156] Sylvester married, 27 August 1930 in Eugene, **Aleta Mae Wooley**, born 8 June 1915 near Monroe, Benton County, died 24 December 1992 in Lane County.[157]

---

144. Benton Co. Marriages; Amos Cadwalader household, 1900 Census, Benton Co., Ore., Blodgett Twp., E.D. 6, sh. 3, dwelling 43, family 43.
145. State of Oregon, Certificate of Death 902, Marion Co., Oregon State Archives.
146. Transcription of a death certificate found under "vital records" at the Jackson Co., Ore., USGenweb Archives webpage: http://www.usgwarchives.net./or/jackson/vitals/deaths/.
147. SSDI; Clackamas Co., Ore., cemetery records at www.findagrave.com.
148. Clackamas Co., Ore., cemetery records at www.findagrave.com.
149. U.S. Selective Service System, Lane, Co., Ore., World War I Draft Registration Cards 1917-1918 (FHL film #1,852,059); exact date of death from the report of the accident, which appeared in the *Eugene Register-Guardian*, 15 Aug. 1980, p. 1.
150. From funeral notice stating both Edna's name and their marriage date in the files of Mary J. Drake.
151. Ambrose W. Canaday household, 1930 Census, Lane Co., Ore., Spencer pct., E.D. 20-107, sh. 4A, dwelling 77, family 77; birth and death dates from SSDI.
152. Lane Co. burials at www.findagrave.com.
153. Ambrose W. Canaday household, 1930 Census, prev. cited.
154. Birth from SSDI and Ambrose W. Canaday household, 1930 Census, prev. cited; marriage date and place from her obituary in the *Eugene Register Guardian*, 23 April 2003, found at Google News Archives.
155. SSDI.
156. Cal R. Wooley household, 1930 Census, Lane Co., Ore., Coyote pct., E.D. 20-19, sh. 1B, dwelling 18, family 18; birth and death dates from SSDI.
157. Obituary, *Eugene Register-Guardian*, 27 Dec. 1992, p. 3B.

Sylvester in 1930 was a sawyer at a lumber mill.[158] His brother Marion was boarding in the same household and was working as a truck driver perhaps for the same lumber mill. Sylvester and Aleta had nine children. Oldest was Hazel Laverne Canaday, born 12 July 1941, died as Hazel Bradshaw in December 1987, Lane County.[159] Their son, William Turner Canaday, was born 29 May 1943 in Lane County, and died in Portland, 25 September 1943.[160] Rosalie Canaday was born 20 January 1951 in Drain, Douglas County; she married _?_ Armenta, but died under her maiden name Canaday, 26 November 2007 in Gridley, Butte County, California.[161]

15. **Marion Leroy^4 Canaday** (*Mary^{3}McMurphy, Silas^2, Abner^1*) was born 13 March 1904 in Oregon.[162] He died 16 May 1979 in Lane County and was buried in Gates Cemetery in Crow, Lane County.[163] He married **Opal Wooley** (sister of Aleta Mae), born 21 February 1914, died 23 May 1999 in Lane County.[164]

Marion operated a sawmill and retail lumber sales business for nearly 30 years in Crow. He and his brother Ambrose started the Canaday Sawmills in 1942 and later opened a retail outlet.[165] He and Opal had six children, including daughter Marian Elaine, born in Crow, 6 November 1931, who married Albin Reynolds, born 2 February 1932, died 29 May 2007 in Fairbanks, Alaska. Marian Reynolds died 16 April 2008, also in Fairbanks.[166]

---

158. Cal R. Wooley household, 1930 Census, prev. cited.
159. SSDI, Hazel Bradshaw listing.
160. Information from records in files of Mary J. Drake.
161. *Eugene Register-Guardian,* 30 Nov. 2007, abstracted on "The Free Library" with no page listed.
162. William H. Canaday household, 1920 census, Lane Co., Ore., Coyote pct., E.D. 234, sh. 4A, dwelling 67, family 68; exact birth and death dates from SSDI.
163. SSDI; Lane Co., Ore. burials at www.findagrave.com. Exact dates of birth and death are on headstone.
164. SSDI. Opal and Marion were evidently divorced, since Opal is listed as Opal Hach in the Social Security Death Index and Marion's obituary states his surviving spouse's name is Elizabeth; *Eugene Register-Guardian,* 18 May 1979, p. B3, col. 3.
165. Obituary of Marion Canaday, cited above.
166. Birth and death dates for both Albin and Marian from SSDI.

Wedding photo of William and Mary (McMurphy) Canaday
Courtesy of Mary J. Drake

Kelley Descendancy

John Kelley = Sarah Palmer
(1814 - 1867) (1811 - 1901)

Silas Wright McMurphy = Elizabeth P. Kelley
(1836 - 1908) (1841 - 1909)

James Peter Roussel = Sarah Ellen McMurphy
(1866 - 1934) (1868 - 1919)

Timothy Aloysius Judge = Hazel Agnes Roussel
(1894 - 1961) (1900 - 1988)

Theodore Timothy Judge
(1921 - 2008)

Descendancy of Kelley family to Ted Judge

❧ Descendants of John Kelley and Sarah Palmer

John Kelley, the father of Elizabeth Kelley McMurphy of Lassen County, was born about 1814, either in Pennsylvania, as reported in the 1850 census, or in Ohio, as recorded in 1860.[1] He married in 1837 in Washington County, Ohio, Sarah Palmer.[2] Sarah Palmer was born in New Hampshire, a descendant of several early New England families, including the Palmers, Dressers, Pembertons, Jewetts, and Cheneys. Her brother, Jewett Palmer, Sr., a War of 1812 veteran, was a neighbor and an important figure in the local Underground Railroad.[3]

John, and presumably Sarah, were enumerated in the 1840 census of Fearing Township, Washington County, Ohio, next to her brother Jewett and several doors away from a William Kelly family, perhaps John's parents.[4] About 1855, the Kelleys moved to Mt. Pleasant Township, Henry County, Iowa, where their son Harris was soon born.[5] John farmed his own land there, evidently a large number of acres since it was valued at $1,800.[6]

When John's will was probated in 1867, those family members still living were in Henry County with the exception of daughter Elizabeth, who had moved west with her husband to Lassen County, California, and is followed in greater depth in the McMurphy chapter.[7] Sarah, along with other family members, including her two youngest sons, Alonzo and Scott, remained on the farm at least through 1870, and probably until 1874, when daughters Eunice and Sarah quitclaimed their share of the farm to their brothers.[8] Sarah, their mother, was not found on the 1900 census, but likely had moved with a daughter to Frontier County, Nebraska, where she was buried in Farnam Cemetery.[9]

---

1. John Kelley household, 1850 Census, Washington Co., Ohio, Fearing Twp., dwelling 91, family 94, p. 311; Jno Kelly household, 1860 Census, Henry Co., Iowa, Marion Twp., dwelling 139, family 141, p. 337.
2. Bernice Graham and Elizabeth S. Cottle, comps., *Washington County, Ohio, Marriages, 1789-1840* (Baltimore: Genealogical Pub. Co., 1989), 41.
3. *History of Washington County, Ohio, 1788-1881* (Knightstown, Ind.: The Bookmark, 1976), 493, (Reprint of the original 1881 printing); obituary of Jewett Palmer, *Marietta Register,* 2 Oct. 1873 (no page no. available). See also, "Underground Railroad Stations in Southeastern Ohio" posted by the Underground Railraod Research Center of Southeastern Ohio at www.rootsweb.ancestry.com.
4. John Kelly household, 1840 Census, Washington Co., Fearing Twp., p. 24.
5. John Kelley household, 1856 Iowa State Census, Marion Twp., dwelling 19, family 23, p. 333.
6. Jno Kelly household, 1860 Census, Henry Co., Iowa, Marion Twp., dwelling 139, family 141, p. 337.
7. Henry County Probate Court, *Record of Heirs and Estates of Decedents, Heir List, 1862-1896.* (FHL film #964,934, item 2).
8. Sarah Kelley household, 1870 Census, Henry Co., Iowa, Marion Twp., dwelling 58, family 54, p. 8; Henry Co., Iowa, deeds, vol. Z, p. 586 (FHL film #964,090, item 2).
9. See www.nebraskagravestones.org, where a photo of headstone and transcription are available.

The descendants of John and Sarah Kelley and their children are followed here only through the children's generation, at which point daughter Elizabeth married into the McMurphy family. Those who are interested in descendants along these Kelley lines or in the ancestry of John and Sarah should contact the California Genealogical Society, where this information is archived.

Genealogical Descendancy

1. **John[1] Kelley** was born about 1814, either in Pennsylvania or in Ohio.[10] John died in Henry County, Iowa, 21 April 1867, and was buried in Oak Grove Cemetery.[11] He married in Washington County, Ohio, 31 December 1837, **Sarah Palmer**, daughter of John Pemberton Palmer and his second wife, Elizabeth Harris.[12] Sarah was born in New Hampshire, some say in Wentworth, Grafton County, 11 February 1811; she died 15 January 1901 and was buried in Farnam Cemetery, Frontier County, Nebraska.[13]

John and Sarah were recorded in the 1840 census of Fearing Township, Washington County, Ohio.[14] About 1855, they moved to Mt. Pleasant Township, Henry County, Iowa, where they farmed and had their youngest child.[15] John died there in 1867 and left his property to be divided among his surviving family.[16] Sarah, along with other family members, remained on the farm at least through 1870, and probably until 1874.[17] She evidently then moved to Frontier County, Nebraska, where she died.

John and Sarah Kelley had the following children:

i. James[2] Kelley, b. abt. 1840 in Ohio.[18] He d. 20 May 1864 and was bur. in Oak Grove Cemetery, Marion Township, Henry Co., Iowa.[19]

2 ii. Elizabeth P. Kelley, b. 1841 m. Silas Wright McMurphy.

3 iii. Eunice M. Kelley, b. abt. 1843, m. Robert Alvin Chandler.

10. John Kelley household, 1850 Census, Washington Co., Ohio, and Jno Kelly household, 1860 Henry Co., Iowa, Marion Twp., cited above.
11. Henry County, Iowa, *Record of Heirs*; Martha E. Godbey, coll., Amy Noll, ed., *Henry County Grave Records* (Grinnell, Iowa: Daughters of the American Revolution, 1936), 66.
12. Graham and Cottle, *Washington County, Ohio, Marriages, 1789-1840*, 41.
13. Birth date calculated from her age at death. The information that she was born in Wentworth, New Hampshire, comes from an unverified online family genealogy. Sarah probably died in Frontier Co., since that is where the family was living even after her death and where her burial was found (www.nebraskagravestones.org). Her sister, Annie A. Leedham, was buried next to her.
14. John Kelly household, 1840 Census, Washington Co., Ohio, cited above.
15. John Kelley household, 1856 State Census, Marion Twp., cited above.
16. Henry Co. probate, *Record of Heirs, 1862-1896*, prev. cited.
17. Sarah Kelley household, 1870 Census, Henry Co., prev. cited. In 1874, daughters Eunice and Sarah sold their share in the farm to their brothers, and one might presume that their mother probably followed daughter Sarah Stevens to Nebraska. See Henry Co., Iowa, deeds, Z: 586, prev. cited.
18. John Kelley household, 1850 Census, Washington Co., Ohio.
19. Godbey, *Henry County Grave Records*, prev. cited.

iv. George W. Kelley, b. abt. 1845 in Ohio.[20] George d. 15 July 1867, and was buried in Oak Grove Cemetery, Henry Co.[21] During the Civil War, he served two years in Company K, 4th Iowa Cavalry.[22]

4 v. Alonzo Kelley, b. 1847, m. Mary F. Johnston.

5 vi. Sarah E. Kelley, b. 1849, m. George Stevens.

vii. Harris Scott Kelley, b. 1855 in Iowa; he d. in 1930 in Lewis Co., Idaho, and was bur. there in Old Craigmont Cemetery.[23] In 1874, Scott and his brother Alonzo paid $1,400 and obtained a quitclaim deed from two of their sisters and their husbands for land that their father had owned.[24] By 1887, Alonzo had moved to Nebraska, where son Edwin was born.[25] In 1900, Scott appears to have been in Harney County, Ore., near his sister Elizabeth and her family, since in July 1900 he was listed along with S. W. McMurphy as the recipient of warrants for bounty on mountain lions, wolves and coyotes.[26] By 1910, he had moved to Idaho, when he was enumerated in Nez Perce County, unmarried and a hostler on his own place. He removed to Lewis County, Idaho, before 1920 and worked as a horse breeder until his retirement.[27]

Generation 2

2. **Elizabeth P.**[2] **Kelley** (*John*[1]) was born 3 May 1841 in Ohio and died 4 September 1909 in Benton County, Oregon.[28] Elizabeth married in Henry County, Iowa, 21 February 1861, **Silas Wright McMurphy**, born in New York in July of 1836, died in Benton County, 20 February 1908.[29] Silas and Elizabeth, with a two-month-old daughter, left Iowa for California in 1864. They first settled in Lassen County, where he farmed and three more children were born. For more information on this family, see the McMurphy chapter.

3. **Eunice M.**[2] **Kelley** (*John*[1]) was born about 1843 in Ohio and died in Kansas in 1898.[30] On 11 April 1870, in the home of Thomas Mann, Henry County, Iowa, J.W. Chaffin officiating, Eunice married **Robert Alvin Chandler.**[31] Robert was born 11 July 1842 in Mt.

---

20. John Kelley household 1850 Census, Washington Co., Ohio, previously cited.
21. Henry County probate, *Record of Heirs, 1862-1896;* Godbey, *Henry County Grave Records,* prev. cited, 66.
22. Godbey, *Henry County Grave Records,* 66; W. M. Forse Scott, *Roster of the 4th Iowa Cavalry* (New York: J. J. Little & Co., 1902), 175.
23. Margaret Nell Longeteig, et. al., comp., *Lewis County, Idaho, Cemetery Records* (Lewiston, Idaho: Ilo Register Publishing, 1985), 10.
24. Henry Co., Iowa, deeds, vol. Z: 586, prev. cited.
25. Son Edwin in Mary Kelley household (widow of Alonzo), 1900 Census, Washington Co., Arkansas, Center Twp., E.D. 100, sh. 3, dwelling 35, family 37, p. 48A.
26. F. I. Dunbar, *Biennial Report of the Secretary of State of Oregon to the Legislative Assembly—21st Regular Session, for fiscal years ending December 31, 1899 and December 31, 1900* (Salem, Ore.: W. H. Leeds, State Printer, 1901), 101: Statement No. IV, Exhibit No. 247, State Scalp Bounty Fund.
27. Scott Kelly household, 1920 Census, Lewis Co., Idaho, Fletcher Pct., E.D. 134, sh. 11A, dwelling 8, family 9.
28. Oregon Death Certificate No. 2368, (1909), Oregon State Archives.
29. Marriage from Henry County, Iowa, Clerk of the District Court, "Marriage Records, 1836-1880," (FHL film #965,926); Silas's birth and death from Benton County, Oregon, Cemetery transcriptions, at www.orgenweb.org.
30. John Kelley household, 1850 Census, Washington Co., Ohio, Fearing Twp., previously cited; John Brown Jr. and James Boyd, ed., *History of San Bernardino and Riverside Counties,* 2 vols. (Chicago: Western Historical Assn., of Lewis Publishing Co., 1922), 2: 1041.
31. Henry County Geneal. Soc., *Henry County, Iowa, Marriages,* 9 vols. (Mt. Pleasant, Iowa: Iowa Genealogical Soc., 1998), 2: ? (vol. 2 covers 1868-1873; received unpaginated from Allen Co. Public Library).

Pleasant, Henry County, Iowa, the son of Ebenezer and Lucinda (Niles) Chandler, and died 15 July 1918 in Los Angeles County, California.[32]

Robert fought in the Civil War in Company I, 14th Regiment Iowa Volunteers. He served more than three years and was captured at Pittsburg Landing in the Battle of Shiloh.[33] In 1880 Eunice and Robert were living in Centre, Smith County, Kansas, where he was the postmaster and at one point cashier of the Smith County National Bank, and she was a member of Rebeckah Lodge No. 47.[34] Following Eunice's death, Robert married Ella J. (_?_) and moved to California, where he died.[35]

Robert and Eunice had the following children:

i. John Smith[3] Chandler, b. 7 Mar. 1871 in Keytesville, Chariton Co., Missouri, d. 16 May 1924 in Los Angeles Co., Calif.[36] John m. 17 Nov. 1901 in Ventura Co., Calif., Angie May Carpenter.[37] He was employed by Standard Oil for most of his life, and he and his family lived at various times in San Francisco, Richmond and Los Angeles.

ii. Walter S. Chandler, b. 1 Oct. 1872 in Keytesville, Chariton Co., Missouri. He served in the Spanish American War and, in 1905, was on duty in the Philippines. [38]

iii. Mary Luella Chandler, b. 11 Jan. 1875 in New London, Henry Co., Iowa.[39] He d. 15 Jan. 1954 in Los Angeles Co., Calif.[40] Mary m. Ernest Earl Wright, b. 18 Feb. 1874 in Missouri, d. 11 July 1959, Los Angeles Co.[41] Ernest was a jeweler and owned a shop in Los Angeles.

iv. Grace Lucinda Chandler, b. Dec. 1877 in Center, Smith Co., Kan.[42] She d. 27 Apr. 1968 in Redlands, San Bernardino Co., Calif. and was bur. there in Hillside Memorial Park.[43] Grace m. 27 Nov. 1906, Percy Dean Stanley, b. 1872 in Wisc., d. 10 Oct. 1911 in Redlands, San Bernardino Co., bur. there in Hillside Memorial Park.[44] Grace earned a B.S. from Stanford University in 1903. She taught school for several years in various districts, from 1915 to 1922 was county Superintendant of Schools and in 1922 to 1924 was State Commissioner of Elementary Education. In her later years, she operated a private school.

4. **Alonzo[2] Kelley** (*John*[1]) was born 19 May 1847 in Ohio and d. in Arkansas, 29 October 1899; he was buried in Farmington Cemetery, Washington County, Arkansas.[45] Alonzo mar-

32. California Death Index, 1905-1929, at www.vitalsearch-ca.com.
33. Charles H. Chandler, *Descendants of Roger Chandler of Concord, Mass., 1658* (Provo, Utah: Herald Printing Co., 1949), 95.
34. Robert A. Chandler household, 1880 census, Smith Co., Kansas, Centre Twp., E.D. 310, p. 40, dwelling 282, family 288, p. 40; Chandler, *Descendants of Roger Chandler of Concord,* 95; Kansas State Historical Soc., "Death Notices of Members of Fraternal Orders," at www.kshs.org.
35. Robert Chandler household, 1910 Census, Los Angeles Co., Calif., city of Long Beach, E.D. 38, sh. 4A, dwelling 86, family 89. Ella _?_ was b. abt. 1853 in Ohio and appears from the California Death Index to have died 28 Dec. 1932 in Los Angeles Co.
36. Chandler, *Descendants of Roger Chandler of Concord,* 95; California Death Index, 1905-1929.
37. Ventura Co. Calif., Marriage Records, bk. 5, p.16, at www.venturagensoc.org.
38. Chandler, *Descendants of Roger Chandler of Concord,* 95.
39. *Ibid.*
40. Abstracts of California Deaths, 1940-2000, at www.vitalsearch.com (hereafter CDA).
41. CDA.
42. Chandler, *Descendants of Roger Chandler of Concord,* 95.
43. *Redlands Daily Facts,* 29 Apr 1968, p. 4, col. 6.; burial from www.findagrave.com.
44. Information on this family unless otherwise noted is from Brown and Boyd, *History of San Bernardino and Riverside Counties,* 2: 1041 and burials from www.findagrave.com.
45. John Kelley household, 1850 census, Washington Co., Ohio, Fearing Twp., dwelling 91, family 94, p. 311; birth and death from gravestone, photo at www.arkansasgravestones.org.

ried in Henry County, Iowa, 18 March 1875, **Mary F. Johnston.**[46] Mary was born in Iowa, 21 April 1852; she died 3 January 1919, and was buried in Farmington Cemetery, Washington County.[47]

Alonzo and his family moved to Frontier County, Nebraska, around 1887, where his last child, Edwin, was born, and next, before 1899, to Washington County, Arkansas, where he died.

Alonzo and Mary had the following children:

i. Johnny W.[3] Kelley, b. 21 Jan. 1876 in Iowa, d. 31 Dec. 1878 in Iowa, bur. in Oak Grove Cemetery, Henry Co.[48]

ii. Frank Pearl Kelley, b. 15 June 1878 in Iowa.[49] Frank d. 7 Dec. 1936 in Ark. and was bur. in Farmington Cem., Washington Co., Arkansas.[50]

iii. Minnie Sarah Kelley, b. 10 Aug. 1880 in Henry Co., Iowa.[51] She d. 1 Apr. 1961 and was bur. in Farmington Cem., Washington Co., Ark.[52] Minnie m. John Thomas Giles, b. 4 Sep. 1877 in Ark.; d. 6 Mar. 1937 and was bur. in Farmington Cem.[53]

iv. Ida Mae Kelley, b. 30 Sep. 1883 in Iowa, d. 4 Dec. 1922 and was bur. in Farmington Cem.[54] In 1920 Ida was the owner of a truck farm in Ark.; her brother Edwin was working as a laborer on the farm and her brother Frank was doing "public work."[55]

v. Edwin Earl Kelley, b. 6 Nov. 1887 in Moorfield, Frontier Co., Neb., d. 1 Sep. 1971, bur. in Farmington Cem.[56]

5. **Sarah E.[2] Kelley** (*John*[1]) was born in August 1849 in Ohio.[57] Sarah died in 1927 in Nebraska, and was buried there in Farnam Cemetery, Frontier County.[58] Sarah married 25 November 1868, in her parents' home in Henry County, **George P. Stevens**, born 28 April 1840 in Indiana.[59] George died 15 May 1893 and was buried next to Sarah in Farnam Cemetery.[60]

---

46. Henry County Geneal. Soc., *Henry County, Iowa, Marriages*, 9 vols. (Mt. Pleasant, Iowa: Iowa Genealogical Soc., 1997), bk. F.
47. Photo of headstone, source for both birth and death data, at www.arkansasgravestones.org, Mary F. Kelly listing.
48. Godbey, *Henry County Grave Records*, 67. Birthdate calculated from age shown on grave record.
49. Birthplace from census (Frank P. Kelley household, 1930 Census, Washington Co., Ark., Marrs Hill Twp., E.D. 72-19, sh. 6B, dwelling 123, family 125).
50. Photo of headstone at www.arkansasgravestones.org, source for both birth and death data.
51. Henry Co., Iowa, Geneal. Soc., *Henry Co., Iowa Birth Records*, 2 vol. (Mt. Pleasant, Iowa: Iowa Geneal. Soc., 1991), 1:8.
52. Photo of headstone at www.arkansasgravestones.org, Minnie Sarah Kelley Giles and John Thomas Giles.
53. John Giles household, 1930 Census, Washington Co., Ark., Prairie Grove Twp., E.D. 72-29, sh. 1B, dwelling 22, family 22; birth and death from headstone photograph at www.arkansasgravestones.org.
54. Ida Kelly household, 1920 Census, Washington Co., Ark, Center Twp., E.D. 135, sh. 13B, dwelling 266, family 282. Birth and death from headstone, at www.arkansasgravestones.org.
55. Ida Kelly household, 1920 Census, Washington Co., Ark., cited above.
56. Birth from Washington Co., Arkansas WWI Draft Registration Cards 1917-1918 (FHL film #1,530,649); death from photograph of headstone at www.arkansasgravestones.org.
57. Elmer C. Stevens household, 1900 Census, Frontier Co., Nebraska, Plum Creek Twp., E.D. 180, sh. 7, dwelling 118, family 118.
58. Photo of headstone and transcription at www.nebraskagravestones.org. Her headstone has the Eastern Star symbol. Sarah and George Stevens are on the same headstone.
59. Marr. from Henry Co. Geneal. Soc., *Henry County, Iowa, Marriages, Record Book, 1868-1873*, 9 vols. (Des Moines, Iowa: Iowa Geneal. Soc., 1998), 2: ?. George's birth from headstone.
60. Photo and transcription of headstone at www.nebraskagravestones.org. His headstone has the Masonic symbol. There are two headstones for George F. Stevens. One is with his wife as described and one that stands alone with his birth and death dates. This last is probably where he is actually buried because he died so many years before she did.

George served in the Civil War in the 19th Infantry, Company I, from Van Buren County, Iowa, and was discharged as a corporal, 31 May 1865.[61] Around 1887 the family, along with Sarah's brother Alonzo and his family and probably her mother, moved to Frontier County, Nebraska. By 1910, Sarah was the owner of her farm; her two sons, Elmer Charles and Fred, were living at home and helping her run it.[62] After Fred married and left, Sarah and Elmer continued working the farm. Elmer married after 1920 but died in 1925; Sarah died two years later.[63]

George and Sarah Stevens had the following children, all born in Iowa:[64]

i. Elmer Charles[3] Stevens, b. 11 Oct. 1869; d. 3 Mar. 1925, and bur. in Eustis City Cem., Frontier Co., Neb. Elmer m. Mary A. _?_, b. 11 Oct. 1869, d. 20 Oct. 1941, bur. Eustis City Cem.[65]

ii. Fred A. Stevens, b. 30 June 1872; d. 21 June 1941, bur. Farnam Cemetery, Frontier Co., Neb. Fred m. Della C. Pickering, b. in 1878 in Ill., d. 1968 and bur. in Farnam Cem.[66]

iii. Elizabeth Stevens, b. abt. 1880.[67]

iv. Finley A. Stevens, b. Dec. 1882, d. 1929 in Kan., bur. in Hill City Cem., Graham Co., Kan.[68] Finley m. 12 Oct. 1904 in Frontier Co., Neb., Ethel May Farmer, b. about 1886 in Neb., d. 1962 in Kan., and bur. in Hill City Cem., Graham Co., Kan.

61. From 1893 Nebraska Census of Civil War Veterans, Iowa S-Z at www.alhn.org.
62. Sarah E. Stevens household, 1910 Census, Frontier Co., Neb., Plum Creek Twp., E.D. 68, sh. 9A, dwelling 147, family 147, stamped p. 218.
63. *Ibid.*
64. Births and deaths of children and their spouses are from headstones, photos and transcriptions available at www.nebraskagravestones.org and from census enumerations as noted.
65. Marr. from headstone photograph at www.nebraskagravestones.org; Elmer Stevens household, 1920 census, Frontier Co., Neb., Plum Creek Pct., E.D. 71, sh. 26A, dwelling 24, family 27, p. 238.
66. Marr. from obituary of Robert Stevens, "son of Fred and Della (Pickering) Stevens," in "Abstracts of Nebraska Obituaries" at www.neobits.ancestralwhispers.com; Fred A. Stevens household, 1930 census, Frontier Co, Neb., Plum Creek Pct., E.D. 32-24, sh. 2A, dwelling 25, family 25.
67. Scott Kelly household, 1880 Census, Henry Co., Iowa, Marion Twp., dwelling 195, family 197, p. 254.
68. Elmer C. Stevens household, 1900 Census, Frontier Co., Neb., Plum Creek Pct., E.D. 180, sh. 7, dwelling 118, family 118; death from Graham County Cemeteries at www.ksgenweb.org.

Book Two

The Ancestry of Ellen Sheehy Sanford Judge

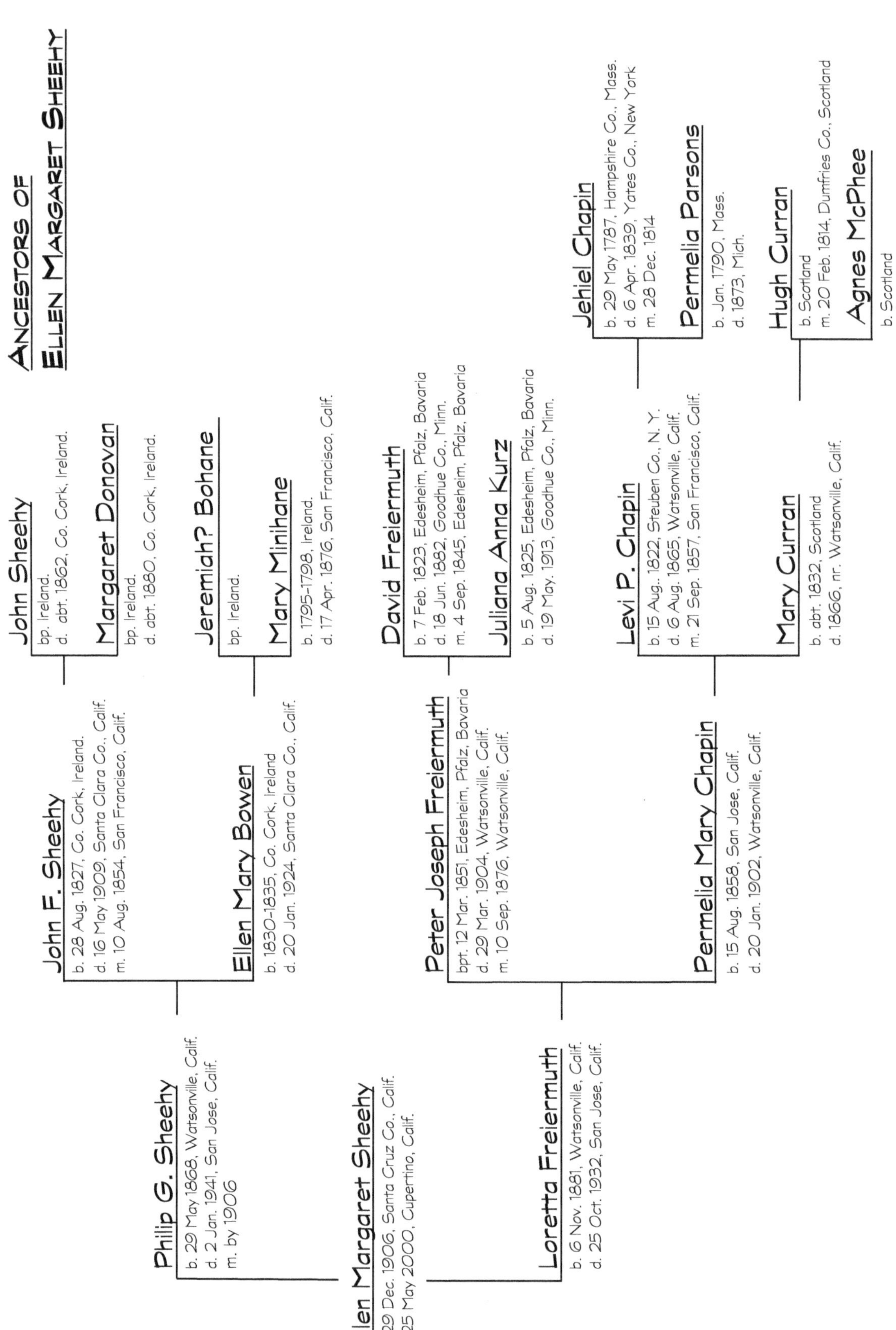
Ancestors of
Ellen Margaret Sheehy
Ellen Margaret Sheehy
b. 29 Dec. 1906, Santa Cruz Co., Calif.
d. 25 May 2000, Cupertino, Calif.
Philip G. Sheehy
b. 29 May 1868, Watsonville, Calif.
d. 2 Jan. 1941, San Jose, Calif.
m. by 1906
Loretta Freiermuth
b. 6 Nov. 1881, Watsonville, Calif.
d. 25 Oct. 1932, San Jose, Calif.
John F. Sheehy
b. 28 Aug. 1827, Co. Cork, Ireland.
d. 16 May 1909, Santa Clara Co., Calif.
m. 10 Aug. 1854, San Francisco, Calif.
Ellen Mary Bowen
b. 1830-1835, Co. Cork, Ireland
d. 20 Jan. 1924, Santa Clara Co., Calif.
Peter Joseph Freiermuth
bpt. 12 Mar. 1851, Edesheim, Pfalz, Bavaria
d. 29 Mar. 1904, Watsonville, Calif.
m. 10 Sep. 1876, Watsonville, Calif.
Permelia Mary Chapin
b. 15 Aug. 1858, San Jose, Calif.
d. 20 Jan. 1902, Watsonville, Calif.
John Sheehy
bp. Ireland.
d. abt. 1862, Co. Cork, Ireland.
Margaret Donovan
bp. Ireland.
d. abt. 1880, Co. Cork, Ireland.
Jeremiah? Bohane
bp. Ireland.
Mary Minihane
b. 1795-1798, Ireland.
d. 17 Apr. 1876, San Francisco, Calif.
David Freiermuth
b. 7 Feb. 1823, Edesheim, Pfalz, Bavaria
d. 18 Jun. 1882, Goodhue Co., Minn.
m. 4 Sep. 1845, Edesheim, Pfalz, Bavaria
Juliana Anna Kurz
b. 5 Aug. 1825, Edesheim, Pfalz, Bavaria
d. 19 May. 1913, Goodhue Co., Minn.
Levi P. Chapin
b. 15 Aug.. 1822, Steuben Co., N. Y.
d. 6 Aug. 1865, Watsonville, Calif.
m. 21 Sep. 1857, San Francisco, Calif.
Mary Curran
b. abt. 1832, Scotland
d. 1866, nr. Watsonville, Calif.
Jehiel Chapin
b. 29 May 1787, Hampshire Co., Mass.
d. 6 Apr. 1839, Yates Co., New York
m. 28 Dec. 1814
Permelia Parsons
b. Jan. 1790, Mass.
d. 1873, Mich.
Hugh Curran
b. Scotland
m. 20 Feb. 1814, Dumfries Co., Scotland
Agnes McPhee
b. Scotland

Overview

The ancestry of Ellen Sheehy Judge is largely a story of immigrants who found prosperity in the post-Gold Rush years of California, in Watsonville and the Pajaro Valley, where Santa Cruz County meets Monterey County. Of her eight great-grandparents, four came from Ireland, two from Germany and one from Scotland. Only one, Levi Chapin, descended from a line that had lived in America over many generations.

The original parameters of this project were to trace descendants starting with the immigrant ancestor or with the great-great grandparents as appropriate. Thus, Ellen's ancestry is presented in four descendancies: Sheehy-Donovan, Bohane-Minihane, Freiermuth-Kurtz, and Chapin-Curran. In the instance of the Sheehy family, her paternal great-great grandparents did not immigrate, but all except one of their children did. The descendants of these immigrant children remained close over subsequent generations and were the subject of a privately published book, *The Sheehys in Ireland and California,* written by Patrick Sheehy in 1994. The work done by Patrick Sheehy is so extensive and interesting that we have chosen to begin in Ireland with the non-immigrant great-great grandparents, John and Margaret Sheehy. However, only the ancestral line of Ellen Sheehy Judge is carried down from John and Margaret Sheehy beyond the second generation.

The Bohanes came from the same area of County Cork as did the Sheehys. Capt. John Sheehy, Ellen Judge's immigrant ancestor, married Ellen Bohane/Bowen, the sister of the wife of a school friend from Baltimore, County Cork. No evidence was found that the Bohanes and Sheehys migrated together, but they managed to find one another in this country. Ellen Bohane Sheehy and her husband remained very close to her sister, Honora, and Honora's husband, James Kelly, who lived in San Francisco. In the hope that descendants of the Kellys may hold information that would add to the Irish history of this family, the descendants of James and Honora Kelly are carried down several generations in the Bohane chapter.

While the Sheehy-Bohane line is entirely Irish, the Freiermuths immigrated to this country from Bavaria. George Anton Freiermuth came first during the large German exodus in the 1840s. Settling first in Massachusetts, he arrived in California in the mid-1850s and left many descendants in both San Francisco and Watsonville. About ten years later his younger brother David immigrated with his family, but settled instead in Minnesota, where he died. Of David's children, however, three made their way to California, and one son, Ellen's grandfather, Peter Joseph Freiermuth, settled in Watsonville, and there married her grandmother, Permelia Chapin.

Mary Curran was born in Scotland, but her husband's Chapin lineage, in contrast, goes back to the earliest days of America. We start with Jehiel and Mary (Curran) Chapin, Ellen Judge's great-great-grandparents, whose son Levi left his family in Michigan to come to California. In order to establish a link between Levi and his family, it was necessary to access old letters written between Levi and his Michigan family. For this information we are grateful to the Rev. Fr. Harry Freiermuth of Watsonville, who willingly shared his private research on both the Chapins and Freiermuths, information that he intends to publish in the near future.

SHEEHY DESCENDANCY

John Sheehy = Margaret Donovan
(? - abt. 1862) (? - abt. 1880)

John F. Sheehy = Ellen Mary Bowen
(1827 - 1909) (1830 to 1835 - 1924)

Philip G. Sheehy = Loretta Freiermuth
(1868 - 1941) (1881 - 1932)

Dudley Phelps Sanford (1899 - 1985) = Ellen Margaret Sheehy (1906 - 2000) = Theodore Timothy Judge (1921 - 2008)

Descendancy from John Sheehy to Ellen

☙ Descendants of John Sheehy and Margaret Donovan

The Sheehy story begins in County Cork, Ireland, along the southwestern coast, southeast of Bantry Bay at the edge of one of the most beautiful lakes of Ireland, a small tidal lake known as Lough Ine (or Lough Hyne). There John Sheehy and his wife, Margaret Donovan (or O'Donovan), perhaps having come from nearby Clonakilty, settled shortly after their first child was born. They farmed land just outside the village of Barloge, in Glannafeen townland, in the parish of Skibbereen and the civil parish of Tullagh.

The second of their ten children was baptized in the cathedral at Skibbereen. It is his baptismal record and that of several younger siblings that help identify where the family lived from 1820 until the Irish famine years, at which time at least eight of the children began the gradual migration to America, eventually arriving in California between 1849 and 1860.

There is no evidence that the parents, John and Margaret Sheehy, ever came to America. John Sheehy died in Ireland in or shortly after 1862.[1] Margaret died in or after 1880, when tenancy rights on the Sheehy land passed from her to another Sheehy.[2] Based upon Irish naming patterns of those times, Patrick Sheehy, in his comprehensive book on the family, has postulated that John's parents were Timothy and Ellen Sheehy and Margaret's parents, Jeremiah and Elizabeth O'Donovan, but this remains speculation.[3]

Those children for whom records have been found were all born in Glannafeen Town, except perhaps oldest child Timothy. Here, an attempt has been made to document down to living descendants the descendants of third son John, the immigrant grandfather of Ellen Sheehy Judge. For additional detail on John's brothers and sisters, the reader should refer to Patrick Sheehy's book.[4] In this account, information on siblings has not extended beyond naming their children, and except in a few circumstances where standard state vital indexes were used, information has been taken directly from the book with only minimal confirmation.

---

1. Surviving land records carry John Sheehy as a tenant farmer on sixty-three acres in Glanafeen until 1862, at which time the land and dwellings were handed over to Margaret. Margaret, in turn, handed over the same land (in tenancy) to a John Sheehy, perhaps a relative but not their son, in 1880.
2. See Patrick E. Sheehy, *The Sheehys in Ireland and California: The Descendants of John Sheehy and Margaret Donovan* (Cupertino, California: self-published, 1994), 26-29.
3. Sheehy, *Sheehys in Ireland and California.* The oldest son was customarily named for his paternal grandfather, the second son after his maternal grandfather, the first-born daughter after her maternal grandmother and the second-born daughter after her paternal grandmother.
4. Sheehy, *Sheehys in Ireland and California.*

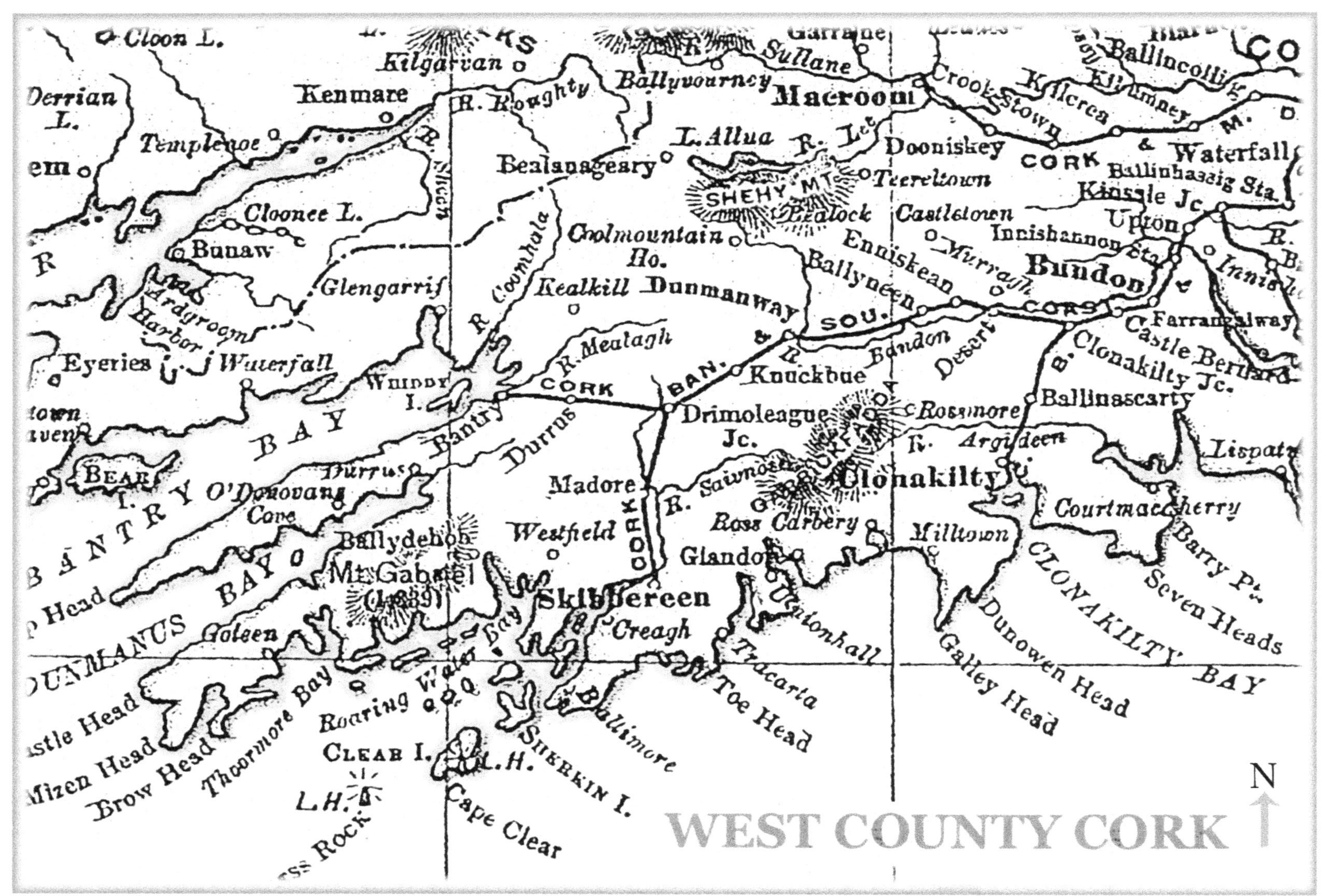

Westernmost part of County Cork: The Sheehy land was located east of Baltimore and southwest of Skibbereen on a saltwater lake fed by the sea

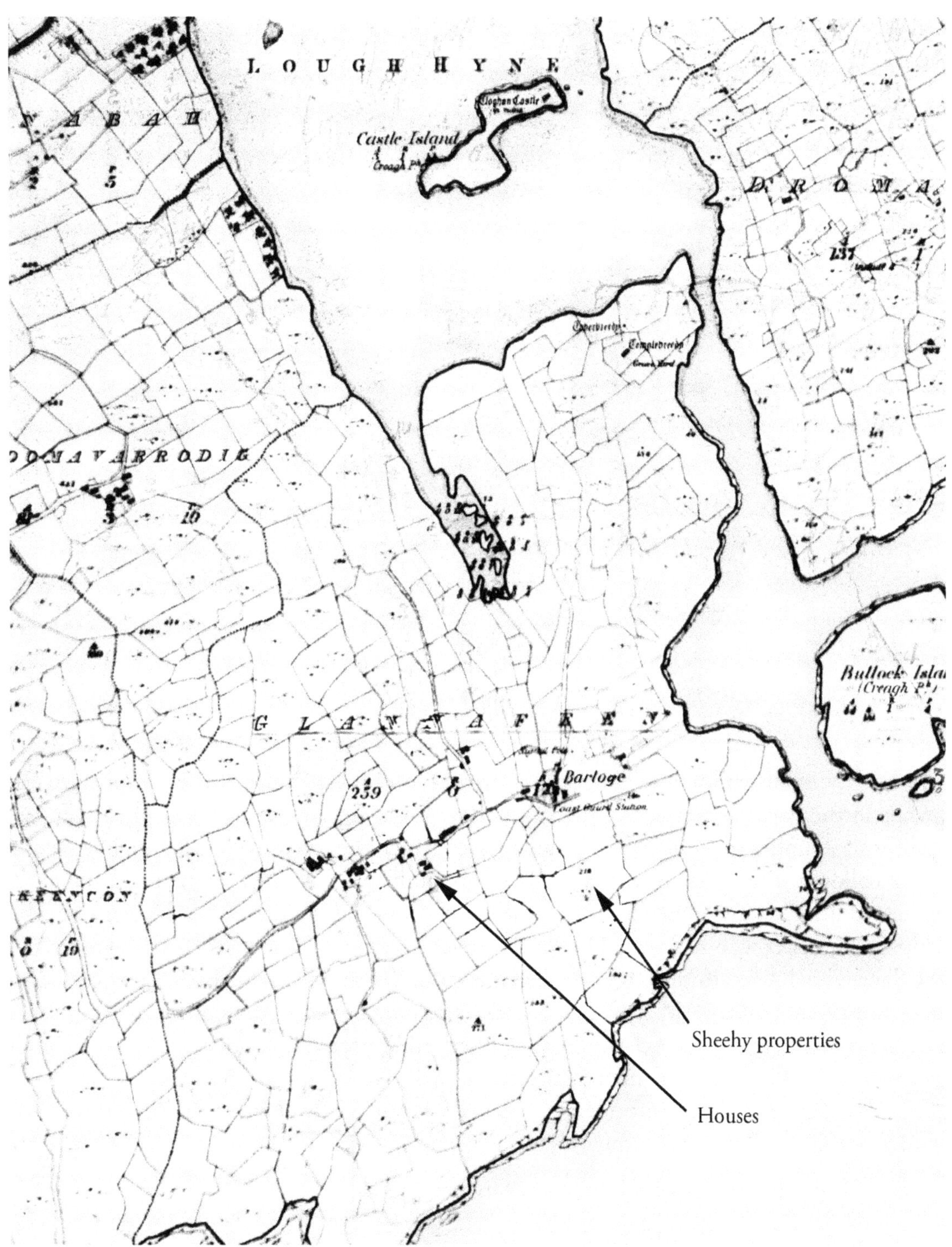

Glannafeen Townland map showing location of Barloge

Abandoned Sheehy cottages in Glannafeen Townland, West Cork
Courtesy of Matt Grul

All the immigrant children of John and Margaret, except for James, settled in or lived for awhile in the Pajaro Valley, along the Pajaro River in and to the east of Watsonville, in the California counties of Monterey and Santa Cruz, which the river divides. James, like several other children, came first to San Francisco, but unlike his siblings, maintained his main residence in that city. Somewhat later, Sheehy cousins and children of Mary Ann Sheehy Shipsey, the sister who had stayed behind in Ireland, came to Pajaro Valley as well. Initially the Sheehys belonged to the old Catholic Church in Watsonville, Our Lady, Help of Christians, commonly called "Valley Church," and many were buried in the small cemetery beside it.[5] Somewhat later, St. Patrick's Catholic Church in Watsonville supplanted Valley Church as the religious center for the many Irish families who settled in the area. Much of the early birth, marriage and death information has been extracted from the records of those two churches and the cemetery nearby.

Thus, we begin in Ireland with John and Margaret Sheehy.

5. This church stands today just east of downtown Watsonville on the north side of Highway 152. Much of the burial information supplied by descendants has been verified in vol. 2 of D. D. Fletcher, *A Tombstone and Vital Records Survey to the Historic Valley Catholic Church Cemetery* (Bonny Doon, Calif.: Bonny Doon Historical Publications, 2002).

Genealogical Descendancy

1. John[1] Sheehy was born in Ireland, and died there in or after 1862.[6][7] About 1818, one or two years before the birth of their first child, John married **Margaret Donovan** or **O'Donovan**.[8] Born in Ireland, perhaps several years after John, Margaret died in or shortly after 1880.[9] In 1880, tenancy rights on the Sheehy land passed from her to another Sheehy.[10]

The land they farmed was located in Glannafeen Townland, in the civil parish of Tullagh. This area lies south of the road from Baltimore to Skibbereen, overlooking the southwest shore of Lough Ine (or Lough Hyne). The family retained tenancy rights until 1945, followed by ownership until 1958.[11]

Known children of John and Margaret Sheehy, all born in County Cork, were as follows:[12]

2 i. Timothy[2] Sheehy, b. 1819 or possibly earlier, m. Mary Ann __?__, and Mary Cunningham.

3 ii. Jeremiah Sheehy, b. late 1820, m. Catherine Carey and Julia Barret.

4 iii. Elizabeth "Bessie" Sheehy, b. 1822, m. John Murphy.

5 iv. Ellen "Ella" Sheehy, b. early 1825, m. Jeremiah Donavan and William Williamson.

6 v. (Capt.) John F. Sheehy, b. 28 Aug. 1827, m. Ellen Bowen (or Bohane).

7 vi. Mary Ann Sheehy, b. April 1830, m. Edward Shipsey.

8 vii. James J. Sheehy/Shea, b. March 1836, m. 22 Jan. 1864, Anna Shipsey.

9 viii. Margaret Sheehy, b. 11 March 1838, m. Thomas O'Connell.

ix. Patrick Sheehy, b. June 1840-1844, d. 22 Sep. 1901, Santa Cruz County.[13] Patrick m. in St. Patrick's Church, Watsonville, 11 Feb. 1879, Elizabeth "Lizzie" Thompson, daughter of John and Mary (Cummings) Thompson, b. May 1857 in California, d. 21 Apr. 1902.[14]

---

6. John Sheehy's year of birth is impossible to estimate from available evidence. If he married about 1818, he likely would have been born about 1795. The last land record found for Timothy, presumed to have been his father, was in 1829. An article published in the *Register Pajaronian* newspaper in Watsonville in 1884 states that son John's grandfather lived to be 104 years old, so it would seem Timothy may have been born about 1758.

7. The approximate year of John Sheehy's death is based upon land records. John Sheehy was a tenant farmer on sixty-three acres in Glanafeen until 1862, at which time the land and dwellings were handed over to Margaret. Margaret, in turn, handed over the same land (in tenancy) to a John Sheehy, perhaps a relative but not their son, in 1880. See Sheehy, *The Sheehys in Ireland and California*, 26-29.

8. Son John's baptismal certificate names his parents as Timothy and Margaret O'Donovan, while the certificates of four other siblings name her Margaret Donovan. The 1829 tithe aplotment valuation shows a Jeremiah Donovan, farming 65 acres in Glannaveen.

9. Timothy, the first child, was likely born in 1819, while the youngest child of record, Patrick, was born in June 1840. Since Patrick was born only two years after his sister Margaret, we assume the mother Margaret had not yet passed her mid-forties. Helen Chalmers Hellman, a descendant of James and a major contributor to the family history, when interviewed in 2006 concurred with these estimates.

10. See Sheehy, *Sheehys in Ireland and California*, 26-29.

11. *Ibid.*

12. If not otherwise noted, information was taken from *Sheehys in Ireland and California*.

13. The 1900 census records his birth in Ireland as June 1840. Other records suggest 1844. See Patrick Sheehy household, 1900 census Santa Cruz Co., Pajaro Twp., city of Watsonville, E.D. 85, sh. 11A, dwelling 240, family 244, p. 99. A brief obituary appeared in the *Santa Cruz Daily Surf*, 24 Sep. 1901, p. 4, col. 6.

14. Records of Valley Church and St. Patrick's Catholic Church, Watsonville; marriage reported in the *Santa Cruz Sentinel*, 15 Feb. 1879, p. 3, col. 7.

They lived in Watsonville, where Patrick was partner in the dry goods firm Atteridge and Sheehy. Patrick and Lizzie were childless and were buried in the cemetery next to Valley Church in Watsonville.

x. EDWARD SHEEHY, b. perhaps in 1843, or in the gap 1831-1835. Great-uncle Edward was identified in family photographs and served as a witness at the 1879 wedding of his brother Patrick, but has not been definitively found in other records. A number of Edward Sheehys of the approximately correct age arrived in New York 1863-1874, but destinations were not included on surviving passenger lists. He was not found in the 1880 census, and descendants speculate he may have come later and then returned to Ireland when his mother became ill or died. Nothing more has been found.

Generation 2

2. TIMOTHY² SHEEHY (*John*¹) was born 23 May, perhaps 1819 but perhaps sooner, in County Cork, Ireland. He died in Watsonville, California, 5 November 1904 and was buried in the cemetery next to Valley Church.[15] Timothy married first, 17 April 1849, **MARY ANN SHEEHY?**, in Boston, Massachusetts.[16] Mary Ann, from census enumerations born about 1830 or sooner in either Boston, Mass. or Ireland, died in California, 23 January 1869. The birth record of her daughter Mary states that the mother was born in Boston, and her tombstone in the cemetery at Valley Church reads, "native of Boston," but the 1860 census reads born in Ireland.[17] In February 1878, Timothy married **Mary CUNNINGHAM**. She was born January 1830 in Ireland, died 14 September 1903 in Watsonville and was buried at Holy Cross Cemetery in Colma, California.[18]

Timothy, as the oldest, was likely the first to leave Ireland, settling for a short time in Massachusetts, where he married. His short obituary states he came to California in 1849, but that seems unlikely given the record of his marriage in 1850 and birth of a daughter in 1852, both in Boston.[19] He was not found in the 1850 census or in the state census of 1852. A biography of one of Timothy's grandsons relates that Timothy crossed "the great plains" and his obituary calls him a pioneer.[20]

Family lore also relates that Timothy and his younger brother John, after locating each other in the Sierra foothills in 1853-54, went to the San Francisco area, where they worked and saved their money. The 1872 *Great Register of Voters*, extracted for foreign-born voters throughout the state, records that Timothy Sheehy, forty-five (a bit young) was naturalized 24 September 1856 in Shasta County, and notes he registered to vote 1868-72 in Monterey County.[21]

---

15. A brief obituary appeared in the *Santa Cruz Daily Surf*, 7 Nov. 1904, p. 2, col. 2. His tombstone reads age 89 at death. The estimate 1819 for year of birth is fairly consistent with census enumerations. No baptismal record was found in Skibbereen records.
16. Mary Ann's surname was either Sheehy (her marriage record in Boston and the baptismal record of daughter Margaret) or Donovan (1867 baptismal record of daughter Annie). Timothy's sister Ellen married a Donovan.
17. Timothy Sheehy household, 1860 census, Santa Cruz Co., Pajaro Twp., dwelling 322, family 297, p. 35.
18. Their San Francisco marriage on 16 Feb. was reported in the Sacramento Daily Union, 26 Feb. 1878, p. 2, col. 2. The obituary of Mary Cunningham Sheehy, *San Francisco Call*, 16 Sep. 1903, p. 13, col. 5, states she was born in Carrickmacross, Co. Monaghan, Ireland.
19. *San Francisco Call*, 6 Nov. 1904, p. 47, col. 4.
20. Account of Gerald Sheehy, son of Jeremiah, appearing in Rolin G. Watkins, ed., *History of Monterey and Santa Cruz Counties, California*, 2 vols. (Chicago: S. J. Clarke Publ. Co., 1925), 275.
21. *The Foreign-Born Voters of California in 1872*, microfiche 1005, published by Jim Faulkinbury. The index to this publica-

Deed

William Dunphy & Thomas Hildreth
To
Timothy Sheehy & John Sheehy

This Indenture made the fourth day of January A D one thousand eight hundred and fifty nine Between William Dunphy and Thomas Hildreth both of the County of Santa Cruz State of California parties of the first part and Timothy Sheehy of the said County of Santa Cruz and John Sheehy of the City and County of San Francisco State aforesaid parties of the second part Witnesseth that the said parties of the first part for and in consideration of the Sum of Two Thousand Two Hundred dollars lawful money of the United States of America to them in hand paid by the said parties of the second part at and before the ensealing and delivery of these presents the receipt whereof is hereby acknowledged Have granted bargained sold and conveyed and by these presents do grant Bargain sell and convey unto the said parties of the second part and to their heirs and assigns forever All that certain tract piece and parcel of land situate lying and being in the County of Santa Cruz State aforesaid being part of that certain Rancho or farm of land which is known as the Bal-si-puedes Rancho and comprising the following fractional sections of the Westerly division of a survey of a portion of said Bal-si-puedes Rancho made by T. W. Wright County Surveyor of said County of Santa Cruz as shown on a map or plat

First Sheehy Land Purchase: Joint purchase by brothers Timothy and John Sheehy along the Pajaro River in Santa Cruz County, January 4, 1859

Early Monterey/Santa Cruz Co. Ranchos: The earliest purchases by Timothy and John Sheehy lay along the Pajaro River in Rancho Salsapuedes
Drawn by Bill O'Neil

Timothy and John together, on 4 January 1859, for $2,200, purchased property along the Pajaro River in Rancho Salsipuedes, Santa Cruz County.[22] This was only the first of a number of large purchases by the two brothers over the next fifteen years in both Santa Cruz and Monterey counties along both sides of the river.[23] In addition to his Pajaro Valley purchases, Timothy bought property in San Francisco, which he willed to his two surviving daughters. One of his many ranch properties in Pajaro was left to his son Edward, another to his son Patrick and one adjacent to his brother John was left to his son Jerry. His estate, which was not mentioned in San Francisco papers, was probated in Santa Cruz County in 1904 but was not obtained. Timothy's short obituary in the *San Francisco Chronicle* mentions a "fortune" estimated at $250,000.[24]

---

tion is online at www.jwfgenresearch.com.

22. Santa Cruz Co. Deeds, 4: 209.
23. See also, Santa Cruz Co. Deeds, 4:512; 7:420; 10:519, 753; and 11:92, 99; and Monterey Co. Deeds, bk. F, p. 343.
24. *San Francisco Chronicle*, 6 Nov. 1904, p. 19, col. 2.

Timothy and his first wife Mary Ann had the following children, all but the first born in California:

i. MARY ANN[3] SHEEHY, b. 11 Dec. 1852 in Boston, Mass., d. Santa Cruz Co., California, 27 Oct. 1926 at 74.[25] She m. 1 Jan. 1878 at St. Patrick's in Watsonville, ARTHUR J. ATTERIDGE, who d. in 1888.[26] Their children, surname Atteridge, were: Robert E., b. Oct. 1878; Arthur J., b. Dec. 1880; John T., b. Mar. 1882; Genevieve M., b. Mar. 1884; and Leo J. (or James Leo), b. June 1886.[27]

ii. JAMES W. SHEEHY, b. abt. 1855, d. 31 Aug. 1887, bur. Valley Church Cemetery.[28] James m. in 1880, KITTY F. CONLAN.

iii. TIMOTHY SHEEHY, b. abt. 1857, d. 26 June 1873, probably in Watsonville, where he was buried in the cemetery at Valley Church.

iv. JEREMIAH J. "Jerry" SHEEHY, b. according to the 1900 census, Sep. 1859, d. in Monterey Co., 15 January 1911.[29] Before 1886, Jerry m. KATHERINE WALLACE, who d. in 1890. Jerry m. second, about 1892-3, FANNY M. MCGOVERN, b. 1858, d. 1909. Jerry and his first wife Katherine had William, b. Sep. 1886 and James, b. Nov. 1890; Jerry and second wife Fannie had Gerald, b. Nov. 1893 (who m. Elsie Regan); Theresa, b. Nov. 1894; Mary, b. 1896; and Albert, b. June 1899.

v. EDWARD W. "Eddie" SHEEHY, b. abt. 1861 in Watsonville, d. there 22 June 1917. Eddie m., 28 Sep. 1889 in St. Mary's Cathedral in San Francisco, AGNES KEARNEY, b. 1867, d. 1925. They had Loretta, b. 23 Mar. 1891; Arthur T., b. 1893; Harold E., b. 23 Nov. 1895; Edward, b. 19 Dec. 1899; Richard Patrick, b. 17 Apr. 1902; Henry G., b. 9 Mar. 1905; Gerald, b. 2 Apr. 1907; and Leo L., b. 20 May 1911.[30]

vi. MARGARET T. "Maggie" SHEEHY, b. in Aug. 1863, d. 6 Feb. 1892.

vii. PATRICK HENRY "Paddy" SHEEHY, b. 12 Oct. (or Aug.) 1865, d. in Santa Cruz County, 11 Oct. 1913.[31] Paddy m. abt. 1898, ISABEL "Belle" ADAM, b. abt. 1865, d. 17 July 1931 as Belle A. Mann.[32] Both Patrick and Belle were buried in Valley Church Cemetery. They had Gladys, b. July 1899, alive in 1900 census but evidently d. bef. 1910; Elizabeth, b. abt. 1900; Kenneth, b. 18 Jan. 1901; William, b. 16 June 1902; Isabella, b. 8 Nov. 1907; and evidently one other child who died between 1900 and 1910.[33]

viii. ANNIE GERTRUDE SHEEHY, b. acc. to her death record, 22 Nov. 1866, d. San Francisco, 17 May 1954. Annie m. in St. Patrick's in Watsonville, 30 Oct. 1894, CHARLES FARDON LANGLEY,

---

25. Massachusetts Vital Records, 1841-1910, vol. 65, p. 82; database at www.newenglandancestors.org.
26. Records of St. Patrick's Catholic Church, Watsonville.
27. Arthur's death is taken from D. D. Fletcher, comp., *A Tombstone and Vital Records Survey to the Historic Valley Catholic Church Cemetery* (Bonny Doon, Calif.: Bonny Doon Hist. Pubs., 2002), 1: 626; the children's births are from the 1900 census, Mary Atteredge household, Santa Cruz Co., Pajaro Twp., city of Watsonville ward 5, E.D. 95, sh. 22A, dwelling 500, family 508, p. 110.
28. Fletcher, *Tombstone and Vital Records Survey*, 1: 626.
29. Jerry Sheehy household, 1900 census, Monterey Co., Pajaro Twp., E.D. 12, sh. 4B, dwelling 76, family 78.
30. Children's births from Edward W. Sheeky (Sheehy) household, 1910 census, Monterey Co., city of Salinas ward 2, E.D. 3, sh. 15A, dwelling 171, family 176, p. 27-28; see also, Abstracts of California Deaths, 1940-2000, a database at www.VitalSearch-ca.com (hereafter, CDA).
31. Death certificate of Patrick H. Sheehy, age 47, died Santa Cruz Co., in possession of Patrick Sheehy of Cupertino.
32. Belle A. Mann household, 1930 census, Santa Cruz Co., Watsonville Twp., E.D. 4-27, sh. 33B, dwelling 320, family 320, p. 143.
33. Children's births from Patric(k) H. Sheehy household, 1910 census, Santa Cruz Co., city of Watsonville ward 2, E.D. 135, sh. 1B, dwelling 25, family 20, p. 43, and 1900 census, Monterey Co., Pajaro Twp., E.D. 12, sh. 4B, dwelling 58, family 67; CDA.

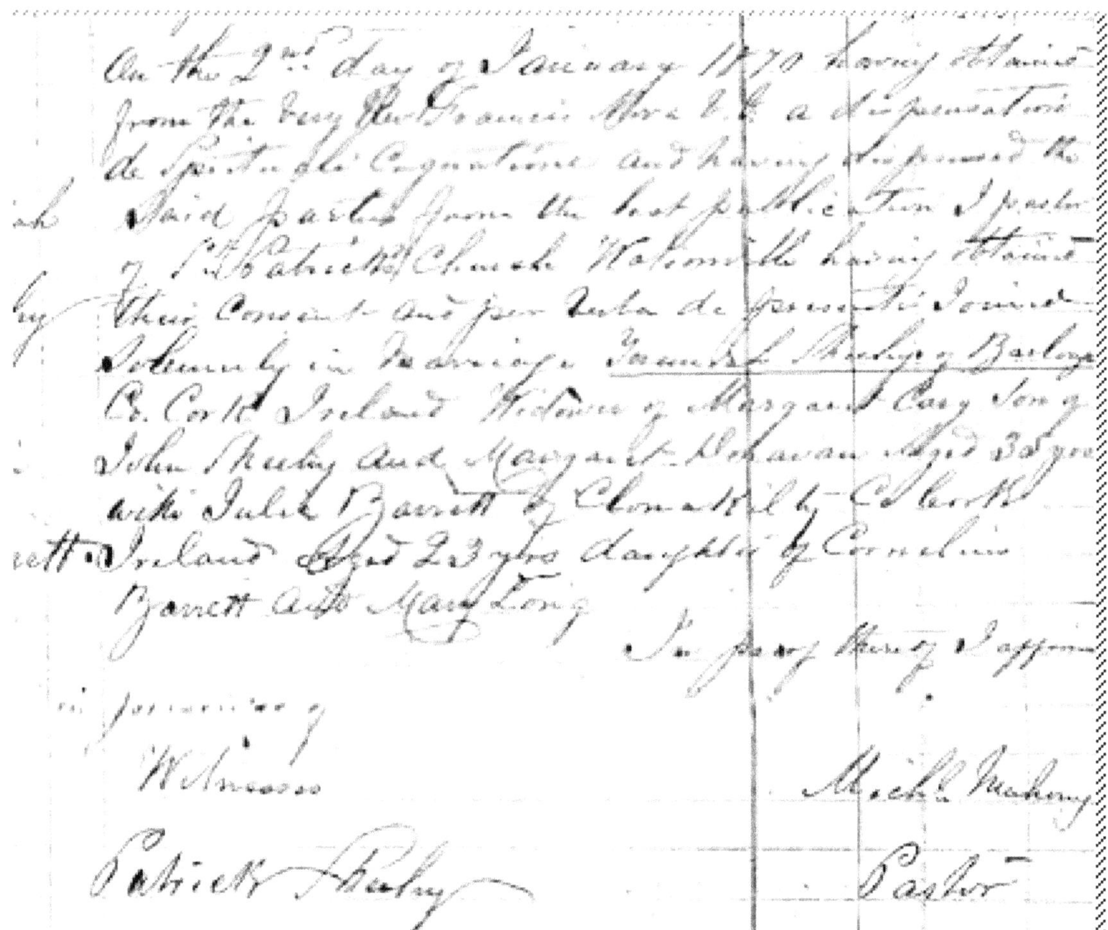

Marriage Record of Jeremiah Sheehy and Julia Barrett: This entry in the St. Patrick's Catholic Church ledger of their marriage, 2 January 1870, led to the identification of the Sheehy homeland near the village of Barloge in Glannafeen Townland, West Cork.
Courtesy of Patrick Sheehy

b. Nov. 1857, d. 31 Oct. 1935, San Mateo Co. They had three daughters, surname Langley: Ethel, b. Sep. 1895; Esther, b. Oct. 1896; and Jeanette Ruth, b. 3 Feb. 1897-8.[34]

3. **Jeremiah**[2] **("Jerry") Sheehy** (*John*[1]) was born about December 1820 in Glannafeen and was baptized January 1821 in Skibbereen Cathedral.[35] Jerry died in California, likely at his ranch in Pajaro Township, in July 1879.[36] He married first, at Valley Church, 7 July 1864, **Catherine Carey**, born about 1837, Co. Cork, who died following childbirth in March 1869. Jerry, "born in Barlogue," married second, January 1871 in St. Patrick's in Watsonville, **Julia Barret**, born 1841 in Clonakilty, County Cork, died in Watsonville, 27 February 1909.[37]

---

34. Annie's death from CDA; Children's birth records are from Charles Langley household, 1900 census, (Monterey Co., Castroville Twp., E.D. 4, sh. 10B, dwelling 188, family 188, p. 177) and from CDA.
35. Birth from baptismal records, Skibbereen Cathedral, obtained by Patrick Sheehy. His date of death in family records was 3 July; however, his obituary, which appeared in the *Santa Cruz Sentinel* (19 July 1879, p.2, col. 4), states he died 5 July.
36. Family records state that he died 3 July, and this date is given upon the 100th anniversary of Jerry's death in the Watsonville *Register Pajaronian*, 9 July 1979.
37. The church ledger entry of Jeremiah's marriage to Julia provided the first clue to the Sheehy homeland: "Jeremiah Sheehy of Barlogue, Co. Cork, Ireland, widower of Margaret Cary…"

Jerry and Catherine's children were as follows:

i. Margaret Ann[3] "Maggie" Sheehy, b. acc. to her death record, 3 July 1865, d. unm. in Santa Cruz County at 88, 6 Mar. 1953.

ii. John Sheehy, b. Aug. 1868 in Watsonville, died less than a year later.

iii. Catherine Josephine "Josie" Sheehy (twin), b. acc. to the 1900 census in Mar. 1869, d. in Watsonville, 6 Dec. 1935. Josie, raised by her aunt Bessie Murphy, m. 24 May 1896 in St. Patrick's, Watsonville, Charles Michael Cassin, son of Charles and Annie (Daly) Cassin, b. 1868, d. 1924.[38] Charles and Josie Cassin had Kathryn, b. 1897-98; Charles Jr., b. 1900 (poss. d. young); Marion, b. 5 May 1901; Gerald, b. 6 Apr. 1903; Anne, b. 10 Apr. 1906; and Robert, b. 25 Mar. 1909.[39]

iv. Unnamed (twin), b. Mar. 1869, d. shortly afterwards.

Jerry and his second wife Julia had the following children, all born in Pajaro Township:[40]

v. Mary Ellen Sheehy, b. 14 Jan. 1871, d. Monterey Co., 4 May 1920.

vi. Joseph A. Sheehy, b. 19 Apr. 1872, d. Monterey Co., 14 Oct. 1916.

vii. James F. Sheehy, b. 6 Sep. 1874, d. Monterey Co., 22 Dec. 1908.

viii. George E. Sheehy, b. 3 July 1876 (or 1878 acc. to death record), d. 11 Sep. 1955, Santa Cruz Co.; evidently unmarried.

4. **Elizabeth[2] "Bessie" Sheehy**, (*John*[1]) was born in June 1822, Glannafeen Townland, County Cork, and was baptized 20 June 1822 in Skibbereen Cathedral. She died in Watsonville, 15 February 1892, and was buried in the Valley Church.[41] About 1852-53, Bessie married **John Murphy**. He was born about 1822 in Ireland; he died in Watsonville, 25 January 1892, and was buried next to Bessie in the old cemetery next to Valley Church.

The Murphys had a large ranch along the Pajaro River near the various Sheehy holdings. There they raised not only Jeremiah's daughter Josie, but six of their own children:

i. Margaret[3] "Maggie" Murphy, b. 24 Oct. 1853-54, d. San Francisco, 6 Sep. 1945.[42] Maggie m. at St. Patrick's, Watsonville, 29 Oct. 1878, James Tynan, b. abt. 1835, d. 27 Aug. 1892. James and Maggie had five daughters, surname Tynan: Maude, b. 29 July 1879; Mollie, b. 8 Oct. 1882; Jessie, b. 7 Mar. 1883; Phileta, b. 7 May 1885; and Annie, d.y.[43]

ii. John D. Murphy, b. 22 June 1855, d. Santa Clara Co., 20 Dec. 1926 and was bur. in the cemetery at Valley Church. John m. abt. 1897, Mary A. Driscoll, b. 1860, d. 1946. They had two sons: John W. Murphy, b. Sep. 1897, and Eugene F. Murphy, b. 21 Sep. 1899.[44]

---

38. Records of St. Patrick's Catholic Church, Watsonville.
39. Children's births are from 1900 census enumeration of Charles Cassin household, Santa Cruz Co., city of Santa Cruz, ward 2, E.D. 127, sh. 6B, dwelling 175, family 182, p. 136; and also from CDA.
40. Exact dates from CDA.
41. Death certificate obtained by Patrick Sheehy.
42. CDA.
43. Children's births from Margaret Tynan household, 1900 census, Santa Clara Co., city of San Jose, ward 2, E.D. 66, sh. 18A, dwelling 363, family 410, p. 28.
44. John Murphy household, 1900 census, Monterey Co., Pajaro Twp., E.D. 12, sh. 1A, dwelling 8, family 10, p. 276.

Margaret Donavan Cupid O'Donovan Kennedy with her son Albert Cupid
Courtesy of Patrick Sheehy

iii. (Sister) Mary Frances Murphy, b. abt. 1857. Mary Frances, a nun, may have been the Mary Murphy in Grass Valley, Nevada County, 1900, in the Sisters of Mercy Orphan Asylum, b. Feb. 1857.[45]

iv. Ellen "Ella" Murphy, b. in 1859, d. in Santa Cruz Co., 5 Aug. 1932, bur. in the cemetery next to Valley Church.

45. Grass Valley Orphan Asylum, 1900 census, Nevada Co., Calif., city of Grass Valley, E.D. 144, sh. 3B, p. 237.

v. Anna J. "Annie" Murphy, b. 27 Nov. 1860, d. Santa Cruz Co., 23 Feb. 1946, bur. in the cemetery next to Valley Church.

vi. Julia Murphy, b. in 1862, d. 21 June 1895, bur. Valley Church Cemetery.

5. **Ellen**[2] **"Ella" Sheehy** (*John*[1]) was born in January or February 1825, County Cork. She died 27 November 1896 and was buried in Valley Church Cemetery.[46] According to family members, Ella married 8 January 1850, in Boston, **Jeremiah Donavan**, born abt. 1822 in Ireland.[47] He died about five years later, and Ella married second, about 1863-1864, **William J. Williamson**, born May 1824-25, in Kentucky, died 29 July 1907, in Monterey County.[48]

The Victorian-style Williamson home, although no longer in the family, still stands along San Juan Road, adjacent to one of the John Sheehy Company farms. Ella had at least three Donavan children by her first marriage and four Williamson children by her second marriage.

Known children of Ella and her first husband Jeremiah Donavan:[49]

i. Jeremiah[3] Donavan, b. 8 Aug. 1849 in Boston, Mass., d. 15 July 1861, bur. in Valley Church Cemetery, Watsonville.[50]

ii. Margaret Donavan, b. 19 Nov. 1850 in Boston, Mass., d. abt. 1930, bur. in Watsonville.[51] Margaret survived three husbands by at least thirty years. In 1867, she m. at Valley Church, William H. Cupid, b. 1831, d. two years later in Watsonville, 16 Sep. 1869. By William Cupid, Margaret had Albert, b. 1868, d. 20 Feb.1914.[52] She next m., 5 Aug. 1873 in St. Patrick's Church, Watsonville, Jeremiah O'Donovan, b. abt. 1846, Ireland, d. 14 Dec. 1873.[53] This very short marriage evidently produced a daughter, Mollie Donavan, born after her father's death. Mollie died at age four and a half, 22 Nov. 1878.[54] Margaret married third, 26 Dec. 1878, Thomas Kennedy, son of Thomas and Mary (Garland) Kennedy, b. abt. 1838 in Sligo Town, Co. Sligo, Ireland, d. Watsonville, 20 Nov. 1898.[55] By her third husband, Margaret had a son George Kennedy, b. 25 Sep. 1879, d. 21 Oct. 1959.[56]

Margaret's second husband, Jeremiah O'Donovan, belonged to a secret fraternal organization, the Knights of the Red Branch. His death was noted in the church ledger: "Death: age thirty, all Sacraments, but blocked from church by [because a member of] Knights of Red

46. Ellen's birth estimated from her baptism, 27 Feb. 1825; her death is from Valley Church records.

47. Massachusetts Vital Records, 1841-1910, vol. 47, p. 103; database at www.newenglandancestors.org. In the Boston vital records, the name is spelled Donovan.

48. Information on this family obtained from the Sheehy book was supplemented by the 1870, 1880 and 1900 census enumerations of Pajaro Twp., Monterey Co.: William Williamson household, 1870, dwelling and family 81, p.12; 1880 E.D. 51, sh. 7; and 1900 E.D. 12, sh. 4A. They probably married first in a civil ceremony, for they were married in St. Patrick's in a religious ceremony, 30 Dec. 1879.

49. In 1850 the Donavans may have been in Boston with a daughter Catherine, age 3, and a son Jeremiah, age 1. If so, Catherine died young. See 1850 census, Suffolk Co., Mass., Boston ward 5, dwelling 166, family 1318, p. 279. The list of known Donavan children was provided by Patrick Sheehy, obtained in interviews with family members.

50. Massachusetts Vital Records, 1841-1910, vol. 36, p. 174; database at www.newenglandancestors.org.

51. Massachusetts Vital Records, 1841-1910, vol. 44, p. 78.

52. California Death Index, 1905-1929, digitizations at www.vitalsearch-ca.com; William Williamson household, 1870 census, Monterey Co., Pajaro Twp., dwelling 81, family 81, p. 12.

53. Records of St. Patrick's Church; marriage and death from Santa Cruz Sentinel, 27 Dec. 1873, p. 2, col. 7. Jeremiah, "age 27" left a will naming Maggie, his father Peter of Co. Cork, and a brother Michael; Patricia Edwards and Janet Jones, abstr., *Santa Cruz County, California, Probate Records* (Santa Cruz: Santa Cruz Co. Geneal. Soc., 1995), 1: 24-25.

54. Records of St. Patrick's Church.

55. *Ibid.*

56. CDA.

Bran[ch]." Family members evidently tried to pursuade Jeremiah to separate himself from this organization but were unsuccessful.

iii. HANNAH T. DONAVAN, b. 1855, Calif., d. 1927; m. 1 May 1878 at St. Patrick's, Watsonville, BYRON N. ALLISON, b. 1857 in Calif., d. in 1937.[57] They had four children, surname Allison: William, b. Jan. 1879; Robert B., b. July 1882; poss. Dorothy (?); and Loretta, b. June 1889.[58]

Ellen and her second husband, William Williamson, had the following children:

iv. DAVID C. WILLIAMSON, b. 9 Dec. 1864-65 in Pajaro Township, d. 29 May 1941, Monterey Co., bur. at Valley Church Cemetery.[59] David m. abt. 1901, ORALIA _?_ and had a daughter Bernice, b. abt. 1903. They were separated by 1910, and Oralia called herself "widow" by 1920.[60]

v. MARY ELLEN "Ella" WILLIAMSON, b. 21 Feb. 1868 in Calif., d. unm. 14 May 1940, Monterey Co., bur. in the cemetery at Valley Church.

vi. JOHN HENRY WILLIAMSON, b. 7 July 1870-71 in Calif., unm. in 1910, bur. in cemetery at Valley Church.

vii. JAMES WILLIAMSON, b. June 1873 in Calif., unm. in 1900, bur. in cemetery at Valley Church.

6. (CAPTAIN) JOHN F.[2] SHEEHY (*John*[1]), the immigrant ancestor of Ellen Sheehy Judge, was born 28 August 1827, in County Cork, and baptized in Skibbereen, 2 September 1827.[61] He died in the city of Santa Clara, 16 May 1909, and was buried at Santa Clara Mission Cemetery.[62] John married, 10 August 1854 at St. Patrick's Church in San Francisco, **ELLEN MARY BOWEN** (likely Bohane or Bohan in Ireland), born in County Cork, perhaps April 1829 or 1830-1835.[63][64] Ellen died in Santa Clara, 20 January 1924.[65]

Family lore relates that as a young man, John attended private school in nearby Baltimore and then shipped out as a seaman from Bantry Bay, County Cork, in 1846. He quickly rose to ship's master, a remarkable accomplishment for a young man, and proceeded to see a bit of the world. In 1852, he left the sea at New Orleans, opting for the life of a miner in the

57. Records of St. Patrick's Catholic Church; his death from California Death Index, 1930-1939.
58. Children's births from Byron Allison household, 1900 census, San Benito Co., San Benito Twp., E.D. 19, sh. 1A, dwelling 10, family 10, p. 314.
59. Birth and death from CDA.
60. Adolph Mautner household, 1910 census, San Francisco, Assembly Distr. 41, E.D. 278, sh. 7A, dwelling 99, family 103, p. 214; Orelia(?) Williamson household, 1920 census, San Francisco, 2057 Scott St., Assembly Distr. 31, E.D. 156, sh. 14A, p. 219.
61. John's exact date of birth appears on his death certificate; a transcription of his Skibbereen Cathedral baptismal record was obtained by Patrick Sheehy.
62. California death certificate, John F. Sheehy, in possession of Patrick Sheehy of Cupertino. A short funeral notice appeared in the *San Francisco Call*, 17 May 1909, p. 13, while a longer article containing many biographical details appeared in the *San Jose Mercury News* 16 May. The Sheehy section in Mission Cemetery is known as "28 old;" it adjoins the Kelly section and evidently was purchased about 1905.
63. The date of their marriage is from an article that appeared in the *Register Pajaronian*, 14 Aug. 1884, regarding their thirtieth anniversary celebration. The place of their marriage, St. Patrick's Church, is family tradition. The records of St. Patrick's were lost in the 1906 earthquake and fire.
64. Ellen's year of birth is taken from her tombstone, month of birth from the 1900 census. Judging from her ages in census enumerations, she is just as likely to have been born 1830-1835. She married many years after her sister Honora, who appears to have been born about 1830.
65. California death certificate of Ellen Sheehy, "father: J. Bohun" [sic], in possession of Patrick Sheehy. See following chapter for information on Bowen/Bohane.

California Gold Rush. After crossing the Isthmus of Panama and catching a boat northward, he arrived in San Francisco, 7 December 1852. Unsuccessful at mining, he next worked as a laborer and participated in a failed ship salvage venture in Santa Cruz County. He then went to Placer County, where he located his older brother Timothy. The two brothers returned to San Francisco, worked and saved their money in order to buy land. Together, on 5 January 1859, they purchased over 200 acres of land in Santa Cruz County, in Rancho Salsipuedes, along the north bank of the Pajaro River. This was followed by another 70-acre purchase across the river by John only, 3 September 1859.[66] Over the next twenty years, John and his relatives continued to buy land in the area, including a number of parcels on the south (Monterey County) side, where land was deemed more suitable for farming.[67]

John Sheehy, 1827 – 1909
Courtesy of Patrick Sheehy

Reportedly John first met Ellen in Boston; she came from an area in County Cork only a few miles from where he had grown up. Meeting her again in San Francisco, they married 10 August 1854.[68] The name Bohane, spelled in the Irish way, is deduced from a number of records. Many family records tie Ellen to a sister Honorah who married James Kelly of Baltimore, County Cork, who later became president of Hibernia Savings and Loan Company in San Francisco.[69] In 1860 in Pajaro Township, Mary Bowen, age sixty-five and born in Ireland, was enumerated in the household of John and Ellen Sheehy. In the 1870 census, Mary Bowen, age seventy-two and born in Ireland, was a member of the Kelly household.[70] Mary Bowen was the baptismal sponsor at the christening of John and Ellen's twins at Valley Church in Watsonville in 1860. Thus, Mary is presumed here to have been Ellen and Honorah's mother. Neither James nor Honorah, nor Ellen for that matter, were found in the 1850 census, but a birth record for the oldest Kelly child was found in 1850 Boston records.[71]

After the move to Pajaro, John farmed and became active in local civic affairs, serving as a county supervisor for eight years. He owned at least four ranches in Watsonville and Salinas

66. Santa Cruz Co. deeds, vol. 4, p. 209 and pp. 512-513.
67. Monterey Co. deeds, bk. F, p. 343.
68. The Boston connection comes from an article in the *Register Pajaronian* of 14 Aug. 1884 on the occasion of their thirtieth wedding anniversary. Birth records for Honora's first children appear in Boston records.
69. See San Francisco city directory of 1890 and following chapter on Bohane.
70. John Sheehy household, 1860 census, Santa Cruz Co., Calif., Pajaro Twp., dwelling 3, family 3, p. 52; James Kenney [Kelly] household, 1870 census, San Francisco, ward 8, dwelling 1195, family 1352, p. 184/471.
71. See following chapter on the Bohane family.

John and Ellen Sheehy family
Courtesy of Patrick Sheehy

as well as a number of buildings in San Francisco, San Jose and Watsonville, including the Universal Hotel building in Watsonville. In the 1900 census, his occupation is reported as "orchardist."[72] He and Ellen retired to Santa Clara in the late 1890s and in 1901 formed the Sheehy Company, in which he consolidated his real estate and stock holdings. That company has since passed down through family members.[73]

John and Ellen Sheehy had ten children:

i. Mary Ellen[3] Sheehy, b. 26 Mar. 1856, San Francisco, d. 13 Mar. 1941, Santa Cruz Co., buried at Valley Church Cemetery, Watsonville.[74] Mary Ellen m., 20 Sep. 1881 at St. Patrick's Church, Watsonville, Timothy J. Horgan, b. 28 Sep. 1856, d. Santa Cruz Co., 11 June 1933.

Timothy started in the grain and feed business, developed a large fruit shipping business and later became active in real estate and insurance. They evidently did not have any children.[75]

72. John Sheehy household, 1900 census, Santa Clara Co., Santa Clara Twp., E.D. 75, sh. 6B, 1155 Chapman St., dwelling 132, family 132, p. 219.

73. Fragments of John's career, in addition to being part of family lore and appearing in his obituaries, were taken from a biography that appeared in *Monterey County: Its General Features, Resources, Attractions, and Inducements to Investors and Homeseekers* (Salinas: E. S. Harrison, 1889), 86.

74. Birth and death data confirmed in CDA. All marriage information was obtained by Patrick Sheehy from parish registers.

75. Biography of Timothy Horgan in Rolin G. Watkins, *History of Monterey and Santa Cruz Counties, California*, 2 vols. (Chicago: S. J. Clarke Pub. Co., 1925), v. 2, p. 149; see also California Death Index, 1930-1939.

ii. JOHN B. SHEEHY, b. Apr. 1858, San Francisco, d. Santa Clara Co., 7 Sep. 1932, bur. in Santa Clara Mission Cemetery.[76] John m. CATHERINE "Kitty" O'CONNOR, b. June 1865, d. 20 Aug. 1925, Santa Clara Co., bur. Mission Cemetery.[77] In 1900, John B. Sheehy and Catherine were living in Pajaro Township, in Santa Cruz County, where John was a farmer.[78] Married for seventeen years, they reported no children.

iii. JEREMIAH FERDINAND TIMOTHY "Jerry" SHEEHY (twin), b. Apr. or May 1860, Watsonville, bp. Valley Church, perhaps 23 May 1860.[79] Jeremiah d. 24 Oct. 1945 in San Jose and was bur. Mission Cemetery, Santa Clara.[80] Jeremiah, a farmer, never married. In 1920 he was "retired" and living in Santa Clara with his mother "Nellie," his sister-in-law Theresa (widow of Henry), Theresa's daughter Elenore and Jeremiah's younger sister Anne, who was listed as head of household.[81]

10 iv. HENRY M. SHEEHY (twin), b. Apr. or May 1860, m. CATHERINE "Kate" THURWACHTER, and TERESA R. "Tessie" MCGOVERN.

11 v. MARGARET "Madge" SHEEHY, b. 28 Feb. 1862, m. THOMAS J. RIORDAN.

12 vi. JAMES SHEEHY, b. probably 1863, m. (1) MARY E. THURWACHTER, (2) HARRIETT "Hattie" GRAVES, and (3) STELLA MATTHEWS.

vii. ANNE ELIZABETH "Annie" SHEEHY, b. Feb. 1865, Watsonville, d. San Francisco, 24 May 1924, bur. Mission Cemetery, Santa Clara.[82] Anne did not marry. In 1920 in Santa Clara, she headed a household consisting of her mother, older brother, widowed sister-in-law and niece.[83]

13 viii. PHILIP G. SHEEHY, b. 28 May 1868, m. LORETTA FREIERMUTH.

ix. HONORA CATHERINE "Kitty" N. SHEEHY, b. 7 Apr. 1871, christened at St. Patrick's in Watsonville, 27 April 1871; d. unm. Santa Clara, 14 Dec. 1911, bur. Mission Cemetery, Santa Clara.[84]

14 x. EDWARD TIMOTHY SHEEHY, b. 11 June 1873, m. MARY ELLEN KELLY.

7. **MARY ANN² SHEEHY** (*John¹*) was born in April 1830 in Glannafeen Townland, County Cork, Ireland. She died 27 March 1916, Cape Clear Island, County Cork, and was buried at

76. Birth and death data confirmed in CDA.
77. *Ibid.*.
78. John B. Sheehy household, 1900 census, Santa Cruz Co., Pajaro Twp., E.D. 84, sh. 2B, dwelling 25, family 25, p. 64.
79. Peggy Larson transcribed the baptismal record from the register at Valley Church. It is not clear, however, if the date corresponds to the baptismal date or the date the information was posted. Family records suggest the baptism took place 12 May. The source of the date of birth, 14 April, has been lost. Witnesses at the twins' baptism were John Murphy, Mary Bowen, Timothy Sheehy and Mary Petit.
80. Birth and death data confirmed in CDA.
81. Ann Sheehy household, 1920 census, Santa Clara Co., Chapman Pct., E.D. 152, sh. 11A, dwelling 247, family 263, p. 80.
82. A year of birth of 1865 is consistent with the entry of her death in the California Death Index at www.vitalsearch-ca.com and with the 1870 census (see ref. below). The source of the month of her birth comes from the 1900 census, in which the year was incorrectly reported as 1870. See John Sheehy household, 1900 census, Santa Clara Co., Santa Clara Twp., E.D. 75, sh. 6B, dwelling 132, family 132.
83. Ann Sheehy household, 1920 census, Santa Clara Co., Chapman Pct., E.D. 152, sh. 11A, dwelling 247, family 263.
84. Kitty's birth was given as April 1874 in the 1900 census (see ref. above), which evidently was incorrect. The entry in the California Death Index, 1905-1929, says died 14 Dec. 1911 at age 32, implying born 1879. In the 1880 census Catherine was 9, which suggests an 1870-71 birth year. In 1910, her age was given as 30. Here the most weight has been given to the earliest records. The source of the exact birthdate is unknown; the christening date is from church records.

North Harbour, Cape Clear Island. Mary Ann married about 1850–1852, **Edward Shipsey**, born about 1827, Skull, County Cork, died Cape Clear Island, about 1882.

They had the following children, all born in Ireland:

i. Margaret[3] Shipsey, n.f.i.

ii. Joanna Shipsey, b. abt. 1853.

iii. Ellen Shipsey, b. abt. 1856.

iv. Edward C. Shipsey, b. abt. 1858-60, d. South Pasadena, Calif., 2 Mar. 1939, age 60.[85] Edward immigrated about 1879, worked for his uncle, James Shea, in San Francisco, and then went to Kern Co. where he had purchased a gold mine. He m. abt. 1892 in Kern Co., Henrietta McGuirk, b. Calif., July 1865, d. Los Angeles Co., 28 Aug. 1938.[86]

v. William Shipsey, b. abt. 1860-61, d. Sierra County, Calif., 31 Oct. 1915, age 53.[87] Family sources say that he married Eliza McGuirk and had three children. These would have been Edward Shipsey, b. Aug. 1892; Annie Shipsey, b. Dec. 1893; and William Shipsey, b. Sep. 1895. By 1900 the marriage had ended in divorce.[88]

vi. John Shipsey, b. abt. 1862, d. 12 Nov. 1924, Kern Co.[89] According to family, John died in a mining accident while working for his brother.

vii. Mary Ann Shipsey, b. 15 Aug. 1864, d. Cape Clear Island, Co. Cork, abt. 1917. Mary Ann m. abt. 1885, Jeremiah Sweeney, b. abt. 1866, Baltimore, Co. Cork, d. Cape Clear Island, Co. Cork.

viii. Thomas Shipsey, b. 14 Sep. 1866.

ix. Charles Shipsey.

x. Ellena Shipsey, b. abt. 1869.

xi. Elizabeth Shipsey, b. Jan. 1871.

xii. Ann "Annie" Shipsey, b. abt. 1877, d. Skibbereen, Co. Cork, 1 Dec. 1968. Ann m. abt. 1902, John Collins, b. abt. 1875/1876, Co. Cork, d. abt. 1960.

8. James J.[2] (Sheehy) Shea (*John*[1]) was born probably June 1835, County Cork, Ireland.[90] James died in San Francisco, 20 October 1902, and was buried at Holy Cross Cemetery in nearby Colma.[91] He married in Old St. Mary's Catholic Church in San Francisco, 22 January 1864, **Anna "Annie" Shipsey**, born June 1839 at Cape Clear Island, County Cork, Ireland, died in San Francisco, 24 September 1919.

---

85. Birth estimated from age at death in California Death Index, 1930-39. The 1900 census of Kern Co. (Edward Shipsey household, Twp. 11, town of Randsburg, E.D. 32, sh. 3B, dwelling 102, family 106) records a birth of March 1860. At this time he listed his occupation as gold mining, and claimed he had immigrated in 1879.
86. Her birth from Edward Shipsey household, 1900 census, prev. cited. They had been married eight years but had no children (nor did they have in 1910). Both Eliza and Henrietta McGuirk, daughters of Andrew and Mary McGuirk, were enumerated with their parents in 1870 in Kern Co. Twp. 1, dwelling 11, family 10, p. 339.
87. California Death Index, 1905-29 (no spouse listed).
88. Lizzie Shipsey household, 1900 census, Kern Co., Twp. 1, E.D. 19, sh. 7A, dwelling 142, family 142, p. 72.
89. California Death Index, 1905-29 (no spouse listed).
90. The birthdate June 1835 is based upon his baptismal record, found at the Skibbereen Heritage Center by Matt Grul, descendant of John and Ellen Sheehy.
91. Obituaries, *San Francisco Chronicle*, 21 Oct. 1902, p. 12, and *San Francisco Call*, 21 Oct. 1902, p. 13, col. 4, and p. 14, col. 4. James and family were all buried in Vault 12 at Holy Cross Cemetery in Colma.

James changed his name from Sheehy to Shea evidently about the time he came to America, which was in 1852 according to his obituary. Descendants of his siblings report that their families were not pleased with the change in spelling. Several family stories relate that James first went to Dublin, either for schooling or to earn money for his passage. Unlike other family members, he came directly to San Francisco. According to city directories, if it was the same James Shea (which is uncertain), he worked as a boatman, a waiter, a drayman and a porter, all before 1866. In 1868 James became a partner and owner of Shea, Bocqueraz and McKee, which a few years later became Shea, Bocqueraz and Co., one of the largest wholesale liquor businesses on the Pacific Coast.

The 1890 Great Register records James Shea was naturalized 6 August 1866 in San Francisco 4th District court, but at age fifty-one, suggesting a birth year some three years after his actual year of birth. The 1872 Great Register accurately recorded his age as thirty.

The Shea family was socially prominent in San Francisco. Two sons attended Santa Clara College. James built a grand house at Golden Gate Avenue and Steiner and a number of other houses, which he gifted to his daughters at marriage. He occasionally traveled abroad and may have returned to Ireland to help settle family affairs. He undoubtedly left a sizeable estate, the details of which were lost in the earthquake and fire of 1906. Annie Shea died in 1919 and left an estate valued at almost $360,000 to be split among her four surviving daughters, Margaret Nolan, Annie Tobin, Ella Chalmers and Elizabeth Murphy, and the two children of her deceased son Leo, Anita McDonald and John Shea.[92]

Over a period of thirteen years, tuberculosis caused the death of five of the Shea children, John, Leo, Mollie, James and Rose. Along with their parents and several more siblings, they were buried in the family vault at Holy Cross Cemetery in Colma. James and Annie Shea had ten children, all born in San Francisco: [93]

i. MARGARET[3] "Maggie" SHEA, b. 23 Nov. 1864, d. 22 Dec. 1938, San Francisco. Maggie m. 26 Sep. 1889 at Sacred Heart Church, San Francisco, JAMES CLAIR NOLAN, b. 14 July 1852, d. 30 Nov. 1924.[94] They had three children, surname Nolan: James Clair ("Clair"), b. 17 Aug. 1894; Mary Estelle, b. 1899; and Lloyd B., b. 11 Aug. 1902, an accomplished actor who starred in the *Dr. Kildare* television series, but perhaps is best remembered for his portrayal of Captain Philip Queeg in the television adaptation of *The Caine Mutiny Court Martial,* for which he won an Emmy.[95] James Jr. and Mary had two children, one of whom is living.

ii. ELLA TERESA SHEA, b. 18 May 1866, d. 22 July 1940 in San Mateo Co., bur. in St. John's Cemetery, San Mateo. Ella Teresa m. 25 Feb. 1889, Dr. WILLIAM PATRICK CHALMERS, b. 18 Dec. 1865 in Watsonville, d. in San Mateo Co., 22 Aug. 1907. They had three children, surname Chalmers: Dorothy, b. 25 Nov. 1890, d. 12 Feb. 1971, San Mateo Co.; John, b. 20 Sep. 1892, d. 25 Mar. 1972, San Mateo Co.; and William, b. 18 Sep. 1894, d. 8 Oct. 1927, San Mateo Co.

iii. LEO W. SHEA, b. 9 Apr. 1868, d. in San Francisco, 20 Feb. 1898. Leo m. 8 Apr. 1891, CATHERINE "Kate" MITCHELL, b. Aug. 1869/1870 in Calif., d. in Los Angeles, 21 Mar. 1951. They had: Anita Shea, b. July 1892, and Jack Shea, b. Oct. 1895.

92. San Francisco Superior Court probate file #027066.

93. Birth and death dates for all children and their spouses and grandchildren were taken from the CDA, from the California Death Index (for years earlier than 1940) and the California Birth Index at www.vitalsearch-ca.com.

94. James Nolan obituary, *San Francisco Examiner*, 2 Dec. 1924, p. 4, col. 6.

95. The Lloyd Nolan obituary appearing in the *Los Angeles Times,* 28 Sep. 1985, p. 2, col. 1, offers a more complete biography.

iv. JOHN W. SHEA, b. 9 July 1870, d. 20 Sep. 1892.

v. MARY AGATHA "Molly" SHEA, b. 18 Aug. 1872, d. 22 Mar. 1904.

vi. ANNA "Annie" SHEA, b. 24 July 1874, d. Arlington, Virginia, 30 Mar. 1959. Annie m. 22 May 1899, ALFRED ALOYSIUS TOBIN, b. 6 Jan. 1878, San Francisco, d. in Burlingame, San Mateo Co., 10 Sep. 1957. Their only child, Aileen Tobin, was b. 31 May 1918.

vii. ROSE E. SHEA, b. 20 June 1876, d. San Francisco, 8 Apr. 1905.

viii. ELIZABETH AGNES SHEA, b. 19 Mar. 1878, d. San Francisco, 2 Aug. 1949. Elizabeth married about 1905, Dr. JAMES D. MURPHY, b. 1 Jan. 1875, d. San Francisco, 6 May 1922. According to family records, they had a daughter Elizabeth, but no additional record was found.

ix. Unnamed daughter SHEA, b. 1880, died in infancy.

x. JAMES SHEA Jr., b. 19 June 1881, d. 17 June 1904.

9. MARGARET[2] SHEEHY (*John*[1]) was born 11 March 1838 in County Cork, Ireland. She died in Watsonville, Monterey County, 27 July 1926, and was buried there in Valley Church Cemetery.[96] Margaret married in 1864, probably in Watsonville, **THOMAS O'CONNELL**, born in 1824 in Ireland, died in 1892 in Salinas, Monterey County.

Thomas came to this country in 1860 and for a short time was a partner in a lumber mill. He then tried farming in Watsonville, where he met Margaret, mined unsuccessfully in Nevada City, Nevada County, California, settled in Salinas, and finally purchased a ranch in nearby San Miguel Canyon.[97]

Thomas and Margaret O'Connell had the following children:

i. JOHNNIE[3] O'CONNELL, b. Jun. 1866 in Nevada, d. in Monterey Co., 25 May 1929, probably unm., bur. Valley Church Cemetery, Watsonville.

ii. THOMAS O'CONNELL, b. abt. 1867, d. Monterey Co., 4 Dec. 1920, bur. Valley Church Cemetery; not found in census records after 1880.

iii. ELLEN O'CONNELL, b. Jan. or May 1870. No information found.

iv. EDWARD O'CONNELL, b. 26 July 1874, d. San Francisco, 27 Aug. 1953. Edward m. in St. Patrick's Church, Watsonville, 25 Apr. 1898 ANNA MARIE FORD, b. 3 June 1870, d. 11 Feb. 1966, bur. Valley Cemetery. They had at least four children: Edward, who died as an infant; Cecile, b. abt. 1901; Edmund, b. 13 April 1902, d. Santa Cruz Co., 27 Mar. 1987; and Willis Ford, b. 20 May 1903, d. 4 Nov. 1951, Watsonville.[98] Willis m. Ellen Sheehy Judge's sister, Annita Sheehy.

v. MARGARET O'CONNELL, b. 20 June 1876, d. 22 Aug. 1959, San Francisco. Margaret m. STEVEN HAUSER. Steven was in the real estate business. They appear not to have had any children.

vi. MOLLIE O'CONNELL, b. 20 Jan. 1880, d. 1954, San Luis Obispo Co., Calif. Mollie m. JOHN BROWN.

---

96. The 1900 census, at which time the widowed Margaret lived in Castroville, records that she was born June 1839. See Margaret O'Connell household, 1900 U.S. Census, Monterey Co., Castroville Twp., E.D. 4, sh. 10B, dwelling 189, family 189, p. 176. Her death certificate was obtained by Patrick Sheehy.

97. Information on the family was also taken from a lengthy obituary in the *Salinas Weekly Index*, 21 Jan. 1892.

98. The three younger children appear with their parents in the 1920 census of San Francisco (Edward O'Connell household, 26th Assembly District, E.D. 95, sheet 5A, p. 176). Birth and death dates from CDA.

vii. ANNIE O'CONNELL, b. May 1886 or, from her death record, 20 Sep. 1884, d. 18 Dec. 1965, Monterey Co. Annie m. 1908-09, HENRY C. CLAUSEN.[99] They had two daughters, surname Clausen: Catherine, b. abt. 1909, and Dorothy, b. 4 Dec. 1910, who died as Dorothy Smith, 25 Nov. 1987, in Monterey Co.

Generation 3

10. **HENRY M.**[3] **SHEEHY** (*John*[2,1]) was born perhaps 14 April 1860, in Watsonville, and died in Santa Cruz County, 10 October 1912.[100] Henry married first, at St. Patrick's in Watsonville, 13 October 1885, **CATHERINE "Kate" THURWACHTER**, daughter of Frederick T. and Catherine (Sweeney) Thurwachter.[101] Kate was born in March 1865 and died in Watsonville, 1 May 1894.[102] Henry married second, also at St. Patrick's, 7 January 1897, **TERESA R. "Tessie" McGRATH** or **McGOVERN**, born 15 April 1865, died in San Jose, 22 January 1929, buried at Santa Clara Mission Cemetery. The St. Patrick's marriage entry reads McGovern (with no parents), but this may have been a name from a previous marriage. Evidence seems to point to a maiden name of McGrath.[103]

Henry, as recorded in every census, was, like most of his relatives, a "farmer." He and Kate had two children:[104]

i. RAYMOND ALFRED[4] SHEEHY, b. 28 Oct. 1886, d. in Monterey Co., 1 Nov. 1940, bur. Valley Church Cemetery, Watsonville. Raymond was still single at the time of the 1930 census, living in Watsonville with his maiden aunt, Ella Thurwachter.[105]

ii. MARGUERITE SHEEHY, b. 17 Nov. 1888. She is believed by family members to have married ROY OWENS, but neither she nor Roy was found in census enumerations 1910 or later.

Henry and his second wife, Teresa ("Tessie"), had one child:

iii. ELLEN NORA M. (or ELENORE) SHEEHY, b. 2 May 1902, d. unm. 18 Nov. 1974, bur. Mission Cemetery, Santa Clara.[106]

---

99. Annie was enumerated in 1900 with Stephen and Margaret Hauser in Salinas, and recorded as born May 1886. In 1910 in Salinas, Henry C. Clausen, wife Annie, age twenty-five and married one year, were enumerated with daughter Catherine. See 1910 census, Monterey Co., Alisal Twp., E.D. 2, sh. 14A, dwelling 148, family 148, p. 26. Anne G. Clausen, maiden name O'Connell, died 18 Dec. 1965 (CDA).

100. Birth year and death date were confirmed in the California Death Index, 1905-1929. The exact date of birth was obtained from descendant Patrick Sheehy.

101. Marriage data for both marriages obtained from records of St. Patrick's Catholic Church by the late Helen Chalmers Hellman; also, see *Santa Cruz Daily Surf*, 14 Oct. 1885, p. 3, col. 2; Kate's parents from death certificate of her unmarried sister Ella, died 6 Feb. 1963, Watsonville.

102. Her death following a carriage accident was reported in the *Santa Cruz Daily Surf*, 1 May 1894, p. 3, col. 1.

103. Descendants thought she was Teresa McGovern. Yet on her daughter Ellen Nora's baptismal record in St. Patrick's Church, Watsonville, Ellen Nora's mother is called Teresa McGrath. Tessie, from the 1900 census, was born in April 1868 in California. She was called Tessie, Teresa and Elissie at various times. William McGrath was a farmer in Watsonville in 1875 (directory); there were no McGovern families there then, in 1880 or in 1900. In the 1870 census, when Teresa would have been between one and two, there were two relevant Teresa McGraths in San Francisco (daughters of Mary and of Patrick/Harriet) and one in Contra Costa Co. (dau. of John/ Margaret). In 1880 there were two in San Francisco and one in Contra Costa, two with fathers named John. In both 1880 and 1900 there were no McGovern families in either Santa Cruz Co. or Monterey Co. Tessie's last name remains unresolved.

104. Birth dates for children who died after 1939 from CDA.

105. Ella Thurwachter household, 1930 census, Santa Cruz Co., Calif., Watsonville Twp., E.D. 44-35, sh. 2A, dwelling 21, family 21, p. 243.

106. Baptismal certificate for Ellen Nora Sheehy obtained in 1967 from St. Patrick's Church in Watsonville; California Death Certificate, Elenore Marie Sheehy.

11. Margaret[3] **"Madge" Sheehy** (*John*[2,1]) was born 28 January 1862 in Watsonville. She died in San Jose, 10 November 1952, and was buried in Mission Cemetery, Santa Clara.[107] Madge married at St. Patrick's, 5 October 1884, **Thomas J. Riordan**, son of Michael and Margaret (Coughlin) Riordan, born 15 November 1859 in San Francisco, died in Salinas, 30 January 1902.[108]

Thomas attended St. Mary's College in San Francisco and worked at various jobs until eventually starting his own grain business. He was active in civic affairs, serving as Monterey County Auditor in 1882 and, subsequently, three terms as Monterey County Clerk.[109] He was injured in and later died from a tragic accident in January 1902, falling from a railroad depot platform while trying to control his team of horses, spooked by a passing train.[110]

Thomas and Madge Riordan had eight children, likely in Monterey County, where they lived for most of the pre-1900 years:[111]

15 i. John H.[4] Riordan, b. 28 Sep. 1885, m. first, Vivian Sheehan and second, Virginia van Zant.

ii. Aileen Frances Riordan, b. December 1887 or 1 Jan. 1888, d. Santa Clara Co., 21 Apr. 1958, bur. Santa Clara Mission Cem.[112] Aileen married Jack Palmtag (divorced, no ch.).

16 iii. Madeline Riordan, b. 8 Oct. 1889, m. Maurice J. Rankin.

17 iv. Thomas Justin Riordan, b. 14 Apr. 1891, m. Elva Pointer.

v. Anita Riordan, b. 1 Jan. 1893 (death record incorrectly says 1896), d. 9 May 1959, bur. Mission Cemetery, Santa Clara. Anita married Weir Losse, b. 7 Nov. 1887, d. 16 Feb. 1969. No ch. Both were interred in the mausoleum at Santa Clara Mission.

vi. Harold Joseph Riordan, b. 7 Oct. 1895, d. San Mateo Co., 16 Feb. 1985, bur. Mission Cemetery, Santa Clara.

18 vii. Kathryn Riordan, b. 3 Mar. 1899, m. William H. Grul.

viii. Robert Kenna Riordan, b. 9 May 1902, d. 16 Feb. 1978, bur. Santa Clara Mission Cemetery. Robert married Auzerais Portoll.

12. James[3] **Sheehy** (*John*[2,1]) was born 5 July, probably 1863, in Watsonville. He died in Salinas, Monterey County, 9 July 1935, and was buried in Mission Cemetery, Santa Clara.[113]

107. Birth and death data of Margaret from family records, confirmed in CDA.

108. Records of St. Patrick's Church, Watsonville; death reported in *San Francisco Call*, 31 Jan. 1902.

109. Henry D. Barrows, *A Memorial and Biographical History of the Coast Counties of Central California* (Chicago: Lewis Publishing Co., 1893), 437.

110. His death, which occurred several weeks after the accident, was reported in the *San Francisco Call*, 31 Jan. 1902, p. 9, col. 3.

111. Birth and death information and births of children and grandchildren are from the California 1905-1929 and 1930-1939 Death Index digitizations, CDA and the Social Security Death Index at www.vitals.rootsweb.ancestry.com (SSDI). Some adjustments in birth years were made according to the 1900 census. It records son John's birthdate as Sep. 1885, Aileen's as Dec. 1887, Madeline's as Oct. 1889, and Anita's as Oct. 1893. See Thomas Riordan household, 1900 census, Monterey Co., Alisal Twp., city of Salinas, E.D. 2, sheets 18A and B, dwelling 371, family 379, pp. 139-40.

112. California and Social Security death records provide a birthdate of 1 January 1889. However, the 1900 census of Alisal Twp., Monterey Co., where her parents were living, states she was born December 1887, and the spacing of the Riordan children seems to suggest she was probably born either the last day of 1887 or shortly into 1888.

113. Birth and death data confirmed in California Death Index, 1930-1939. The date of death and age at death (68) together suggest an 1867 birth. The 1900 census provides the birthdate Oct. 1862, but this follows too closely his sister Madge's birth. The date 5 July was obtained from an unrecorded source by Patrick Sheehy, who located a baptismal record sug-

James married first, about 1890 in San Francisco, **Mary E. Thurwachter**, born June 1866, died 26 March 1895.[114] James married second, 3 May 1899, in St. Patrick's, Watsonville, **Harriett "Hattie" Graves**, born October 1866, died 3 July 1933, Santa Cruz County.[115] Following her death, James married third, **Stella Matthews**, born 1 September 1883, died 24 February 1976.[116]

James and Mary had two children:

19 i. Leontine Geraldine[4] Sheehy, b. Dec. 1892, m. William Nelson Cumming.

ii. John Fredrick "Bud" Sheehy, b. 23 Jan. 1895, d. Piedmont, Calif., 27 June 1977.[117] John m. first, abt. 1930 in Reno, Nevada, Rose __?__, and second, at an unknown date, Helen __?__.

James and Hattie had one child:

iii. Edward Sheehy, b. Nov. 1899 in California, not alive at the time of the 1910 census.[118]

13. Philip G.[3] Sheehy (*John*[2,1]) was born 29 May 1868 in Watsonville and died in San Jose, Santa Clara County, 2 January 1941.[119] Philip married first, **Loretta Freiermuth**, daughter of Peter Joseph Freiermuth and Permelia Chapin, who was born 6 November, 1881, and died in San Jose, 25 October 1932 at age forty-nine.[120] In 1937, Philip married second, **Josephine Cribari**. Philip and Loretta are buried at Santa Clara Mission Cemetery.

Philip attended Santa Clara University and the University of California Hastings School of Law, and was admitted to the bar in 1901. A prominent lawyer, he argued many cases in the California Supreme Court, in federal district courts and, ultimately, the Supreme Court of the United States. He served six years as the City Attorney of Watsonville and as deputy collector of internal revenue and later became senior partner in the accounting firm Sheehy & Helwig.[121]

He and Loretta had five children:[122]

i. Ellen Margaret[4] Sheehy, b. 29 Dec. 1906, Santa Cruz Co., d. at The Forum retirement home in Cupertino, Calif., 25 May 2000. Ellen m. 5 July 1932 at St. James Cathedral in

---

gesting 1863. See Jim Horgan household, 1900 census, Santa Cruz Co., city of Watsonville, ward 4, E.D. 85, sh. 16A, dwelling 374, family 381, p. 104.

114. Death reported in The *Santa Cruz Daily Surf*, 27 March 1895, p. 4, col. 4.

115. Marriage from records of St. Patrick's Catholic Church, Watsonville; death from California Death Index, 1930-1939.

116. Birth and death from CDA.

117. Both the SSDI and John's World War I draft card provide a birth of 23 Jan. 1895. He served as an Army pilot.

118. James Sheehy household, 1910 census, Santa Cruz Co., city of Watsonville, ward 3, E.D. 136, sh. 9A, dwelling 207, family 236, p. 78. He must have died shortly after 1900, for Harriet reported in 1910 that she had had no children and Edward's death is not in the 1905-1929 California Death Index.

119. Birth and death from CDA. Philip was two at the time of the 1870 census; thus, the information in his biography, published in the *History of Santa Clara County* by Eugene T. Sawyer, is not correct. See John Sheehy household, 1870 census, Monterey Co., Pajaro Twp., dwelling 22, family 22, p. 369; also Eugene T. Sawyer, *History of Santa Clara County, California, with Biographical Sketches of the Leading Men and Women of the County Who Have Been Identified with Its Growth and Development from the Early Days to the Present* (Los Angeles: Historic Record Co., 1922), 862.

120. California Death Index, 1930-1939. Loretta's date of birth from family information is consistent with the 1900 census, Philip Sheehy household, Santa Clara Co., Calif., Santa Clara Twp., E.D. 75, sh. 6B, dwelling 132, family 132. Her daughter Ellen's 1906 birth certificate states that Loretta was twenty-five at the time.

121. Eugene T. Sawyer, *History of Santa Clara County, California,* 862.

122. Unless otherwise cited, information on all the children, provided by Patrick Sheehy, was confirmed where possible in the California Death Indexes for 1905-1929 and 1930-1939, the CDA, the California Birth Index and the SSDI.

Philip Sheehy
Courtesy of Patrick Sheehy

Seattle, Dr. Dudley Phelps Sanford, b. 8 Nov. 1899, died Carmel Valley, Calif., 4 July 1985.[123] They divorced in 1944, and the marriage was formally annulled by the Catholic Church in 1976.

Following her divorce in 1944, Ellen returned to school and earned her B.A. and teaching credential from San Jose State in 1955. She taught for a number of years in Watsonville and then went to work for the Pillsbury Food Co., which is how she met her future husband, Theodore Timothy Judge. Ted then worked for Pillsbury in Minnesota, but they managed to maintain a long-distance friendship for many years until Ellen was able to obtain an annulment from the Catholic Church and felt free to marry. Their marriage took place 18 Dec. 1976 at St. Christopher's Convent in San Jose.[124]

123. Certificate of marriage, prepared 10 Aug. 1976, evidently needed for church annulment.
124. Annulment document found among the papers of Ellen and Theodore Judge. Marriage certificate of Theodore Judge and Ellen Sanford, found among the papers of Theodore Judge.

Philip Sheehy children: Ellen, John Jerome and Annita on bench, Philip and Rosemarie in back
Courtesy of Patrick Sheehy

Ted's childhood and career are covered in the biographical section. He outlived Ellen by eight years. Both are buried at Santa Clara Mission Cemetery.

20 ii. Rosemarie Sheehy, b. 4 Sep. 1909, m. Frank Gummer.

iii. Philip G., Jr., b. 7 Feb. 1912, d. unm. San Jose, Santa Clara Co., 23 Nov. 1933, bur. Mission Cemetery, Santa Clara.

iv. Annita Sheehy, b. 24 Oct. 1913, d. Watsonville, 9 Oct. 1992, bur. at sea, Monterey. Annita m. first, in Nevada, Willis Ford O'Connell, son of Edward O'Connell and Anne Marie Ford, b. 20 May 1903, d. Watsonville, 4 Nov. 1951, and second, Tony Rogers, b. poss. 18 Jan. 1899, d. Santa Cruz Co., 9 Oct. 1986. No children.

21 v. John Jerome Sheehy, b. 16 Nov. 1916, m. Hope Boyd.

14. **Edward Timothy^{3} Sheehy** (*John^{2,1}*) was born 11 June 1873 in Watsonville and died there, 21 September 1943.[125] Edward married in the Santa Clara University chapel, 30 November 1910, **Mary Ellen Kelly**, born in 1874, died in Santa Cruz County, 4 January 1936.[126] Both are buried in the cemetery adjoining Valley Church in Watsonville.

Edward and Mary Ellen had the following children:[127]

22 i. John Edward "Ed" Kelly^{4} Sheehy, b. 25 April 1912. Edward m. Betty Mylott.

23 ii. Kathleen Helen "Katie" Sheehy (twin), b. 8 June 1913, m. Edward Alexander Palmer.

24 iii. Thomas Eugene "Bud" Sheehy (twin), b. 8 June 1913, m. Pearl Huston.

Generation 4

15. **John H.^{4} Riordan** (*Margaret^{3} Sheehy, John^{2,1}*) was born 28 September 1885, and died 17 July 1981, in San Francisco. John married first, **Vivian Sheehan** and second, **Virginia van Zant.**

John Riordan served as secretary and a director of the John Sheehy Company. He wrote a history of the family and the company in the 1960s upon which much of the family history is based.

He and Vivian had three children, all born in San Francisco:[128]

25 i. John H.^{5} Riordan, Jr., b. 27 June 1916, d. 17 Mar. 1971, Alameda Co. John m. Ruth Bloch.

26 ii. Catherine Ann Riordan, b. 15 Sep. 1920, m. William L. Ferdon.

iii. Thomas Riordan, b. 10 Dec. 1921, d. 19 Mar. 1990, San Francisco.

---

125. CDA.
126. California Death Index, 1930-39.
127. California Birth Index and SSDI.
128. Unless otherwise cited, information in Generations 4 and 5 have been taken from information provided by Patrick Sheehy, from the California Birth Index, from the various California death indexes and abstracts previously cited and from the SSDI. In this instance, information was supplemented from the John Riordan household enumeration, 1930 census, San Francisco, E.D. 38-208, sh. 26A, p. 274. Children are named only with permission.

Children of Edward and Mary Ellen Sheehy: l. to r. Bud, Ed and Katie Sheehy
Courtesy of Patrick Sheehy

16. Madeline[4] Riordan (*Margaret[3] Sheehy, John[2,1]*) was born 8 October 1889 and died 3 September 1978. Madeline married San Jose attorney **Maurice J. Rankin**, born 5 March 1888 in Kansas, died 12 May 1975. Both Madeline and Maurice are buried at Santa Clara Mission Cemetery.

John and Madeline Rankin had one child:

27 i. John Alden[5] Rankin, b. 19 September 1917, m. Mary Elizabeth Brady.

17. Thomas Justin[4] Riordan (*Margaret[3] Sheehy, John[2,1]*) was born 14 April 1891 and died in Santa Clara County, 23 October 1984. Thomas m. **Elva Pointer**, born 14 March 1895, died 26 November 1980. Thomas was a graduate of the University of Santa Clara.

Thomas and Elva had two daughters:

28 i. Kathleen Patricia[5] Riordan, b. 12 November 1921, Santa Clara Co., m. Clark Edward Guinan

29 ii. Suzanne Marie Riordan, b. 4 January 1926, San Francisco; m. Robert B. Cahill.

18. Kathryn[4] Riordan (*Margaret[3] Sheehy, John[2,1]*) was born 3 March 1899. She died 19 September 1978 and was buried at Valley Church Cemetery, Watsonville. Kathryn married in Texas before 1919, **William H. Grul**, born 2 January 1898, died at Watsonville, 13 January 1971.

William and Kathryn Grul had two children:

i. WILLIAM[5] GRUL JR., b. 7 April 1919, d. Santa Cruz Co., 17 Nov. 1966; m. NANCY COCKRAN.

30 ii. TIMOTHY JEROME GRUL, b. 7 Aug. 1929, m. ADELE GRETCHEN WAHLSTROM.

19. LEONTINE GERALDINE[4] SHEEHY (*James*[3], *John*[2,1]) was born in December 1892. She died in Salinas, 25 February 1967, and was buried at Valley Church Cemetery. Leontine married 9 June 1915 in Valley Church, **WILLIAM NELSON CUMMING**, born 6 March 1891, died 28 July 1958.

William and Leontine Cumming had three children, all born in Santa Cruz County:

31 i. WILLIAM NELSON[5] CUMMING, b. 16 Nov. 1916, m. MARGARET MARIE GLENSOR.

ii. JAMES D. CUMMING, b. 22 June 1921, d. San Francisco, 22 Nov. 2000.

iii. LEONTINE "Mary Lee" CUMMING, b. 8 Mar. 1928. n.f.i.

20. ROSEMARIE[4] SHEEHY (*Philip*[3], *John*[2,1]) was born 4 September 1909, and died 4 September 2002. She married **FRANK GUMMER**, born 13 August 1911, died 14 March 1989.

Frank and Rosemarie Gummer had one child:

32 i. FRANCIS GREGORY[5] "Frank" GUMMER, JR., b. 19 Mar. 1938, Santa Clara Co., m. DIANE DOWNING and JERI HELM.

21. JOHN JEROME[4] SHEEHY (*Philip*[3], *John*[2,1]) was born 16 Nov. 1916 and died 18 February 2003 at Yuba City, California. He married **HOPE BOYD**, daughter of Donald and Nadine (Sherwood) Boyd, born 26 February 1919, died 2 February 2004.

John and Hope Sheehy had two children, both born in Sutter County:

i. LORETTA ANN[5] "Lorie" SHEEHY, b. in Marysville, Calif., 22 Jan. 1944. Lorie m. 11 Sep. 1965, DENNIS WESTERBERG (divorced), and 9 Aug. 1980, PAUL CRONAN CRESS.

ii. JOHN JEROME SHEEHY, b. 11 Sep. 1946, d. 6 Dec. 1955, Marin Co., Calif.

22. JOHN EDWARD KELLY[4] SHEEHY (*Edward*[3], *John*[2,1]) was born 25 April 1912 in Watsonville and died in Ventura County, 12 August 1962. John married, 22 April 1939, at Sierra Madre, California, **BETTY MYLOTT**, born 28 June 1911 in Los Angeles, died in Ventura County, 10 December 1982.

John and Betty Sheehy had three children, including:

i. [Name withheld]

33 ii. MAUREEN ELLEN[5] SHEEHY, b. 12 May 1945, m. DANIEL LOFTUS.

iii. [Name withheld]

23. KATHLEEN HELEN[4] SHEEHY (*Edward*[3], *John*[2,1]), the twin of Thomas Eugene, was born 8 June 1913 at the Sheehy Ranch outside of Watsonville and died in Davis, California, 20 September 2004. Kathleen married, 20 December 1945, in San Francisco, her distant cousin, **EDWARD ALEXANDER PALMER,** born 9 July 1913, Alameda County, died 25 May 1987.[129]

---

129. See the following chapter on the Bohane family. Wedding date and place provided by Patrick Sheehy. The license was issued 23 Nov. 1910 and is on file at the San Jose Historical Museum; death from CDA. Their great-grandmothers were

Kathleen's obituary recounts a long and impressive career in nursing, public health and teaching.[130]

Edward and Kathleen lived in Piedmont, Alameda County. They had five children, all born in San Francisco:

34 i. Christine Ann[5] Palmer, b. 9 Nov. 1946, m. David J. Beeby.

35 ii. Timothy Edward Palmer, b. 19 Mar. 1948, m. Constance Curry.

36 iii. Mark Jonathan Palmer, b. 19 May 1951, m. Virginia Nielson (div.).

iv. Aileen Marie Palmer, b. 27 Mar. 1953.

37 v. Philip Sherman Palmer, b. 11 Aug. 1954, m. Bonnie L. Lowrie.

24. Thomas Eugene[4] "Bud" Sheehy (*Edward[3], John[2,1]*), the twin of Kathleen, was born 8 June 1913 at the Sheehy Ranch outside of Watsonville. He died in Salinas, 7 April 2003, and was buried at Valley Church Cemetery, Watsonville. Bud married, in Valley Church, 25 June 1939, **Pearl Mae Huston**, born 16 July 1917, Dayton, Washington, died in Salinas, 19 April 1991. Following Pearl's death, Bud married in Salinas, 1 August 1992, **Grace Johnson,** who survived him.[131]

Bud first ran the Kelly ranch in Pajaro Valley and went on to manage many nearby ranches in the Pajaro Valley and operate a fertilizer business. He and Pearl had four children:

38 i. Patrick Eugene[5] Sheehy, b. 24 Sep. 1940, Watsonville; m. Pauahi Merrill Judd.

39 ii. Ellen Kathleen Sheehy, b. 30 Aug. 1942, Watsonville, m. James G. Ferrasci.

40 iii. Mary Kelly Sheehy, b. 5 Aug. 1947, Watsonville; m. Robert J. Putz and Douglas K. Guerrero.

41 iv. Michael Clarence "Mike" Sheehy, b. 9 Jan. 1953, Salinas; m. 17 July 1976, Kathleen M. Cusack. Michael and Kathleen had a daughter Erin, b. 24 Jan. 1981, Los Gatos, Santa Clara Co.

Generation 5

25. John H.[5] "Jack" Riordan (*John[4] Riordan, Margaret[3] Sheehy, John[2,1]*) was born 27 June 1916, and died 17 March 1971 in Alameda County. John married **Ruth Bloch**. They had two children: John H., born in San Francisco, 28 June 1949, who married Diann McArthur, and Francis Vincent, born in San Mateo, 28 March 1953, who married Jennifer Kirby.

26. Catherine Ann[5] Riordan (*John[4] Riordan, Margaret[3] Sheehy, John[2,1]*) was born 15 September 1920, and died in San Francisco, 29 March 1995. Catherine m. **William L. Ferdon**. Their children included Mary Catherine "Mary Kay" Ferdon, born in San Francisco, 28 January 1954, who married Stephen Edmund Leveroni.

sisters, making them third cousins.

130. *San Francisco Chronicle,* 13 Oct. 2004, online without a page number at www.sfgate.com.

131. Thomas Eugene Bud Sheehy obituary, *San Jose Mercury News,* 9 April 2003 (digitizations at www.GenealogyBank.com).

27. **John Alden**[5] **Rankin** (*Madeline*[4] *Riordin, Margaret*[3] *Sheehy, John*[2,1]) was born 19 September 1917 and died 24 January 2004 in Santa Clara County. He married, 22 July 1942, **Mary Elizabeth Brady.** Their children, all born in San Jose, included: Maureen Ann, born 5 July 1943, married Terrance R. Thomas; Margaret Jane, born 29 October 1946, married John D. Noonan; Mary Louise, born 15 May 1949, married Vernon T. Snowden; Marilyn Sue, born 7 May 1951, married John Daniel Coll; Marcia Kathryn, born 25 March 1953, d. 24 July 1996; and John Alden, born 27 October 1955, married Terri Stone.

28. **Kathleen Patricia**[5] **Riordan** (*Thomas*[4] *Riordan, Margaret*[3] *Sheehy, John*[2,1]) was born 12 November 1921, in San Jose. She married, 17 June 1944, **Clark Edward Guinan,** born in Kern County, 15 June 1921, died in Santa Clara County, 6 January 1988. [Living children, names withheld]

29. **Suzanne Marie**[5] **Riordan** (*Thomas*[4] *Riordan, Margaret*[3] *Sheehy, John*[2,1]) was born in San Francisco, 4 January 1926; she married **Robert B. Cahill.** Their children included Susana Cahill, born 14 December, 1957.

30. **Timothy Jerome**[5] **Grul** (*Kathryn*[4] *Riordan, Margaret*[3] *Sheehy, John*[2,1]) was born 7 August 1929, and died in Santa Cruz County, 29 December 1995. He married 1 September 1952, **Adele Gretchen Wahlstrom,** born in Omaha, Nebraska, 29 August 1928 (div.). They had three children: Jonathan Andrew b. 13 March 1962; Timothy Arnold b. 12 January 1954; Matthew Peter b. 3 May 1957, m. Suzanne Marie Michaud.

31. **William Nelson**[5] **Cumming** (*Leontine*[4] *Sheehy, James*[3], *John*[2,1]) was born 16 November 1916, and died in Monterey County, 14 January 1990. He married, 30 December 1941, **Margaret Marie Glensor.** William and Margaret Cumming had two children, both born in San Jose: Margaret Leontine, born 24 October 1942, who married Robert Owen Hebert, and William Nelson, born 8 January 1945, who married Veeda M. James, born Shelton, Washington, 23 January 1948 (their ch: Janelle Cumming Fandrick, b. 4 Aug. 1969, and Sean Cumming, b. 19 June 1973).

32. **Francis Gregory**[5] **Gummer, Jr.** (*Rosemarie*[4] *Sheehy, Philip*[3], *John*[2,1]) was born in Santa Clara County, 19 March 1938. The owner of a liquor store in Campbell, Frank, Jr., was shot and killed during a store robbery, 27 February 1980.[132] He married first, **Diane Downing** (div. 1966) and second, [name withheld]. By his first marriage, Frank, Jr., had one son, Eric M. Gummer, born 11 October 1965.

33. **Maureen Ellen**[5] **Sheehy** (*John Edward*[4], *Edward*[3], *John*[2,1]) was born 12 May 1945, in Santa Clara County. She married, 24 February 1968, **Daniel Loftus.** Their children included Stephen Loftus, born in Santa Clara County, 30 September 1974.

34. **Christine Ann**[5] **Palmer** (*Kathleen*[4] *Sheehy, Edward*[3], *John*[2,1]) was born in San Francisco, 9 November 1946. Christine married, 20 December 1969, **David J. Beeby** and had Elizabeth Aileen Beeby, b. 15 February 1981, and Maureen Margaret Beeby, b. 11 November 1982, d. 19 July 2008.

---

132. *San Francisco Chronicle,* 28 March 2009, B1, regarding parole for murder.

35. **Timothy Edward**[5] **Palmer** (*Kathleen*[4] *Sheehy, Edward*[3], *John*[2,1]) was born in San Francisco, 19 March 1948. Tim married, 4 June 1971, **Constance Curry**. [Living children, names withheld]

36. **Mark Jonathan**[5] **Palmer** (*Kathleen*[4] *Sheehy, Edward*[3], *John*[2,1]) was born in San Francisco, 19 May 1951.

37. **Philip Sherman**[5] **Palmer** (*Kathleen*[4] *Sheehy, Edward*[3], *John*[2,1]) was born in San Francisco, 11 August 1954. Philip married, 17 June 1978, **Bonnie L. Lowrie** (div.).

38. **Patrick Eugene**[5] **Sheehy** (*Thomas*[4], *Edward*[3], *John*[2,1]) was born in Watsonville, 24 September 1940. Patrick married, 15 June 1963, **Pauahi Merrill Judd**, born in Honolulu, 8 May 1941. Patrick and Pauahi have four children: Patrick Edward, born 6 December 1964; Julie P., born 14 February 1967; Peter H., born 7 December 1970, married Martha M. Padgett; and Matthew J., born 7 January 1976.

39. **Ellen Kathleen**[5] **Sheehy** (*Thomas*[4], *Edward*[3], *John*[2,1]) was born in Watsonville, 30 August 1942. She married, 26 June 1971, **James G. Ferrasci**. James and Ellen Ferrasci had a daughter Margaret, born 19 November 1973, who married Jason Roger Bales.

40. **Mary Kelly**[5] **Sheehy** (*Thomas*[4], *Edward*[3], *John*[2,1]) was born in Watsonville, 5 August 1947. Mary married, 15 June 1971, **Robert J. Putz** (div.) and secondly, **Douglas K. Guerrero**. Children from her marriage to Robert Putz included Jennifer M., b. 19 August 1971, who m. James Christopher Barry.

41. **Michael Clarence**[5] "Mike" **Sheehy** (*Thomas*[4], *Edward*[3], *John*[2,1]) was born in Salinas, 9 January 1953. Mike married, 17 July 1976, **Kathleen M. Cusack**. Their children included Erin, born in Los Gatos, Santa Clara County, 24 January 1981.

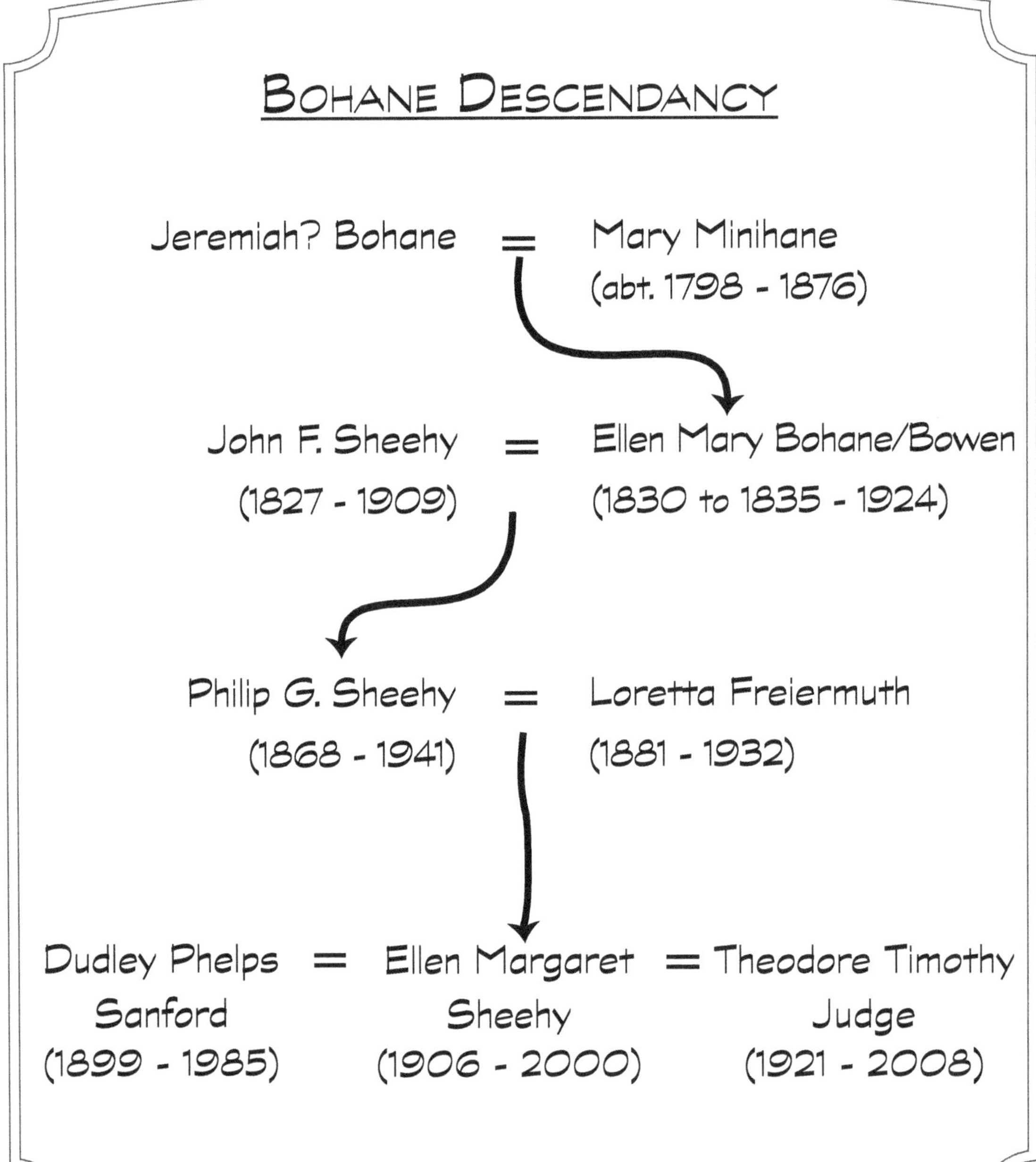

Descendancy from Jeremiah? Bohane to Ellen

Descendants of Jeremiah? Bohane and Mary Minihane

Capt. John F. Sheehy, the immigrant Sheehy ancestor of Ellen Sheehy Judge, married in San Francisco, 10 August 1854 at St. Patrick's Church, Ellen Mary Bowen (Bohane or Bohan in Ireland), born in County Cork, Ireland, between 1830 and 1835. Ellen likely came from a large Irish family, but the only members thus far identified have been her sister Honora Bowen Kelly, who lived in San Francisco, their mother, Mary, and two probable sisters who also came to San Francisco: Catherine and Margaret Bowen.

Thus, we start this descendancy in Ireland with Mary Bohane (likely née Minihane) and her husband, believed by the family to have been named Jeremiah. The choice of the name Jeremiah, tenuously chosen by descendants, was based upon traditional Irish naming patterns. Each of the two known daughters who married and bore children named her second son either Jeremiah or Jerome, as would have been expected in families who clung to tradition, even in a new land. Ellen's death certificate names her father as "J. Bohun."

Genealogical Descendancy

1. **Jeremiah?**[1] **Bohane** was born in Ireland and perhaps died there. He married, probably in Ireland, a woman named **Mary** __?__, written on her daughter Ellen's death certificate to be **Minihane**, born there about 1798, who came to this country and appears to have been the mother of the sisters Honora(h) and Ellen, with whom she lived at various times.[1]

In the 1870 census of San Francisco, the James Kelly household included James's wife Honora(h) and an older woman, Mary Bowen, age seventy-two, born in Ireland.[2] The 1860 census of Santa Cruz County, household of John and Ellen Sheehy, included Mary Bowen, age sixty-five, born in Ireland.[3] Mary Bowen served as a godparent at the baptism of Ellen and John's twins.[4] The assumption is made here that Mary was the mother of Ellen and Honora.

1. See John Sheehey [Sheehy] household, 1860 U.S. Census, Santa Cruz Co., California, Pajaro Twp., dwelling 3, family 3, p. 1; and James Kenney [Kelly] household, 1870 Census, San Francisco, ward 8, dwelling 1195, family 1352, p. 184.
2. James Kenney [Kelly] household, 1870 Census, San Francisco Co., San Francisco ward 8, dwelling 1195, family 1352, p. 184.
3. John Sheehey [Sheehy] household, 1860 Census, Santa Cruz Co., cited above.
4. Valley Church register (more accurately, Our Lady, Help of Christians Church in Watsonville). The register, in Latin, was examined by Patrick Sheehy of Cupertino.

California State Board of Health
DUPLICATE CERTIFICATE OF DEATH

1 PLACE OF DEATH Dist. No. 4361 — County of SANTA CLARA — City or Town of College Park — (No. 915 Chapman St.) — Reg. No. 68 — Local Registered No. 4

2 FULL NAME Ellen Sheehy

PERSONAL AND STATISTICAL PARTICULARS
SEX Female — COLOR OR RACE White — SINGLE, MARRIED, WIDOWED, OR DIVORCED Widow
If married, widowed, or divorced HUSBAND of John Sheehy (deceased)
DATE OF BIRTH April 1829
AGE 95 years
OCCUPATION at Home
BIRTHPLACE Ireland
NAME OF FATHER J. Bohun
BIRTHPLACE OF FATHER Ireland
MAIDEN NAME OF MOTHER Minihan
BIRTHPLACE OF MOTHER Ireland
LENGTH OF RESIDENCE At Place of Death 90 years; In California 70 years
Informant Neil Sheehy; Address 10 Martin [illegible]
Filed Jan 21 1924

MEDICAL CERTIFICATE OF DEATH
DATE OF DEATH Jan 20 1924
I HEREBY CERTIFY, That I attended deceased from Jan 20 1924 to Jan 20 1924, that I last saw h[er] alive on Jan 20 1924 and that death occurred on the date stated above at 7.30 a.m.
The CAUSE OF DEATH was as follows: Myo cardial degeneration due to age
(Duration) unknown
Contributory nothing
Did an operation precede death? No
Was there an autopsy? No
What test confirmed diagnosis? Physical Exam.
(Signed) [illegible] M.D.
1-21 1924 (Address) San Jose Cal
PLACE OF BURIAL OR REMOVAL S P Catholic Cem. — DATE OF BURIAL 1-22 1924
UNDERTAKER [illegible] — ADDRESS Santa Clara Cal — EMBALMER'S LICENSE No. 883

Death Certificate of Ellen Sheehy: Note her father's surname given as Bohun and her mother's maiden name as Minihan.

Also in 1860, two unmarried Bowen females were enumerated in the James Kelly household: Margaret, twenty-three, and Catherine, twenty, born about 1836-1840, both described as dressmakers.[5] That census does not indicate relationships; they may have been sisters, cousins or even granddaughters of Mary. City directories indicate that Mary Bowen, widow, and Miss Catherine Bowen, seamstress, joined the James R. Kelly household at 42 Ritch Street in 1860-61. In 1862, Miss Kate Bowen and Mary Bowen, widow, were listed at 5 Minna Street, after which they were no longer together. No listing was found at any time for Margaret. A "Mrs. Mary Bowen," age seventy-eight, died in San Francisco, 17 April 1876, with no identifying information in her death notice.[6]

Parental names remain unproven, but the surname Bohan(e) (or Bouhane) is certain. The death certificate of Ellen Sheehy names her father "J. Bohun." Bohan was appended by family members as a middle name to Honora Kelly's unmarried daughter, Margaret.[7] Griffith's

5. James R. Kelly household, 1860 census, San Francisco, tenth district, dwelling 1608, family 1635, p. 352.
6. *Sacramento Daily Union*, 19 April 1876.
7. Letter of Kathleen Sheehy Palmer directed to the director of the Mission Santa Clara Cemetery in 1978. Margaret,

Valuation (an Irish tax roll) records a number of families with this surname in the area surrounding Skibbereen. The online website of the Irish Family History Association indexes several Ellen Bouhans, an Honora Bouhan, a Margaret Bouhane and a number of Catherines baptized between 1830 and 1840, the years in question.

Ellen Bowen Sheehy
Courtesy of Patrick Sheehy

Ellen's death certificate names her mother _?_ Minihane. Skibbereen baptismal records include the baptisms of five daughters to Jeremiah Bohane and Mary Minihane: Anne (1814), Margaret (1817), Honora (1819), Mary (1822), and Catherine (1825), but these birth years are ten to fifteen years before those of the Bowen girls.[8] Nonetheless, the older Margaret, Honora and Catherine may have died and the names given to younger daughters for whom no record was found. Related Irish families, moreover, often used the same set of names for their children; inasmuch as the surnames were common in the area, the coincidence is not considered unusual.

As to immigration, a Jeremiah Bohane evidently came to this country from the village of Kilcrohane via Quebec in 1847 with his brother Denis, with ages, unfortunately, not stated. An unnamed sister, placed an advertisement in the *Boston Pilot*, requesting any news of him.[9] The 1850-1853 tax list of Kilcrohane (slightly west of the Sheehy ancestral home) lists a Jeremiah Bohane, perhaps or perhaps not the father, still in Ireland.

Likely daughters of Jeremiah? and Mary Bohane were:

2 i. ELLEN MARY[2] BOHANE, born Apr. 1830-35, m. JOHN F. SHEEHY.

3 ii. HONORA BOHANE, b. abt. 1830, m. JAMES ROBERTS KELLY.

Possible daughters were:

iii. CATHERINE? BOHANE, b. abt. 1836-37, Ireland.[10]

iv. MARGARET? BOHANE, b. abt. 1839-40, Ireland.[11]

---

however, was recorded in records as Margaret A. Kelly.

8. Information provided by the Skibbereen Heritage Center.
9. Ruth Ann Harris and Donald M. Jacobs, ed., *The Search for Missing Friends: Irish Immigrant Advertisements Placed in the Boston Pilot, 1831-1920,* 8 vols. (Boston: New England Historic Genealogical Soc., 1999), 1: 475.
10. James R. Kelly household, 1860 U.S. Census, San Francisco, previously cited.
11. *Ibid.*

Generation 2

2. **Ellen Mary[2] Bohane/Bowen** (*Jeremiah?[1] Bohane*) was born in County Cork, Ireland, April 1830-1835, depending upon which census is to be believed. Ellen died 20 January 1924, in Santa Clara County, California.[12] She married, according to family members, at St. Patrick's Catholic Church, San Francisco, 10 August 1854, **John F. Sheehy**, son of John and Margaret Sheehy, born 28 August 1827 in Glenafeen (or Glanafeen) Townland, County Cork, died 16 May 1909 in Santa Clara.[13] John and Ellen had ten children, and are described in much greater detail in the preceding chapter on the Sheehy family.

3. **Honorah[2] Bohane/Bowen** (*Jeremiah?[1]Bohane*) was born about 1830 in Ireland, most likely County Cork, and died 24 March 1893 in San Francisco.[14] She married, either in Ireland or in Boston, about 1848-1849, **James Roberts Kelly**, born 9 September 1827 in Baltimore, County Cork, died 28 September 1912 in San Francisco.[15]

According to his obituary, James was educated in Ireland to be a barrister. Recorded as a "painter" in Boston in 1850, James, after coming to San Francisco in 1855, first was a partner in several painting supply import businesses.[16] About 1870 he became a director of the Hibernia Bank, along with his many other businesses, which included at the time of the 1880 census, a fruit dealership.[17] In 1890 he was named president of Hibernia Savings and Loan Society. James was buried in Mission Cemetery in Santa Clara, but there is no record of Honora there. Honora had died in 1893 and according to her obituary, was buried in old Calvary Cemetery. Her remains presumably were reinterred in Holy Cross Cemetery in Colma when the San Francisco cemeteries were relocated.

James and Honorah had six children as follows:

i. William J.[3] Kelly, b. 27 Mar. 1850, Boston, Mass., not mentioned in his mother's 1893 obituary and not enumerated with the family in 1880.[18]

ii. John Jerome Kelly, b. Dec. 1852, Mass., d. 21 Jan. 1906, Stillwater, Shasta Co., California.[19]

---

12. Ellen's year of birth is taken from her tombstone at Santa Clara Mission Cemetery. Judging from her ages in decennial census enumerations, she is just as likely to have been born 1830-1835. She married five or six years after her sister Honora. Ellen's death certificate, in the possession of Patrick Sheehy, names her father as "J. Bohun."
13. See chapter on Sheehy. Their marriage date is from a newspaper account of their 30th wedding anniversary, the location from family lore. The records of St. Patrick's were lost in the 1906 earthquake and fire.
14. Honora's ages in the decennial censuses suggest birth years ranging from 1825 to 1835. Her age at death in 1893 was reported as sixty-three; obituary, *San Francisco Call*, 25 March 1893, p. 7, col. 4.
15. Their marriage year is estimated from the birth record of their first child, William, born in Boston, 27 March 1850. James's death: California Death Index, 1905-1929, digitization of state index at www.vitalsearch-ca.com; obituary, *San Francisco Call*, 29 Sep. 1912, p. 46, cols. 2-3. His obituary and funeral notice mistakenly identify Baltimore, his birthplace, as in Co. Limerick. This most likely should have read West Cork, unless there is a townland named Baltimore in Limerick. Baltimore, Cork, lies southwest of Skibbereen, where a baptismal record dating to Oct. 1831 was found for a James O'Kelly, son of James O'Kelly and Sara Roberts.
16. James Kelley [Kelly] Household, 1850 Census, Boston Ward 11, Suffolk Co., Mass., dwelling 61. family 76; San Francisco city directories 1855-1870.
17. James R. Kelly household, 1880 Census, San Francisco, E.D. 91, sh. 2 -3, dwelling 13, family 17.
18. Massachusetts Vital Records, 1841-1910, vol. 44, p. 30; database at www.newenglandancestors.org. The spelling in the original register was William J. Kelley (son of James, painter, and Honora, both parents born in Ireland). Boston birth records were not found for John and Sarah, although census enumerations suggest they were born in Massachusetts.
19. John Jerome Kelly household, 1900 Census, Shasta Co., Buckeye Twp., E.D. 117, sh. 11A, dwelling 194, family 198, p. 178. He was a "farmer" and single. Death information is from cemetery records, Santa Clara Mission Cemetery.

4 iii. SARAH M. KELLY, b. abt. 1855, Massachusetts, m. WILLIAM S. LYLE.

5 iv. ALFRED ROBERTS KELLY, b. Aug. 1857, San Francisco, m. FRANCES RALEIGH.

v. MARGARET A. KELLY, b. 1859, probably San Francisco, d. 24 June 1905, San Francisco.[20]

vi. MARY J. KELLY, b. abt. 1866, probably San Francisco, d. aft. 1893, but bef. 1912, and perhaps bef. 1900.[21]

Generation 3

4. **SARAH M.**[3] **KELLY** (*Honora*[2] *Bowen, Jeremiah?*[1] *Bohane*) was born about 1855 in Massachusetts and died in San Francisco, 16 June 1937.[22] About 1889, Sarah married **WILLIAM SIMPSON LYLE**, son of Joshua and Ann (Simpson) Lyle, born 21 March 1842 in Machias, Maine, died 27 November 1915 in San Francisco.[23] William was described in the 1900 census as "mining expert," but in 1910 as "farmer."[24] His mother-in-law's obituary describes her son-in-law as "the well-known mining capitalist of the Nevada block." William was buried at Santa Clara Mission Cemetery.

William and Sarah Lyle had the following children, both born in San Francisco:[25]

6 i. GEORGE BLAKE[4] LYLE, b. 23 Aug. 1892, m. LOUISE QUEEN.

ii. WILLIAM SIMPSON LYLE, b. 20 Oct. 1897, d. after 1937.[26]

5. **ALFRED ROBERTS**[3] **KELLY** (*Honora*[2] *Bowen, Jeremiah?*[1] *Bohane*) was born in August 1857, probably San Francisco, and died 14 September 1940, San Francisco.[27] He married about 1883, **FRANCES E. "Fannie" RALEIGH**, born 1858 in Oregon, died 25 June 1922, Marin County, California.[28] Both Alfred and Fannie were buried at Santa Clara Mission Cemetery. Alfred, like his father, was a banker.

---

20. Margaret was seven months old in the 1860 Census, ten years old in 1870 and seventeen in 1880. Her years of birth and death are consistent with the Margaret Kelly buried at Santa Clara Mission Cemetery in the Kelly plot.
21. Mary was six in the 1870 Census, fourteen in 1880. She was evidently alive (but unnamed) at the time of her mother's death in 1893, but was not found in the 1900 Census with either her father or her sisters Margaret and Sarah.
22. Sarah's birth was not found in Boston, Mass., records; her birth is estimated from the 1860-1910 census enumerations, except for 1900, which was an obvious mistaken entry. Her death is from the California Death Index, 1930-1939 (digitization of the state index at www.vitalsearch-ca.com) and from her obituary, which appeared in the *San Francisco Chronicle,* 13 June 1937, p. 11, col. 4. See James R. Kelly household, 1900 Census, San Francisco, Assembly District 39, E.D. 188, sh. 6B, dwelling 65, family 72. William Lyle's short obituary (*San Francisco Chronicle*, 28 Oct. 1915, p. 35, col. 8) describes him as an associate of Fair and Mackay in the early mining days.
23. James R. Kelly household, 1900 Census, San Francisco, cited above; 1850 Census, Washington Co., Maine, East Machias Twp., family 176, and J. B. Lyle household, 1860 Census, San Francisco, District 10, family 498. Postings at Ancestry.com for this family identify William's mother as Ann Simpson. Obituary, William S. Lyle, *San Francisco Chronicle,* 28 Nov. 1915, p. 35. His obituary identifies his wife as the daughter of James Kelly and names both sons.
24. James R. Kelly household, 1900 Census, above.
25. Birth months and years in the 1900 enumeration of the James R. Kelly household, cited above, are consistent with details shown for each son.
26. William was mentioned in both his mother's and father's obituary, but without a residence or occupation. He may have been the William S. Lyle born 26 Oct. 1895 who died in San Joaquin Co., 21 May 1979.
27. Abstracts of California deaths, 1940-2000, a database available online at www.vitalsearch-ca.com (hereafter CDA), lists a date of birth, 8 Aug. 1857, while descendants have posted the date 15 Aug. 1857 online.
28. Alfred Kelly household, 1900 Census, San Francisco, E.D. 238, sh. 11A, dwelling 192, family 218. At that time it was recorded that Alfred and Frances had been married seventeen years. Fannie's year of birth was misreported as 1863. She appears to have been the daughter of Patrick and Mary Raleigh, age 12 in the 1870 census of Portland, Multnomah Co., Ore., p. 124, and of So. Fork Pct., Yamhill Co., Ore. (p. 685) in 1860. The California Death Index (1905-1929) entry

Alfred and Frances Kelly had at least seven children, all born in San Francisco:[29]

7 i. MARY IRENE[4] "Renee" KELLY, b. Oct. 1884, m. EDWARD ALEXANDER PALMER.

8 ii. ETHEL KELLY, b. Mar. 1885, m. JOHN G. EWING.

9 iii. JAMES RALEIGH KELLY, b. Mar. 1885, m. ELLEN COOK.

iv. ALFRED ROBERT KELLY, b. 26 Jun. 1889, d. 26 Sep. 1966, Marin Co., California; m. LAURETTA TWOHEY.[30] They evidently did not have children. Alfred was a real estate developer in San Francisco and active in the building of the Carquinez Bridge.[31]

10 v. CYRIL STANLEY KELLY, b. 8 Jan. 1891, m. MARY BELINDA KINSEY.

11 vi. WILLIAM HAROLD KELLY, b. 19 Jan. 1894, m. HARRIETTE WOOD and LOUELLA _?_ .

12 vii. MARGARET C. KELLY, b. 19 Aug. 1900, m. JEAN LOUIS BRINDAMOURE.

Generation 4

6. GEORGE BLAKE[4] LYLE (*Sarah M.[3] Kelly, Honora[2] Bowen, Jeremiah?[1] Bohane*) was born 23 August 1892 and died 6 March 1940.[32] He married **LOUISE G. QUEEN**, born in Kentucky, 18 January 1892, died 11 November 1983.[33] George was a commercial artist. He and Louise had three daughters, all of whom were evidently living in 1997, and a son, George Blake Lyle, Jr., born 26 September 1931 and died 21 August 1959.[34]

7. MARY IRENE[4] KELLY (*Alfred Roberts[3] Kelly, Honora[2] Bowen, Jeremiah?[1] Bohane*) was born October 1884, died as "Renee" K. Palmer in the Spanish Flu epidemic, 14 March 1919, Portland, Oregon. She is buried in the Kelly family lot at Santa Clara Mission Cemetery, Santa Clara.[35] Renee married in San Francisco, April 1910, **EDWARD ALEXANDER PALMER**, son of Warren Sherman Palmer of Oakland.[36] Edward, a University of California graduate in engineering, was born 18 June 1885, and died November 1965 in or near Edgewood, New Jersey.[37]

The newly married couple was enumerated in 1910 in Klamath Falls, Oregon, where his occupation was recorded as civil engineer.[38] At the time of the 1920 census, Edward was a "widower" in Lafayette County, Oregon, but married again within the year, Josephine Hum-

(25 June 1922) calls her "Fannie."

29. Unless otherwise referenced, birth years and months of the Kelly children are from the 1900 census and from CDA.
30. The Lauretta Kelly death entry at CDA, provides a birthdate of 29 Aug. 1898, a date of death of 7 May 1980 in Alameda Co. and the maiden name Twohey. This is consistent with her age in the 1930 Census, which suggests they married about 1921. See Alfred Kelly household, 1930 Census, San Francisco, Assembly District 27, E.D. 38-182, sh. 13A, p. 172.
31. *San Francisco Chronicle*, 10 Dec. 1922, p. B17.
32. CDA. His date of birth coincides with that on his World War I draft registration card, available at Ancestry.com.
33. CDA. Louise is named Louise Queen Kelly in her husband's obituary, *San Francisco Examiner*, 7 March 1940, p. 11, col. 7.
34. California Birth Index; CDA.
35. Renie's date of birth is from the 1900 Census, Alfred Kelly household, previously cited; her death is from the Oregon State Death Index at Ancestry.com and cemetery records. In 1920 Edward A. Palmer was enumerated as a widower (Edward A. Palmer household, Yamhill Co., Oregon, city of Lafayette, E.D. 455, sh. 2B, dwelling 56, family 56).
36. *San Francisco Chronicle*, 27 April 1910, p. 7; photo *Oakland Tribune* 26 April 1910, p. 8.
37. Social Security Death Index at ssdi.rootsweb.ancestry.com (hereafter, SSDI); 1900 census, Alameda Co., city of Oakland, ward 4, E.D. 365, sh. 7B, dwelling 136, family 155.
38. Edward A. Palmer household, 1910 Census, Klamath Co., Oregon, city of Klamath Falls, ward 3, E.D. 33, sh. 15B.

mel.[39] According to family members, Edward then left for South America on an engineering assignment and did not maintain contact with his family. The children were raised in the homes of various relatives.[40]

Edward is mentioned as deceased in the 1937 University of California alumni directory and in his father's 1940 obituary.[41] Ship passenger lists, however, show that he arrived in New York City, 20 November 1928, on the *SS Harold Walker* from Aruba.[42] He provided full identification and a current address in Edgewood, New Jersey. He later took out a Social Security card in New York and married again, Helen _?_(maiden name Wossell). He died in or near Edgewood; his obituary in the *Trenton Times* does not mention children.[43]

Renee and Edward Palmer had four children:[44]

i. Kathrine Frances[5] Palmer, b. 10 Feb. 1911, d. in San Francisco, 22 Sep. 1959; m. Edward Whitney and had one child [living, name withheld].

ii. Warren Alfred Palmer, b. 24 Apr. 1912, d. 25 Nov. 1994, Sonoma Co.; m. (1) Beatrice Cassidy, d. 27 Feb. 1980, marr. (2) Zoe _?_ .[45] Warren and Beatrice had two children [living, name withheld].

iii. Edward Alexander Palmer, b. 9 July 1913, d. 25 May 1987, Alameda Co.; m. Kathleen Helen Sheehy (see chapter on Sheehy family). Edward and Kathleen had five children [living, names withheld].

iv. Robertson Raleigh Palmer, b. 1 Nov. 1916, d. 5 May 1994, Modesto, Stanislaus Co.; m. Frances Papsin.[46] They had four children (three of whom are living; dau. Michelle d. unm., 29 Oct. 1997).

8. Ethel[4] Kelly (*Alfred Roberts[3] Kelly, Honora[2] Bowen, Jeremiah?[1] Bohane*) was born 10 March 1885 and died 28 May 1951 in San Francisco.[47] Ethel married in San Francisco, 22 May 1906, **John Gillespie Ewing**, son of Philemon and Mary Gillespie Ewing, born in Ohio about 1858, died in the District of Columbia, 2 August 1927.[48]

---

39. See Edward A. Palmer household, 1920 Census, Yamhill Co., Oregon, city of Lafayette, E.D. 455, sh. 2B, dwelling 56, family 56. His second wife, Josephine Hummel, was born in Oregon about 1892, perhaps as Myrtle J. Hummel. When she married Edward she may already have been a divorcee, Myrtle J. Purdin. She died as Josephine Reich in San Clemente, 2 May 1992. Edward and Josephine had a daughter, who is living.
40. In 1930, Warren and Edward were living with their grandfather; see 1930 Census Warren S. Palmer, in Oakland, Alameda Co. (E.D. 1-225, sh. 4A., p. 96). In 1920 son Robertson Raleigh was a "ward" in the Albert A. Robertson household, 1920 Census, Marin Co., San Rafael Twp., town of Ross, E.D. 85, sh. 17A.
41. Warren Palmer obituary, *San Francisco Examiner*, 9 Jan. 1940, p. 11, col. 7.
42. This list is digitized at Ancestry.com. Edward stated he was born in Oakland, 18 June 1886.
43. Trenton *Evening Times*, 29 Nov. 1965, p. 8.
44. Information on the children is patched together from the California Birth Index, CDA and the SSDI.
45. Kathleen Sheehy Palmer's obituary (*San Francisco Chronicle*, 13 Oct. 2004) calls Warren's wife Zoe.
46. Robertson R. Palmer obituary, *The Modesto Bee*, 7 May 1994 (from unpaginated digitization at GenealogyBank.com). Frances, born in Connecticut, evidently was a captain in the U.S. Air Force. She died in 1999 and was buried in San Joaquin Valley National Cemetery.
47. CDA; obituary, *San Francisco Examiner*, 29 May 1951, p. 11, col. 5.
48. Their marriage was reported in the *Los Angeles Times*, 23 May 1906, p. 3. For his obituary see, *New York Times*, 4 Aug. 1927, p. 21. In the 1930 census, Ethel, a widow, was enumerated in her father's household. See Alfred R. Kelly household, 1930 census, Marin Co., California, San Rafael Twp., city of Larkspur. E.D. 21-9, sh. 10B-11A, dwelling 315, family 320.

They were married just following the 1906 earthquake and fire in a newsworthy ceremony that took place in the ruins of St. Dominic's Catholic Church in San Francisco.[49] John Ewing was a graduate of Notre Dame and a professor there for a number of years; he was serving as a Justice Department lawyer at the time of his death. Ethel Kelly Ewing was buried at Santa Clara Mission Cemetery.

The Ewings had two daughters:

i. Audrey[5] Ewing, b. 31 July 1907, Illinois, d. in San Francisco, 5 Oct. 1986; m. (1) _?_ Wheeler, and (2) Grahame Bates. Audrey had two children by her first marriage, both evidently living.[50]

ii. Mary Ewing, b. 10 Sep. 1912, San Francisco, d. 15 May 1988, Solano Co., as Mary McNulty, n.f.i.[51]

9. James Raleigh[4] Kelly (*Alfred Roberts[3] Kelly, Honora[2] Bowen, Jeremiah?[1] Bohane*) was born in March 1885 and died 19 October 1928 in San Francisco.[52] James, a lawyer, married in San Francisco, 24 September 1914, **Ellen Cook**, born 24 May 1887, died 9 July 1978, Monterey County.[53] Both James and Ellen were buried at Santa Clara Mission Cemetery.

James and Ellen Kelly had at least seven children: [54]

i. Joan Mary[5] Kelly, b. 18 July 1915, d. 9 Nov. 1990 as Joan Randall.

ii. James Raleigh Kelly, b. 29 Dec. 1916, d.y.

iii. Ethel Barbara Kelly, b. 18 Feb. 1918, d. 25 Sep. 2003 as Barbara Ransom.

iv. Ellen Patricia Kelly, b. 18 June 1919, d. 20 Mar. 1999, as Ellen Clifford.

v. Living son.

vi. Alfred Robert Kelly, b. 10 Dec. 1925, d. 1 May 1999.

vii. Martin John Kelly, b. 5 Nov. 1927, d. 17 Mar. 1982.

10. Cyril Stanley[4] Kelly (*Alfred Roberts[3] Kelly, Honora[2] Bowen, Jeremiah?[1] Bohane*) was born 8 January 1891 and died 17 December 1964, Santa Cruz County.[55] Stanley married about 1915, **Mary Belinda Kinsey**, daughter of Pryce and Elizabeth Kinsey.[56][57] Mary

---

49. *Los Angeles Times,* 23 May 1906, p. 3.
50. Obituary, Audrey Bates, *San Francisco Chronicle,* 8 Oct. 1986, p. 22, col. 1.
51. CDA.
52. Alfred Kelly household, 1900 Census, San Francisco, E.D. 238, sh. 11A, dwelling 192, family 218. His tombstone reads 1884.
53. Marriage: *San Francisco Chronicle,* 27 Sep. 1914, p. 16; birth and death: California Death Index, 1905-1929, digitization of state index at vitalsearch-ca.com and obituary, *San Francisco Examiner,* 20 Oct. 1929, p. 4, col. 6.
54. All birthdates, unless otherwise noted, are from the California Birth Index, 1905-1995, database at Ancestry.com. Dates of death through 2000 are from CDA, and after 2000 from the SSDI. Married names of daughters were included in their father's obituary.
55. Death certificate, Cyril Stanley Kelly, Sr.
56. Cyril's World War I draft card registration (digitization available at Ancestry.com) states that he was married with one child. This is consistent with the birth of son Cyril, born 17 June 1916 (California Birth Index), mother's maiden name Kinsey. Daughter Mary Belinda was not born until the end of 1917, after the gathering of information but not the filing took place. A specific marriage date, 1 Sep. 1915, is posted at Ancestry.com, but was not confirmed.
57. *Ibid.* For Mary Belinda's parentage, see Pryce Kinsey household, 1910 Census, San Francisco, Assembly District 38, E.D. 205, sh. 8B, dwelling 108, family 172.

Belinda was born 21 December 1891, died 2 September 1975, Santa Cruz County.[58] Both are buried at Holy Cross Cemetery in Santa Cruz.

Stanley was a self-employed real estate broker in Santa Cruz.[59] He and Mary Belinda had two children:[60]

i. CYRIL STANLEY[5] KELLY, b. 17 June 1916, d. 12 June 1986; m. MARGARET ULRICH. They had five or six living children.

ii. MARY BELINDA KELLY, b. 20 Nov. 1917, d. 25 Oct. 1987, Santa Clara Co.; m. (1) KEN CAREY and (2) DONALD HOBBS. Mary Belinda had two children. [both living, names withheld]

11. WILLIAM HAROLD[4] KELLY (*Alfred Roberts[3] Kelly, Honora[2] Bowen, Jeremiah?[1] Bohane*) was born 19 January 1894 and died in San Francisco, 10 June 1979. Harold married about 1920, **HARRIETTE WOOD,** born 10 April 1896, apparently died in Marin County, 4 April 1952.[61] Harold married second, **LOUELLA _?_ .**[62]

At the time of the 1930 census, William was an insurance broker, and the family was living in Woodside, San Mateo County.[63] They had one son, who is living.

12. MARGARET C.[4] KELLY (*Alfred Roberts[3] Kelly, Honora[2] Bowen, Jeremiah?[1] Bohane*) was born 19 August 1900 and died 15 June 1960 in San Francisco. Margaret married about 1927, Dr. **JEAN LOUIS BRINDAMOUR,** born 8 November 1898 in Massachusetts, died 24 March 1967, Santa Clara County.[64] They were living in Holyoke, Massachusetts, in 1930, where their first child was born, but by 1932 the family had moved to San Francisco.[65]

They had four children, none of whom are followed here and two of whom may be living. Son Jean Louis Edmond Brindamour, born 5 October 1933 in San Francisco, died 15 May 2000 in Portland, Oregon.[66] Alfred Kelly Brindamour, born 17 March 1936, San Francisco, died 8 December 1958 in San Francisco.[67]

---

58. Birth and death from CDA.
59. Death certificate; Stanley Kelly household, 1930 Census, San Mateo Co., city of Burlingame, E.D. 41-2, sh. 15A, dwelling 7, family 7, p. 36.
60. Births and deaths are from CDA. Names of spouses are from a posting at Ancestry.com.
61. Birth and death from CDA.
62. Louella's maiden name may have been Quinones (CDA).
63. William Kelly household, 1930 Census, San Mateo Co., Third Twp., Woodside Village, E.D. 41-51, sh. 4B.
64. Birth and death of both Margaret and Jean Louis are from CDA.
65. Jean-Louis Brindamour household, 1930 Census, Hampden Co., Mass., town of Holyoke, E.D. 7-165, sh. 14A, dwelling 234, family 388, p. 41.
66. California Birth Index at www.vitalsearch-ca.com; SSDI; obituary *The Oregonian,* 22 May 2000, p. E10.
67. CDA.

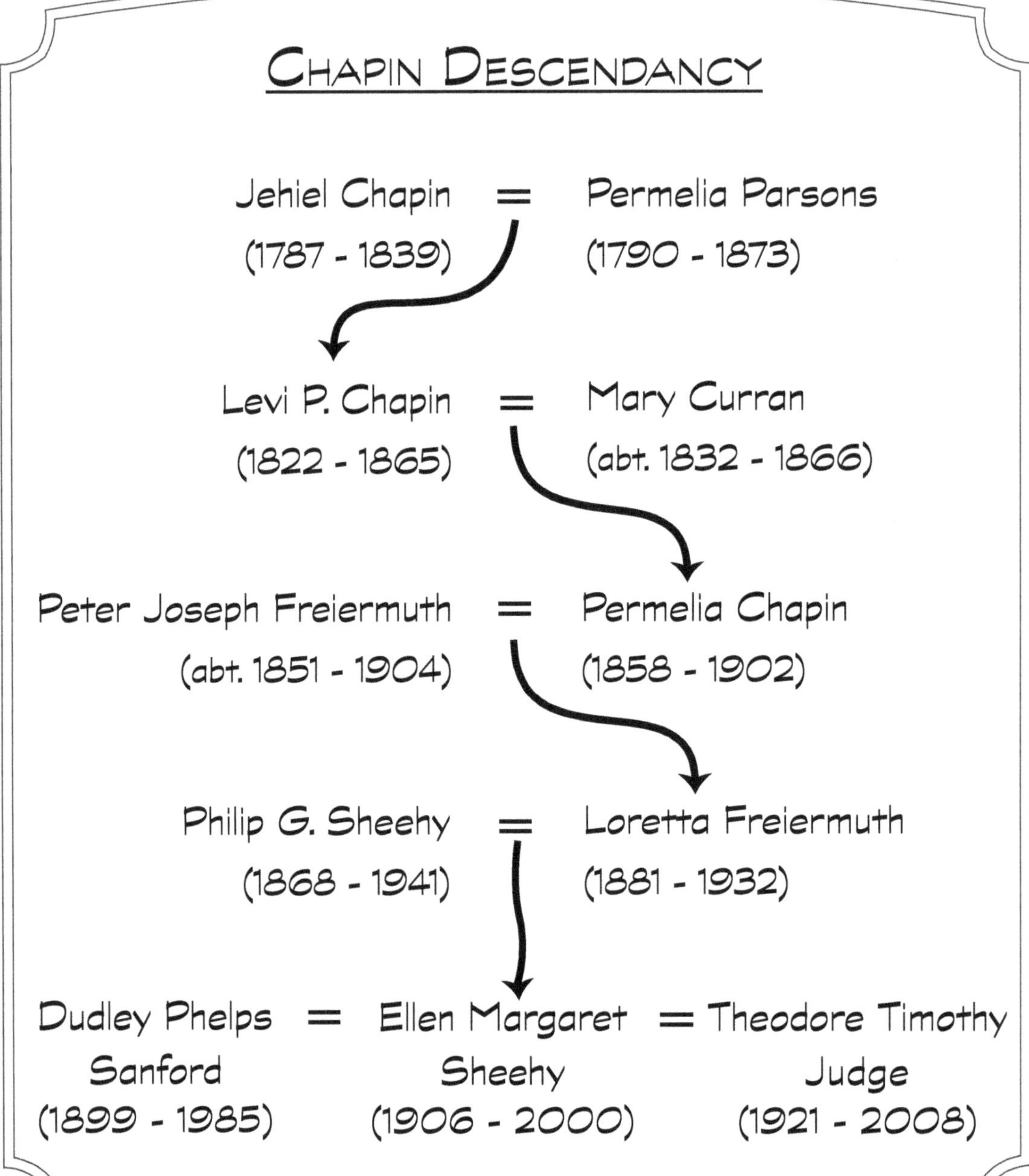

Descendancy from Jehiel Chapin to Ellen Sheehy

❧ Descendants of Jehiel Chapin and Permelia Parsons

"Almost all Chapins in the United States today are descendants of Deacon Samuel Chapin born in Devon, England in 1598." With these words, Jeffrey and Marie Charnley began their family history, based largely upon old family letters and titled, *The Jehiel Chapin (Jr.) – William Clement Johnson Family History and Reunion Story: Seven Generations in Michigan.*[1] The information in this publication is all that has been found to document the connection between Levi Chapin, son of Jehiel and Permelia (Parsons) Chapin, who came to Pajaro Valley in Monterey County, California, and the siblings he left behind in Michigan.[2]

Following his father's death in an accident near their home in Yates County, New York, Levi followed an uncle and several of his brothers to Michigan, arriving between 1844 and 1848. After the group reached Michigan, all stayed except Levi. He moved on to California a few years later, arriving in 1852. Because only Levi came to California, his Michigan siblings are followed in this history very minimally, through their lives and those of their children whom we can identify. Those who wish to trace the Chapins back to the immigrant are referred to the Charnley book and to two more comprehensive Chapin genealogies.[3]

Unless otherwise confirmed and noted, information has been taken from the Charnley book and from documents in the possession of Fr. Harry Freiermuth of Watsonville. We start our Chapin history, then, four generations back from Ellen Sheehy Judge, with Levi's parents, Jehiel and Permelia Chapin of Yates County, New York.

Genealogical Descendancy

1. **Jehiel[1] Chapin** was born 29 May 1787 in Hampshire County, Massachusetts, and died in Italy Hollow, Yates County, New York, 6 April 1839.[4] Jehiel married, 28 December 1814,

1. Jeffrey and Marie Charnley, *The Jehiel Chapin (Jr.)—William Clement Johnson Family History and Reunion Story: Seven Generations in Michigan* (Stevenson Lake, Mich.: privately publ., 1982). Only thirty copies were printed, one of which made it into the hands of descendant Father Harry Freiermuth of Watsonville, California. We are most grateful to Fr. Freiermuth that he permitted us to photograph his copy.
2. See Charnley, *Chapin-Johnson Family History*, pp. 16-17.
3. Gilbert Warren Chapin, comp., *The Chapin Book of Genealogical Data, with Brief Biographical Sketches of the Descendants of Deacon Samuel Chapin*, 2 vols. (Hartford: Chapin Family Association, 1924); also, Orange Chapin, *The Chapin Genealogy: Containing a Very Large Proportion of the Descendants of Dea. Samuel Chapin, Who Settled in Springfield, Mass., in 1642* (Northampton, Mass.: Metcalf & Co., 1862).
4. This date, the marriage date, Permelia's birthdate and their children's dates of the birth (and occasionally death) were

Permelia Parsons, daughter of Wareham Parsons of Prattville, Steuben County, New York, born January 1790, also in Massachusetts, died in Michigan, 1873.[5] Following Jehiel's death, Permelia married Jared Watkins. They lived in Grattin Township, Kent County, Michigan, at least through 1870, which is probably where she died.

Jehiel and Permelia Chapin had the following children, all but Horatio born in Prattsburg, Steuben County, New York:

2 i. Horatio[2] Chapin, b. 14 July 1816, New York, m. Elizabeth Lindsley.

3 ii. Jehiel Chapin III, b. Nov. 1819, m. Laura Foskett.

4 iii. Levi P. Chapin, b. 15 Aug. 1822, m. Mary Curran.

iv. Fidelia Chapin, b. July 1826, d. New York, 25 Jan. 1827.

5 v. Flavel Chapin, b. 23 July 1826, m. Mary Jane Johnson.

6 vi. Theodore Newell Chapin, b. 26 Sep. 1828, m. Sarah Ann Underhill.

Generation 2

2. Horatio[2] Chapin (*Jehiel[1] Chapin*) was born 14 July 1816 in New York and died during a typhoid fever epidemic in Kent County, Michigan, 18 December 1856.[6] Horatio, the last of the brothers to settle in Michigan, married about 1839 in New York, **Elizabeth Lindsley**, born about 1823 in Pennsylvania; evidence seems to suggest she married again, William Chipman.[7]

Horatio and Elizabeth Chapin had the following children, all but the last born in New York:[8]

i. Mary S.[3] Chapin, b. abt. 1842, d. Mich., Oct. 1939; m. abt. 1868, Peter DeGlopper.[9] The 1900 census recorded that Mary had four children, none living, but her obituary mentions "two" grandchildren.[10]

ii. Thales S. Chapin, b. Mar. 1844, m. Olivia _?_, b. Mar. 1849, Mich. They had two ch., William, b. Jan. 1867, and Vernon, b. Aug. 1875, next door neighbors in 1900.[11]

iii. Rachel Chapin, b. abt. 1846. Following their parents' deaths, Mary, Thales and Rachel were living in the William Chipman household. She was not found as Rachel Chapin in 1870.

---

entered in a family Bible, all in the same writing and probably at the same time, a photograph of which was donated to the Pajaro Valley Historical Association by an unidentified person.

5. All information unless otherwise noted is from Charnley, *Chapin-Johnson Family Family History.* Documents spell her name in a number of ways: Permelia, Parmelia and Pamelia. Except for census entries, we have standardized the spelling to Permelia.
6. The Charnley family history states born in 1816, while the unidentified Bible record says "July 14, 1816".
7. Elizabeth Chipman appears in the 1860 census with what appear to be several Chapin children. William Chipman household, 1860 Census, Kent Co., Mich., Grattan Twp., dwelling 845, family 766, p. 101.
8. Information from the 1850 and 1860 census enumerations: Horatio Chapin household, 1850 Census, Ontario Co., N. Y., dwelling 270, family 270, p. 264; William Chipman household, above. Later censuses provide slightly different years, but 1842 seems most reasonable.
9. Obituary of Mary DeGlopper, *Belding Banner News,* 12 October 1939 (Belding, Mich.).
10. Peter DeGlopper household, 1900 Census, Alpena Co., Mich., E.D. 13, sh. 10B, dwelling 173, family 212, p. 96.
11. Thayler (Thales) Chapin household, 1880 Census, Montcalm Co., Mich., Fairplain Twp., E.D. 234, family 252; Thales Chapin household, 1900 Census, Emmet Co., Mich., Readmond Twp., E.D. 86, sh. 2A, dwelling 38, family 42, p. 53.

iv. Rosella Chapin, b. abt. 1849, d. Kent Co., Mich., 15 Dec. 1856; Rosella died, as did her father, in the 1856 typhoid epidemic that swept the area.

v. Augusta Chapin, b. May 1854, Kent Co., Mich., d. Oct. 1945; m. abt. 1875, Francis O. Johnson. They had a son, Guy, b. Dec. 1875, Mich., found in 1880 and 1900 enumerations and mentioned in his mother's obituary.[12]

3. **Jehiel[2] Chapin** (*Jehiel[1] Chapin*) was born in November 1819, in Prattsburg, Steuben County, New York, and died in Michigan, 19 April 1901.[13] Jehiel, the third in his family line to be named Jehiel but the second to be followed here, married, 30 March 1847, **Laura M. Foskett**, born 9 April 1809 in Massachusetts, died in Michigan, 8 May 1889.[14] Both were buried in Lakeview Cemetery, Montcalm County.

Jehiel and Laura Chapin had one child:

i. Isadore Emma[3] Chapin, b. Apr. 1848, Ingham Co., Mich., d. 1921 in Mich.; m. Alfred Clement Johnson, b. Apr. 1848, Mich., d. 1924.[15] They had children (surname Johnson) Harry V., b. abt. 1871; Ella M., b. abt. 1873; and Albert E., b. Mar. 1878.[16]

4. **Levi P.[2] Chapin** (*Jehiel[1] Chapin*) was born 15 August 1822, in Prattsburg, Steuben County, New York, and died 6 August 1865, near Watsonville, California.[17] Levi married in San Francisco, 21 September 1857, **Mary Curran**, daughter of Hugh and Agnes Curran of Dumfries, Scotland.[18] Mary was born about 1832 in Scotland and died in early 1866, in or near Watsonville.[19]

Levi followed his brothers and uncle from Steuben County to Yates County, New York, and then on to Michigan. In 1850, still unmarried at twenty-seven, he was living and working as a gunsmith in Marshall, Calhoun County, Michigan.[20] In 1852 Levi joined a large group of Marshall residents, lured by gold fever, and made the difficult trip to the California gold fields, 105 days as he described in a letter home to his brother, Jehiel.[21]

Discouraged by the hard work involved in mining, he first turned to making shingles in the California redwood logging country and then eventually turned to farming, settling first on

12. Obituary, Augusta Johnson, *Belding Banner News*, 19 October 1945, from Charnley book. Her birth and marriage are estimated from the Francis O. Johnson household, 1880 U.S. census, Ionia Co., Mich., Orleans Twp., E.D. 90, sh. 33A, p. 53, and Frank Johnson household, 1900 census, Ionia Co., Mich., Otisco Twp., city of Belding ward 4, E.D. 26, sh. 12B.
13. The undated obituary from Charnley book and the gravestone transcription from the Lakeview Cemetery at www.findagrave.com provide differing days in November for his birth.
14. Gravestone transcription from Lakeview Cemetery at www.findagrave.com.
15. Gravestone transcription, Lakeview Cemetery, at www.findagrave.com; Alfred C. Johnson household, 1900 U.S. census, Isabella Co., Mich., Gilmore Twp., E.D. 70, sh. 2B.
16. A. C. Johnson household, 1880 U.S. census, Montcalm Co., Mich., Lakeview Twp., E.D. 229, sh. 1A, p. 55.
17. Obituary, *Pajaro Valley Times*, 19 August 1865, in possession of Fr. Harry Freiermuth.
18. An online subscription database providing digitizations of old parish registers. ScotlandsPeople.gov.uk carries the marriage entry of a Hugh Curran to Agnes Fee, 20 Feb. 1814, in the parish of Troqueer, which lies adjacent to Dumfries parish. This seems fairly consistent with a hand-drawn descendancy created in 1965 by descendant Irene Gill that names Mary's mother as Agnes MacPhee.
19. Her death was recorded on the back of a photograph of Levi and Mary in the possession of Fr. Harry Freiermuth. It appears to have been taken about the time of their wedding.
20. Information from a letter written by Levi, a copy of which is in the possession of Fr. Harry Freiermuth. Levi was enumerated in the Anne Peterman household, 1850 Census Calhoun Co., Mich., Marshall Twp., dwelling 93, family 98.
21. His description of the trip west, written in a letter to his brother Jehiel, is part of the collection of transcribed correspondence provided by Fr. Harry Freiermuth.

Levi Chapin–Mary Curran wedding photograph
Courtesy of Father Harry Freiermuth

rented land near Mission San Jose. Following his 1857 marriage and the birth of his first child, Permelia, he and Mary moved to a farm near Watsonville, where their second child, John, was baptized in 1860.[22]

In July 1861 Levi purchased property at the mouth of the Salinas River in Monterey County, located in what was called the "City of St. Paul," in 1860 a swampy area more commonly known as Paul's Island. The following day he purchased a ferry boat franchise on the Salinas River, which he later sold.[23] Several years later he briefly held a gold mine claim in Tulare County. During this period he farmed on 160 acres of leased land, part of San Cayetano Rancho in the Pajaro Valley in Monterey County.[24] Levi's land, inherited by his minor children was later sold to their guardians.[25] In 1865, "in his forty-third year," Levi P. Chapin died; less than a year later, Mary died at age thirty-four. Mary's sister Ellen, wife of Thomas Jamieson, and her family arrived from Rhode Island shortly after her death and subsequently raised Levi and Mary's surviving children.

Levi and Mary Chapin had four children:[26]

7 i. PERMELIA[3] (frequently, "Pamelia") CHAPIN, b. 15 Aug. 1858, d. 20 Jan. 1902; m. PETER JOSEPH FREIERMUTH.

8 ii. JOHN HUGH CHAPIN, b. Feb. 1860, d. 23 Nov. 1936; m. LOUISA "Lulu" A. VANWAGNER.

iii. AGNES ELLEN CHAPIN, b. 1862 in Watsonville, d. 3 Aug. 1936, Santa Cruz Co.; m. 25 Apr. 1901, in Watsonville, FRED H. SEIGMAN, b. 5 Jun. 1864 in Calif., d. Santa Cruz Co., 11 Sep. 1943.[27]

iv. LEVI CHAPIN, b. abt. May 1864, d. 30 Oct. 1864.[28]

5. **FLAVEL[2] CHAPIN** (*Jehiel[1] Chapin*) was born 23 July 1826, in Prattsburg, Steuben County, New York, and died in Lakeview, Michigan, October 1901, buried Lakeview Cemetery, Lakeview, Montcalm County, Michigan.[29] Flavel married April 1859 in Grattan, Kent County, Michigan, **MARY JANE JOHNSON**, born in Michigan, October 1835.

Flavel and Mary Jane Chapin had the following children, all born in Grattan, Kent County:

---

22. Records of Valley Catholic Church, Watsonville.
23. Monterey Co. deeds, bk E, pp. 74 and 75, both Paul Leazer to L. P. Chapin. The identity of "St. Paul City" is from the *Annual Report of the Surveyor-General for the Year 1860* (Charles T. Botts, California State Printer, 1860), 86. The sale of the ferryboat franchise is information obtained from Fr. Harry Freiermuth of Watsonville, as is the "gold mine claim."
24. Rancho Bolsa de San Cayetano was a large Mexican land grant located north of the Pajaro River, just south of Watsonville. In the 1870 census (cited below) the orphaned Chapin children owned real estate valued at $3200, but it evidently did not come from this property.
25. Thomas Jamieson household, 1870 Census, Monterey Co., Calif., Pajaro Twp., p. 18, dwelling 133, family 133.
26. Levy P. Chapin household, 1860 Census, Monterey Co., Calif., family 773, p. 98; and Thomas Jamieson household, 1870 Census, Monterey Co., cited above.
27. *Santa Cruz Daily Surf*, 26 April 1901, p. 1, col. 2. Births and deaths also from California death indexes and databases at www.vitalsearch-ca.com.
28. Information provided by Fr. Harry Freiermuth, citing an obituary printed in the *Pajaro Times* (Watsonville), 12 Nov. 1864, stating Levi Jr., son of Levi and Mary Chapin, age 5 mos., had died 30 Oct. He may possibly have been known as Hugh, or may have had Hugh as a middle name.
29. Undated obituary in Charnley book; transcribed gravestone inscription from Lakeview Cemetery at www.findagrave.com.

i. William J.[3] Chapin, b. abt. Mar. 1860, d. 1943; m. abt. 1887, Mary Merriman, b. 1856, d. 1944.[30] In 1900, they had four children. William was buried at Lakeview Cemetery.

ii. Cordelia Chapin, b. abt. 1863.

iii. Permelia Chapin, b. abt 1865.

iv. Harvey Chapin, b. abt 1868, d. Grattan, Kent Co., 1873.

v. Levi Newell Chapin, b. June 1870.

vi. Giles F. Chapin, b. Aug 1872.

6. Theodore Newell[2] Chapin (*Jehiel[1] Chapin*) was born 1828, in Prattsburg, Steuben County, New York, and died in Nashville, Tennessee, 8 June 1863. Theodore married in Courtland, Kent County, 4 July 1857, **Sarah Ann Underhill**, born about 1832 in Canada. Following Theodore's death, Sarah married Charles L. Cleveland.[31]

Theodore and Sarah Ann Chapin had three children, all born in Michigan:

i. Frank[3] Chapin, b. 1858, d. 1859.

ii. Theodore Newell Chapin, b. 10 Dec. 1862, d. Nov. 1925; m. 30 Mar. 1884, Vesta J. Hutchinson. They had Eugene W. Chapin, Minnie M. Chapin, Alonzo V. Chapin (d.y.) and Lewis V. Chapin.[32]

iii. Eugene Frank Chapin, b. abt. 1863.

Generation 3

7. Permelia (or **Pamelia**)[3] **Chapin** (*Levi P.[2], Jehiel[1] Chapin*) was born 15 August 1858 near San Jose, Santa Clara County, California, and died in Watsonville, 20 January 1902.[33] On 9 October 1876, in St. Patrick's Church, Watsonville, Permelia married **Peter Joseph Freiermuth**, born in Edesheim, Pfalz, Bavaria, 15 March 1851, died in Watsonville, 29 March 1904.[34] They had nine children, as described in the chapter on the Freiermuth family. Documents collected over her life call her "Pamelia," "Permelia" and "Amelia." Here we call her Permelia, which is entirely arbitrary.

8. John Hugh[3] Chapin (*Levi P.[2], Jehiel[1] Chapin*) was born in February 1860 and died in Santa Clara County, 23 November 1936.[35] John married in Santa Cruz County, California, 29 April 1886, **Louisa A. "Lulu" VanWagner**, born February 1866 in California, died in Santa Cruz County, 12 March 1921.[36]

30. Gravestone transcriptions of both William and Mary at Lakeview Cemetery, available at www.findagrave.com.
31. Second marriage information from her son Theodore's obituary, cited below.
32. All information on Theodore, Jr., is from his obituary that appeared in the (Michigan) *Bellaire Antrim County Record*, 12 Nov. 1925, p. 1.
33. Cemetery records, Watsonville Catholic Cemetery.
34. Cemetery records, Watsonville Catholic Cemetery; California Death Index, 1930-39, prev. cited.
35. John Chapin household, 1900 Census, Santa Cruz Co., Pajaro Twp., city of Watsonville, E.D. 85, sh. 14B, dwelling 333, family 337.
36. *Santa Cruz Daily Surf*, 30 April 1886, p. 3, col. 4; California Death Index, 1905-1929, prev. cited. The middle name "Hugh" is from their wedding announcement and from notes of Fr. Harry Freiermuth of Watsonville.

John and Louisa Chapin had four children, all probably born in Watsonville:[37]

i. IRENE L.[4] CHAPIN, b. 7 Mar. 1896, d. Santa Clara Co., 25 July 1996; m. G. GILL. They had two children, one of whom may be living. The other was Raymond F. Gill, b. 7 Aug. 1919, d. 30 Oct. 1994 in Marin Co.

ii. ELAINE MARIE CHAPIN, b. 31 July 1899, d. 22 June 1984, Santa Clara Co., m. WILLIAM P. KIELY, born in Australia, 15 Mar. 1896, d. 1 July 1971, Santa Clara Co. [Living children, names withheld]

iii. EDWINA P. CHAPIN, b. 23 Nov. 1902, d. 23 Nov. 1983, San Benito Co., m. JOHN WEHMUELLER, b. 6 July 1902, d. San Benito Co., Jan. 1969. [Living children, names withheld]

iv. JOHN HUGH CHAPIN, b. 6 Mar. 1905, d. 29 Sep. 1967, Santa Cruz Co., m. RUTH MARTIN, b. 10 July 1911, d. Santa Cruz Co., 7 July 1967. [Living children, names withheld]

37. Birth and death dates are from abstracts of California deaths, 1940-2000, prev. cited. In the 1900 census, cited above, John and Louisa had indeed been married fourteen years and she was recorded as having borne two children, both living. Louisa stated she was born in February 1866. Spouses of children are from records of Fr. Harry Freiermuth, who received information and a Curran descendancy chart from Irene Chapin Gill, granddaughter of Levi Chapin. The information as presented has been verified in the 1930 Census; dates are from California vital record indexes.

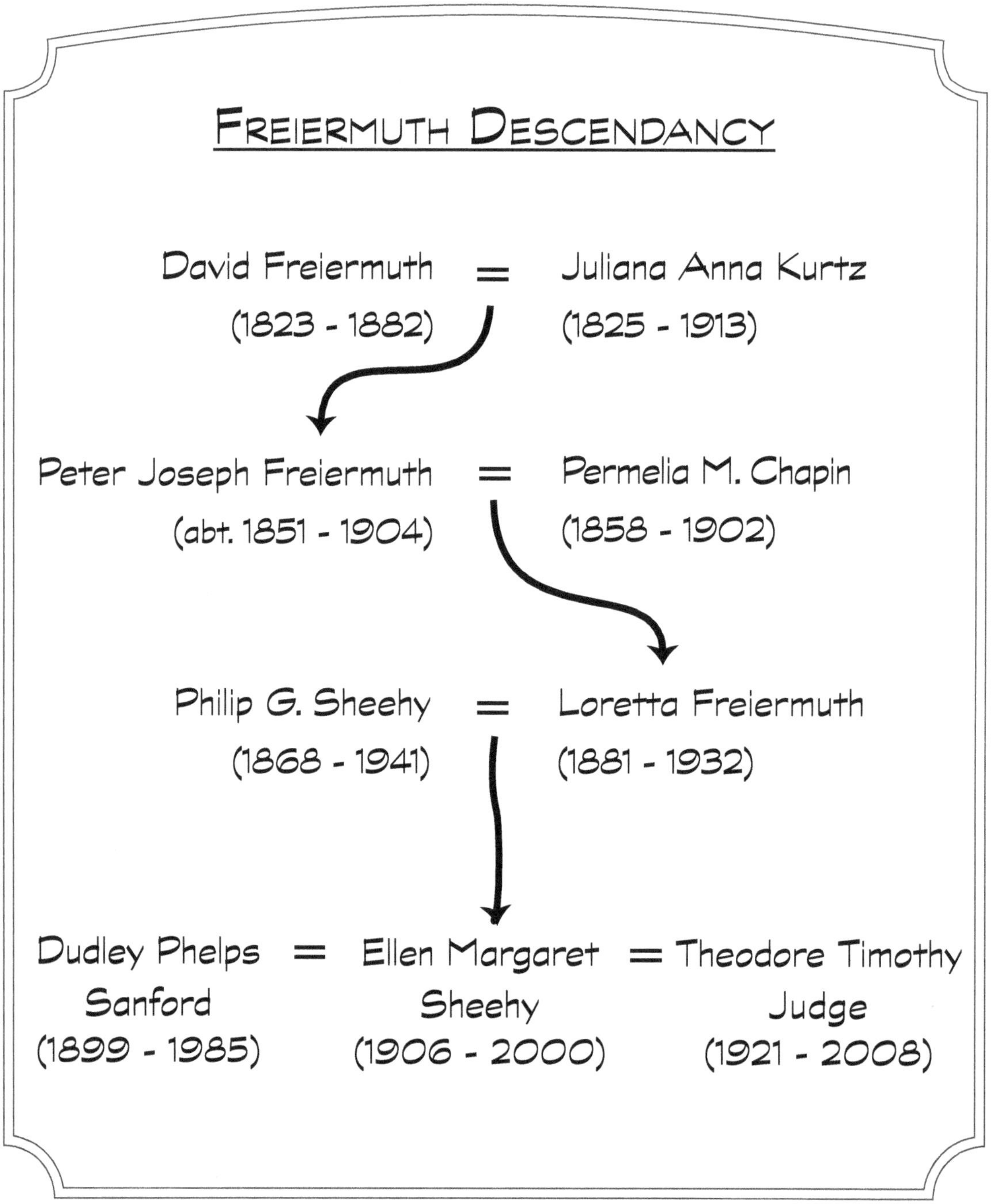

FREIERMUTH DESCENDANCY

David Freiermuth (1823 - 1882) = Juliana Anna Kurtz (1825 - 1913)

↓

Peter Joseph Freiermuth (abt. 1851 - 1904) = Permelia M. Chapin (1858 - 1902)

↓

Philip G. Sheehy (1868 - 1941) = Loretta Freiermuth (1881 - 1932)

↓

Dudley Phelps Sanford (1899 - 1985) = Ellen Margaret Sheehy (1906 - 2000) = Theodore Timothy Judge (1921 - 2008)

Descendancy from David Freiermuth to Ellen Sheehy

❧ Descendants of David Freiermuth and Juliana Kurz

David Freiermuth, the great-grandfather of Ellen Sheehy Judge and the person with whom we begin, came to this country from Bavaria about 1856 and settled in Minnesota. The story of how this German family came to settle in Watsonville, however, starts somewhat earlier with the arrival of David's older brother, who came to this country in the early 1840s and settled in Massachusetts. George A. Freiermuth, a "tinsman," married on 29 January 1843, at Taunton, Massachusetts, Sarah Louisa Lambright.[1] Shortly after 1850, perhaps lured by better prospects in California, the family—by that time including three children—went west. George A. opened a traveling tinware business based in Watsonville which served people over a wide area south of San Francisco.[2] His younger brother David, who had stayed behind and married in Bavaria, came to this country over ten years later with his wife and three children. He settled in Goodhue County, Minnesota, probably before 1857, and some seven years later, fought in the Civil War. In 1869 he was awarded a homestead grant of 160 acres in Hay Creek Township, Goodhue County, and farmed it probably up to his death in 1882. Surely the two brothers must have corresponded, but they may never have seen each other after leaving their homeland.

While David stayed and died in Minnesota, three of his seven identified children went west. The first to leave was Peter J. Freiermuth, the grandfather of Ellen Margaret Sheehy. He left Minnesota about 1868 and arrived in Watsonville in 1871, where he apprenticed as a tinner with his uncle.[3] He and his wife Permelia had eleven children, four of whom died quite young. Peter's sister Katherine may have stayed in Minnesota until her father died in 1882. However, she too went west and in 1883 married Martin Weber in San Francisco.[4] It is not clear when their younger brother Charles followed. His first listing in San Francisco was in the 1886 city directory, as a "tinner," like Peter. Charles remained single for many years in San Francisco, eventually marrying in 1908 a younger woman, who died a few years later.

1. Massachusetts Vital Records to 1850 (Online Database: NewEnglandAncestors.org, New England Historic Genealogical Society, 2001-2008).
2. Isaac L. Mylar, *Early Days at the Mission San Juan Bautista* (Watsonville: Evening Pajaronian, 1929), 113.
3. Obituary of P. J. Freiermuth, *Evening Pajaronian,* 29 March 1904, p. 1; see also, Rolin C. Watkins, *History of Monterey, and Santa Cruz Counties, California: Cradle of California's History and Romance,* 2 vols. (Chicago: S. J. Clarke Publ. Co., 1925), 2: 212; and Edward Martin, *History of Santa Cruz County, California with Biographical Sketches of the Leading Men and Women of the County* (Los Angeles: Historic Record Co., 1911), 292-294.
4. The exact date and a copy of the notice in the *San Francisco Call* (coded as 1883M-1514) is available from Jim Faulkinbury, who offers a service at http://www.jwfgenresearch.com/.

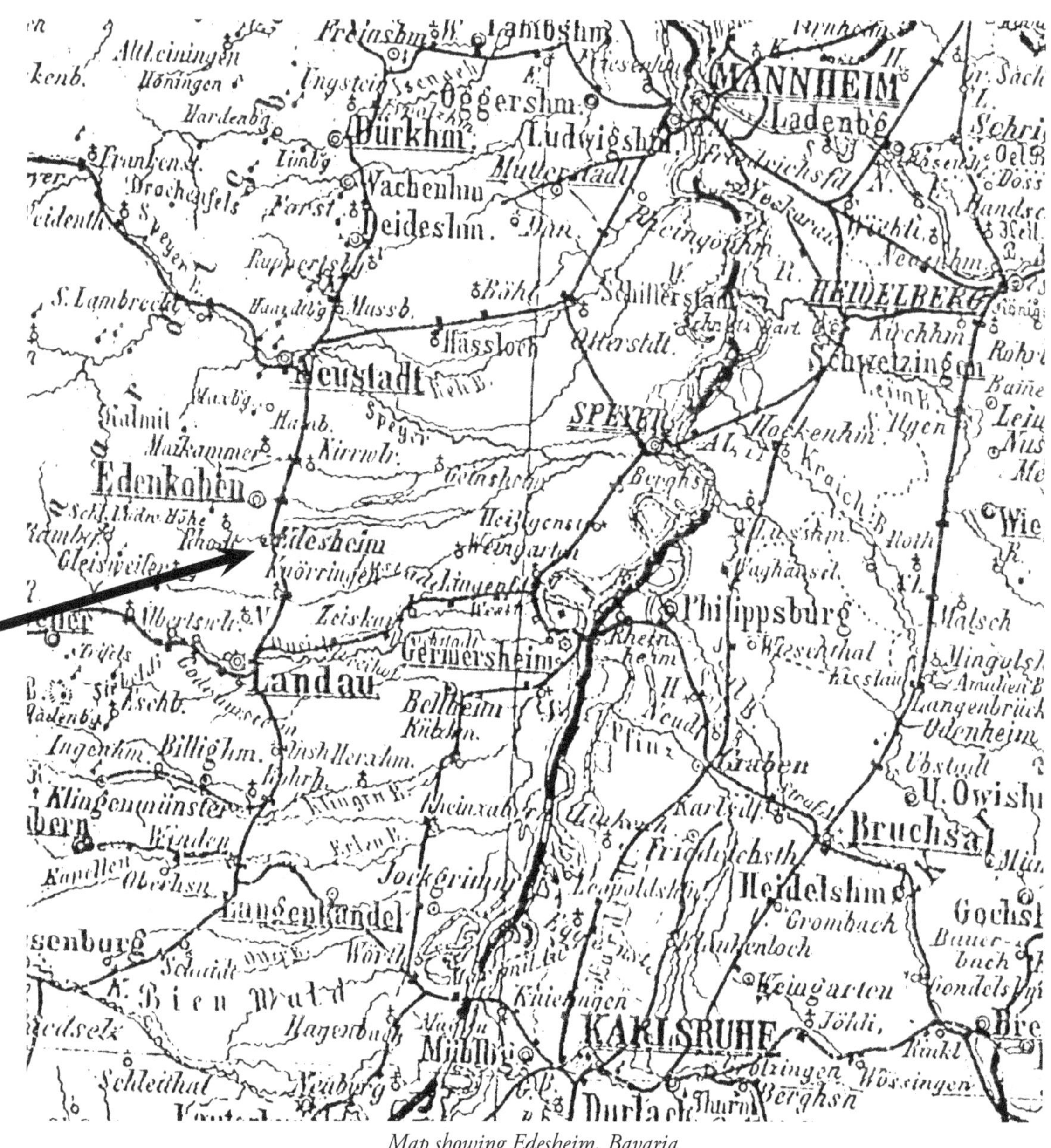

Map showing Edesheim, Bavaria

This story thus begins in Edesheim, Bavaria, a small village located in the southern Pfalz halfway between Neustadt and Landau, and in Minnesota with the immigrant David, the great-grandfather of Ellen Sheehy Judge.

Genealogical Descendancy

1. **DAVID[1] FREIERMUTH** was born 7 February 1823 in Edesheim, Pfalz, Bavaria (Bayern), and died in Hay Creek, Goodhue County, Minnesota, 18 Jun 1882.[5] He married, 4 September

5. Birth: Edesheim church records, St. Peter and Matthew Katholisch Church: baptisms, 1785-1836; Family History Library (FHL) film #367,584 examined by both Julia Sjöberg and Jean Wilcox Hibben and posted at Rootsweb.com. Death: obituary, *Red Wing Advance,* 21 June 1882. His tombstone inscription, transcribed by Julia Sjöberg reads "Feb 8 1823 – June 18 1882."

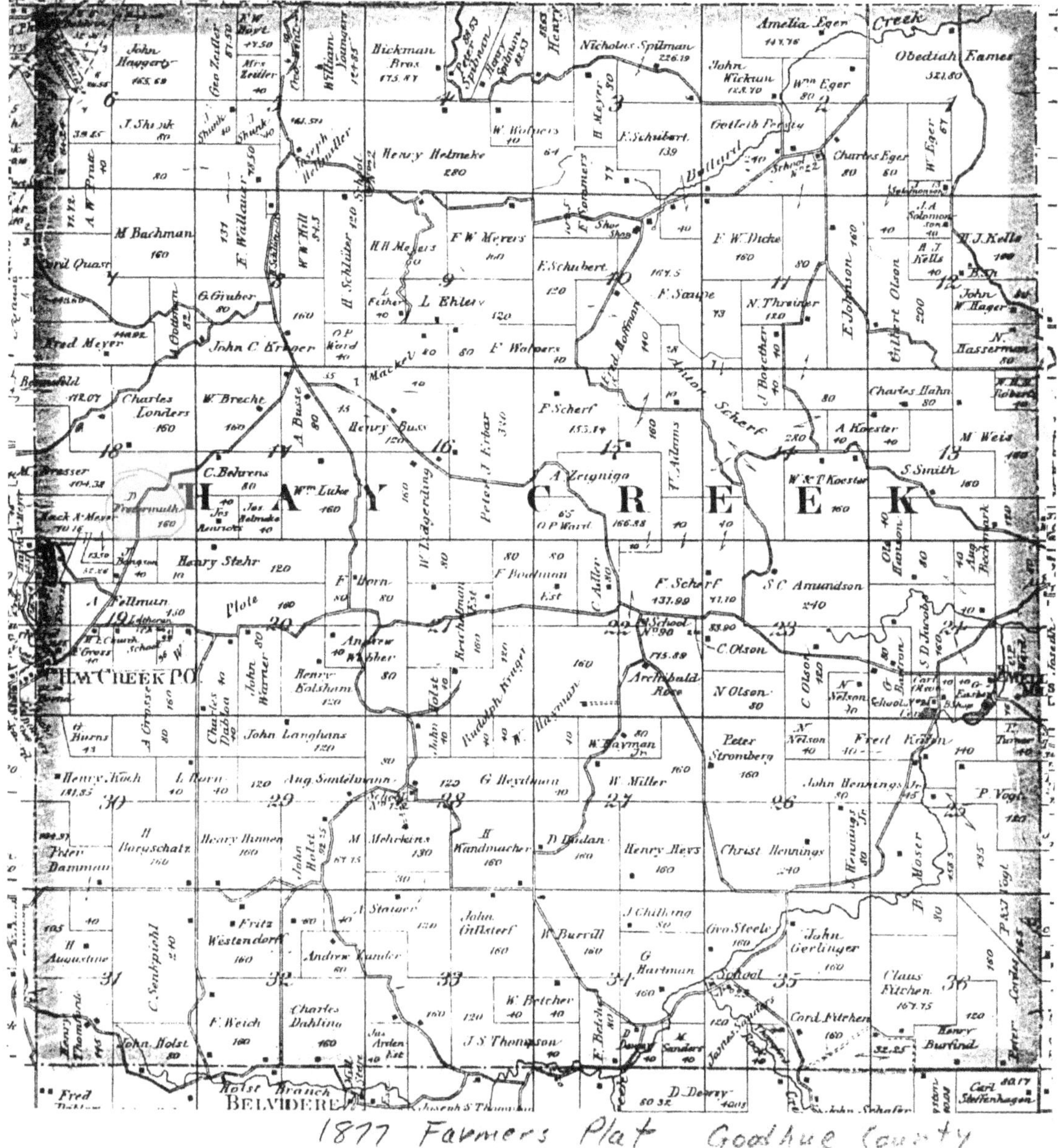

Hay Creek Township, Goodhue County, Minnesota

1845, in Edesheim, **Juliana Anna Kurz**, daughter of Casparo Kurz and Barbara Mees.[6] Born 5 August 1825 in Edesheim, Juliana Anna died in Red Wing, Goodhue County, 19 May 1913.[7]

David and Juliana, along with their three oldest surviving children came to this country between 1851 and 1857.[8] David served in the Civil War in the Second Regiment, Minnesota

6. Edesheim Catholic church records: marriages, 1785-1910 (FHL film #367,586).
7. Information posted by Julia Sjöberg at Rootsweb.com. Her Minnesota death certificate, obtained by Ms. Sjöberg, identifies Juliana's father as "Kaspor" Kurtz. An obituary appearing in the *Red Wing Daily Eagle* 20 May 1913 listed her date of birth as 5 May 1825 and mentioned children Frances Schroeder of Minneapolis and Katie B. Weber and Charles Freiermuth, both of San Francisco.
8. They came after Peter was born in March 1851, but before Katherine was born in 1857. The 1900 census of Peter Freiermuth leaves blank the year of immigration; the enumeration of Francis Schroder records she came in 1856. See John

Infantry Company F, from 28 September 1864 to 11 July 1865.[9] Following the war, in 1869, he applied for and was awarded a homestead grant of 160 acres in Goodhue County, the southeast quarter of Section 18, Hay Creek Township. His service evidently left him somewhat debilitated, for in 1873 he appealed in a notarized letter to the German government to allow two young men named Fitschen to emigrate and help him work his land in Hay Creek.[10] David's occupation was listed as a farmer in the 1870 and 1880 census enumerations.[11] The agricultural schedule of 1870, taken in conjunction with the 1870 census, lists both improved and unimproved acreage each at 80 acres, with a cash value at $3000. At that time he was raising spring wheat and corn; the numbers of livestock were such that they probably were intended for food.[12]

David Freiermuth's estate was probated in Goodhue County beginning in July 1882.[13] Son Anthon(e) and daughter Frances stayed in Minnesota, but within a few years daughter Katie and son Charles went west. Both David and Juliana were buried in Calvary Cemetery in Red Wing.

David and Juliana Freiermuth had seven children:[14]

i. John[2] Freiermuth, b. May 1846?, Edesheim, Pfalz, Bavaria; no information after the 1860 Goodhue Co., Minn., census.[15]

2 ii. Frances (Francisca) Freiermuth, b. 8 Jan. 1849, Edesheim, Bavaria, d. 1935, Minn.; m. John Schroeder.

3 iii. Peter Joseph Freiermuth, b. 12 Mar. 1851, Edesheim, Bavaria; d. 1904, Calif.; m. Permelia Mary (often "Pamelia" or "Amelia") Chapin.

4 iv. Katherine Barbara "Katie" Freiermuth, b. 2 May 1857, Minn., d. 1942, San Francisco; m. Peter Behring and Martin Weber.

v. Charles Freiermuth, b. Dec. 1859, Minn.; d. in San Francisco, 14 Apr. 1920.[16] A tinner and later a plumber, Charles appears to have arrived in San Francisco about 1885. He married about 1908, Minnie Coffey, who died at age 44, childless, in 1911.[17] Following

---

Schroder household, 1900 Census, Hennepin Co., Minn., city of Minneapolis, ward 11, E.D. 113, sh. 4B, dwelling 60, family 82.

9. *History of Goodhue County, Including a Sketch of the Territory and State of Minnesota* (Red Wing, Minn.: Wood, Alley & Co., 1878), 303; Irene B. Warming, *Minnesotans in the Civil and Indian Wars, 1861-1865* (St. Paul: Minnesota Historical Society, 1936), 136.

10. See http://www.lemmermann-genealogie.de/briefeausamerika.htm ("Emigrant Letters from America").

11. David Freirmouth household, 1880 Census, Goodhue Co., Minnesota, Hay Creek Twp., family 86, E.D. 155, sh. 10B.

12. Agricultural schedule, 1870 Census, Goodhue Co., Minn., Hay Creek Twp., E.D. 155, p. 9C, line 10.

13. Index to Probate Registry, 1860-1963, Goodhue Co. (FHL film #1,379,164, items 3-4). This file was not pursued.

14. Births and baptisms from Edesheim Catholic church baptismal records, 1836-1884 (FHL film #367,585). Baptismal records in St. Joseph's Catholic Church, Red Wing, were located by Julia Sjöberg for Katie, Henry and Anton, but not for Charles, although he was in the household through the 1875 Minnesota state census. Information is largely consistent with the 1860 and 1870 census enumerations: David Freemoot [sic] household, 1860 Census, Goodhue Co., Minn., Twp. 112, p. 55/505; also, David Friermuth [sic] household, 1870 Census, Goodhue Co., Hay Creek Twp., p. 186.

15. A baptism of John Freyermuth, 18 May 1846, was found in the Edesheim register by Jean Wilcox Hibben CG, but was accompanied by the notation that he died shortly after. Nonetheless, John appears in the 1860 census in the Freiermuth household, age 14.

16. Birth from Charles Freiermuth household, 1900 Census, San Francisco, Calif., 41st Assembly District, E.D. 234, sh. 6B, dwelling 119, family 124; obituary *San Francisco Chronicle,* 15 April 1920, p. 6.

17. Charles Freiermuth household, 1910 Census, San Francisco, Calif., 41st Assembly Distr., E.D. 272, sh. 10A, dwelling

his wife's death, Charles disappeared from San Francisco city directories for a a number of years and then reappeared in 1918 with the listed occupation "Red Wing Hotel," which he evidently owned.[18]

vi. HENRY FREIERMUTH, b. 15 June 1860, bp. 10 July 1860, St. Joseph's Catholic Church, Red Wing; last record found was the 1865 state census.[19]

5 vii. ANTHON(E) GEORGE FREIERMUTH, b. 13 Aug. 1864, Minn., d. 1907, Minn.; m. LOUISE BREMER.

Generation 2

2. **FRANCES[2] FREIERMUTH** (*David[1]*) was born 9 January 1850 in Edesheim, Pfalz, Bavaria, and died in Minneapolis, Hennepin County, Minnesota, 21 January 1935.[20] Frances married in Red Wing, 28 May 1874, **JOHN SCHROEDER**, born August 1850 in Germany, died in Hennepin County, before 1910.[21]

John appears to have been a man of many talents. On daughter Mathilda's birth record, he is listed as a farmer, whereas in the 1880 census of Red Wing, his occupation appears as "police officer." In 1881 on Pearl's birth record, he was a "cooper." In 1900 he was a city watchman.[22]

John and Frances Schroeder had four children:[23]

6 i. JULIA THERESA[3] SCHROEDER, b. 19 July 1875, m. WILLIAM WEISGERBER.

ii. EMMA MARGARETA SCHROEDER, b. 22 Sep. 1876 in Red Wing, Goodhue Co., Minn.; d. in Minn. between 1885-1900.

iii. MATHILDA SCHROEDER, b. 23 July 1878, Hay Creek, Goodhue Co.; d. bef. 1880, prob. in infancy, since only three births were declared in 1900.

7 iv. PEARL CATHERINE SCHROEDER, b. 18 Jan. 1881; m. CHARLES FLANIGAN.

3. **PETER JOSEPH[2] FREIERMUTH** (*David[1]*) was baptized 12 March 1851, Edesheim, Pfalz, Bavaria, died in Watsonville, Santa Cruz County, California, 29 March 1904, and was buried in Watsonville Catholic Cemetery.[24] On 10 Sep. 1876, in St. Patrick's Catholic Church in Watsonville, Peter married **PERMELIA MARY CHAPIN**. Permelia (or just as often "Pamelia"

124, family 191; obituary, Minnie F. Freiermuth, *San Francisco Chronicle*, 25 Dec. 1911, p. 17.

18. San Francisco Superior Court 1920 probate file 29400. Charles left an estate of about $36,000, with major bequests going to his executor, his nephew Harry of Watsonville; to his lawyer, John Riordan; to the four children of his brother Peter in Watsonville; and to his sister Francis Schroeder in Minnesota.

19. The baptismal record, found by Julia Sjöberg, evidently is the source of the date of birth.

20. Birth from Edesheim baptismal records, 1785-1836 (FHL film #367,585); death from Minnesota Death Index at Ancestry.com.

21. Marriage information copied from Rootsweb site of Julia Sjöberg, citing the *Red Wing Argus*, 4 June 1874. John Schroeder's birth from the 1900 census: John Schroder household, 1900 Census, Hennepin Co., Minn., city of Minneapolis, E.D. 113, sh. 4B, dwelling 60, family 82.

22. John Schroeder household, 1880 Census, Hennepin Co., Red Wing Twp., E.D. 172, p. 25, dwelling 218, family 255; John Schroder household, 1900 Census, Hennepin Co., cited above.

23. Information on Emma and Mathilda was taken from Julia Sjöberg's Rootsweb website. Emma, but not Mathilda, was enumerated in 1880. See John Schroeder household, 1880 Census, Hennepin Co., Minn., prev. cited. In 1900, Francis reported only three children, two living, one of whom would have been Julia Weisgerber and the other, Pearl Flanigan.

24. Birth and baptism from Edesheim Catholic baptismal records (FHL film #367,585); death: *San Francisco Call*, 30 March 1904, p. 15, cols. 6-7, and fuller obituary, *Evening Pajaronian*, 29 March 1904, from files of the Pajaro Valley Historical Association; tombstone from Watsonville Catholic Cemetery.

Wedding photograph of Peter Freiermuth and Permelia Chapin
From Ted Judge archives

or "Amelia") was born 15 August 1858 in nearby San Jose, Santa Clara County, and died in Watsonville, Santa Cruz County, 20 January 1902.[25]

Peter is said by family members to have left Minnesota in 1868.[26] He first appeared in Watsonville in 1872, where he served a short apprenticeship with his uncle, George A. Freiermuth, a tinner who, with his son-in-law, operated a hardware business partnership, Freiermuth & Steigleman.[27] Peter then moved to San Francisco for several years in order to apprentice as a plumber. With his new skills, he returned to Watsonville, where in 1882 he founded his own hardware, plumbing and sheetmetal business, the P. J. Freiermuth Hardware and Plumbing Company.[28]

---

25. Birth and death from transcription of Watsonville Catholic Cemetery records obtained from the Pajaro Valley Historical Association. Her will (see below) reads "Pamelia Freiermuth"; her church funeral notice, "Amelia Mary;" and her death record, "Permelia." For additional information, see the Chapin chapter.
26. Information provided by Fr. Harry Freiermuth of Watsonville.
27. Undated newspaper clippings and mimeographed history of the P. J. Freiermuth Co., written by George Freiermuth in the early 1930s, from the files of the Pajaro Valley Historical Association, Watsonville.
28. P. J. Freiermuth obituary, cited above, and Rolin C. Watkins, *History of Monterey, and Santa Cruz Counties, California: Cradle of California's History and Romance,* 2 vols. (Chicago: S. J. Clarke Publ. Co., 1925), 2: 212. A long article on the company was published in the *Watsonville Morning Sun* 6 May 1939 (files of Pajaro Valley Historical Association).

In 1888, for $400, Peter purchased a small, unimproved city lot on Second Street in Watsonville, which may have been purchased with his wife's inheritance and on which their residence was constructed.[29] The company originally stood where City Hall is now located, but moved to Van Ness Avenue in Watsonville in 1897. Following Peter's death in 1912, the company passed to his son Harry.

Permelia inherited property as a child when her parents died. Interestingly for those times, she must have retained her separate property, for in 1902, shortly before her death, she wrote a short will in which she bequeathed her "house and lot on Second Street" to her daughter Loretta, any separate cash to her sons Vincent and George, and her wedding ring to her son Harry.[30] Harry and Loretta at some point before 1910 assumed the care of their younger siblings.[31]

Peter and Permelia had the following children, probably born in Watsonville, many of whom died of diptheria:[32]

i. Mary Ellen[3] Freiermuth, b. 24 June 1877, d. Watsonville, 1 Jan. 1888.

8 ii. Henry David "Harry" Freiermuth, b. 17 Oct. 1879, m. Lou Henrietta Webb.

9 iii. Loretta Julia Freiermuth, b. 6 Nov. 1881, m. Philip G. Sheehy.

iv. Catherine Mary Freiermuth, b. 26 May 1886, d. in Watsonville, 14 Jan. 1888.

v. Leo Peter Freiermuth, b. 19 Jan. 1888, d. in Watsonville, 18 Aug. 1890.

vi. Irene Cecilia Freiermuth, b. 26 Feb. 1889, d. in Watsonville, 29 Aug. 1890.

vii. Frances Theresa Freiermuth, b. 13 June 1891, d. in Santa Cruz Co., 16 July 1891.

viii. Eva Agnes Christine Freiermuth, b. 13 Dec. 1892, d. in Watsonville, 17 Nov. 1897.

10 ix. George Peter Freiermuth, b. 19 Aug. 1894, m. Adele R. Laporte.

x. Vincent John Freiermuth, b. 8 Nov. 1898, d. Los Altos, Santa Clara Co., 15 Apr. 1973. Vincent John married Eunice Erline Rohrback, b. 7 May 1896 in Calif., d. Santa Clara Co., 27 Aug. 1978. In 1918, Vincent was working as a hardware salesman for the P. J. Freiermuth Company in Watsonville.[33] They evidently had no children.

xi. Theresa Permilia Freiermuth, b. 6 Jan. 1902, d. Santa Clara Co., 27 Jan. 1983. Teresa, at age twenty, became Sister Teresa Bernadette, a nun in the order Sisters of Notre Dame de Namur.[34]

---

29. Copy of original deed, dated 17 Feb. 1888, recorded in vol. 62, p. 272, Santa Cruz County deeds. Presumably women could not purchase property in their own right if married at the time. Permelia ("Pamelia" when she signed her will) bequeathed this property to her daughter Loretta.
30. Copy of will in possession of Patrick Sheehy of Cupertino.
31. Harry Freiermuth and Phil Sheehy households, 1910 Census, Santa Cruz County, city of Watsonville, ward 4, E.D. 136, sh. 12A, dwellings 246 and 247.
32. The births, deaths and burials of Mary Ellen, Catherine Mary, Leo, Irene, Francis and Eva are from a transcription of Watsonville Catholic Cemetery records obtained from the Pajaro Valley Historical Association; their names and dates of birth appear on two sides of a monument in Watsonville Catholic Cemetery. Death records after July 1905 confirmed in the California death indexes available by subscription at www.vitalsearch-ca.com.
33. See World War I draft registration card at Ancestry.com.
34. Apostolic Blessing momentos on the occasion of her Golden Jubilee (1970) and Diamond Jubilee (1980) in possession of Patrick Sheehy of Cupertino.

4. **Katherine Barbara² Freiermuth** (*David*¹) was born 1 May 1857 in Goodhue County, Minnesota, and baptized 10 July 1860, in St. Joseph's Catholic Church, Red Wing. She died in San Francisco, California, 25 April 1942.[35] On 4 May 1875, in St. Joseph's Catholic Church, Red Wing, Goodhue County, Minnesota, Katherine married **Peter Behring.**[36] In 1883 in San Francisco, using the name Freiermuth, Katherine married carpenter, **Martin Weber**, born March 1847 in Hessen-Darmstadt, Germany, died in San Francisco, 24 Jan 1905.[37] Whether the Behring marriage ended in an annulment or a death is not known.[38]

Martin was a carpenter. He and Katherine had the following children, all born in San Francisco:[39]

i. Julia Rose³ Weber, b. 22 July 1885, d. in San Francisco, 2 May 1946; m. abt. 1907, Edward L. Moore, b. abt. 1857 in Iowa, d. abt. 18 May 1928.[40] In May 1942, Julia R. Moore, as the oldest child, was appointed executor of her mother's will.[41] Although not a sizeable estate, the proceeds were evidently used to support her younger sister Frances, an inmate at Napa State Hospital. No children were born to Edward and Julia.

ii. Henry Weber, b. Oct. 1886, d. 15 Oct. 1918.[42]

11 iii. Katherine L. Weber, b. Dec. 1887, m. John Martin Henrich.

iv. Frances Mary Weber, b. 28 Dec. 1889, d. 5 Jul. 1969, Napa Co. In 1942, Frances had been a patient at Napa State Hospital for "several years," and trustees were appointed to manage funds left by her mother for her care. Her sister Katherine was named guardian.[43]

5. **Anthon(e) (Anton) George² "Tony" Freiermuth** (*David*¹) was born about 1864 in Minnesota and died there in Goodhue County, 3 Aug 1907.[44] He married in Minnesota, 12 February 1895, **Louise Bremer** (sometimes "Elizabeth"), born 1 September 1872 in Germany, died 31 January 1933 in Minneapolis. Following Anthon(e)'s death, in about 1910, Louise evidently had a son, Francis, by Gust Gusterson, but according to a descendant, did

---

35. Baptismal records, examined by Julia Sjöberg; California Death Abstracts, 1940-2000, at www.vitalsearch-ca.com (hereafter abbreviated CDA).

36. Goodhue County Marriages, 1854-1878, FHL film # 1,379,159. The marriage was also reported in the *Red Wing Argus,* 6 May 1875 (Julia Sjöberg's Rootsweb website).

37. Original ledger, Odd Fellows Crematory, California Genealogical Society, entry 4466, January 1905. An obituary was pasted into the ledger, but no notation as to what newspaper it was published in was included. He was a native of Hessen-Darmstadt.

38. The only Peter Behring found in the 1880 census was a miner, born in Pennsylvania and age 31, working in Lawrence Co., Dakota Territory. No record was found for a man of this name after 1875 in Minnesota.

39. In the 1900 census of San Francisco (Martin Weber household, 41st Assembly District, E.D. 234, sh. 8B, dwelling 172, family 177) the four listed children are shown. In the 1910 census of San Francisco (41st Assembly District, E.D. 274, sh. 10A, dwelling 195, family 193) Katie B. Weber, then a widowed nurse, declared she had had six children, four of whom were living. Birth and death dates where shown are from CDA.

40. Death notice, *Oakland Tribune,* 18 May 1928, page illegible; Edward Moore household, 1910 census, Alameda Co., Calif., city of Oakland, ward 1, E.D. 79, sh. 14A, dwelling 195, family 232; 1920 Census, Alameda Co., city of Oakland, E.D. 60, sh. 7B, dwelling 179, family 186. Edward in 1910 was a "racetrack reporter," and in 1920, a salesman for a printer/publisher.

41. San Francisco Superior Court 1946 probate file 89957.

42. Henry was mentioned in his father's obituary; his death is from the California Death Index, 1905-1929, at www.vitalsearch-ca.com, and Gantner Bros. Funeral Home Records at http://pilot.familysearch.org/.

43. San Francisco Superior Court probate file #89959.

44. Birth from various census enumerations; death from Minnesota death index at Minnesota Historical Society website: http://people.mnhs.org/.

not marry him.[45] She did marry, about 1914-15, Carl Lofgren, by whom she had a daughter, Lucile, in 1915. Louise died as Louise Lofgren.[46]

Anthon(e) was a tinner. He drowned in a tragic accident on the nearby Mississippi River when his rowboat capsized, leaving not only his wife and four children, but also his aged mother. His obituary names his sisters Frances Schroeder of Minneapolis and Katie Weber of San Francisco, and his brother Charles of San Francisco, but oddly omits his brother Peter.[47]

Anthone and Louise Freiermuth had four children, all born in Minnesota:[48]

i. Pearl Julia[3] Freiermuth, b. 16 Mar. 1897, d. 28 Aug. 1978, Hennepin Co., m. Harold E. Gilmore.[49] n.f.i.

ii. Theresa Margaret Freiermuth, (twin) b. 10 Nov. 1898, d. in Hennepin Co., Minn., 15 Feb 1975; unm.

12 iii. Mary Magdalen Freiermuth, (twin) b. 10 Nov. 1898, m. Basil Van Zanten.

iv. George Anton Freiermuth, b. 17 May 1903, d. Hennepin Co., 22 Dec. 1986; unm. in 1930.[50]

Generation 3

6. **Julia Theresa[3] Schroeder** (*Frances[2], David[1] Freiermuth*) was born 19 July 1875 in Red Wing, Goodhue County, Minnesota, and died in Hennepin County, Minnesota, 3 November 1941. Julia married about 1905 **William Harry Weisgerber**, born 1 September 1874 in Galena, Jo Daviess County, Illinois, died in Hennepin County, Minnesota, 15 December 1936.[51]

William was a salesman throughout all census enumerations. He and Julia had one child, about whom little could be learned:

i. Lester Joseph[4] Weisgerber, b. 5 Aug. 1908, Minneapolis, Hennepin Co., Minn., d. Orange Co., Calif., 24 Feb. 1979.[52]

45. See Louise Lofgren household, 1920 Census, Hennepin Co., Minn., city of Minneapolis, ward 12, E.D. 219, sh. 3B, dwelling 64, family 76. Francis, born 11 July 1909 in Minneapolis, was given the name Francis Gust Freiermuth. Julia Sjöberg, granddaughter of Anthon(e), found Francis's death record in Estherville, Emmet Co., Iowa. Neither Francis nor Lucille, her daughter by Carl Lofgren, is followed in this history.

46. Julia Sjöberg on her Rootsweb website found Louise's burial, 3 Feb. 1933, in St. Mary's Cemetery, Minneapolis, and obtained her death certificate: born 1 Sep. 1872, Hanover, died 31 Jan. 1933, Minneapolis, widow of Carl Lofgren.

47. *Red Wing Daily Republican,* 5 Aug. 1907.

48. Anton Friermuth household, 1900 Census, Goodhue Co., Minn., city of Red Wing, ward 1, E.D. 50, sh. 9, dwelling 175, family 188, p. 182. Louise reported having had three children, all living. Exact birth dates, where given, are from Return of Births, Goodhue County, Minnesota, vol. 3, 1894-1905 (FHL film #1,379,164); deaths are from the Minnesota State Death Index, available at Ancestry.com.

49. Little could be found on Pearl and Harold Gilmore. Harold's name is from Julia Sjöberg, who is in possession of Pearl's wedding ring. Pearl's death is indexed in the Minnesota Death Index at Ancestry.com, but not Harold's. None of the men with similar names who registered for the WWI draft seem to fit, and neither Pearl nor Harold (or Harry) were found in the 1930 census.

50. See Louise Lofgren household, 1930 Census, Hennepin Co., Minn., city of Minneapolis, ward 12, E.D. 27-219, sh. 8A, dwelling 113, family 135, p. 248.

51. Date of birth and death of Julia and William from Julia Sjöberg's Rootsweb website. All information is consistent with census enumerations.

52. Lester, at age twenty-one, working in a gas station, was still with his family in 1930. Julia Sjöberg's website states he

7. **Pearl Catherine[3] Schroeder** (*Frances[2], David[1] Freiermuth*) was born 18 January 1881 in Red Wing, Goodhue County, Minnesota, and died in San Diego County, California, 9 January 1953.[53] Pearl married, perhaps about 1908, Charles P. Flanigan.[54] In 1910, they were in South Dakota and in 1920, Greene County, Alabama. In 1930, Pearl was a "widow" living with her two daughters and managing a hotel in San Diego, California.

Pearl and Charles Flanigan had two daughters, both born in South Dakota:[55]

i. Florence[4] Flanigan, b. 7 June 1909, d. as Florence F. Zalabak in Riverside Co., Calif., 23 Jan. 1997.[56]

ii. Monica Flanigan, b. abt. 1918, alive 1930. n.f.i.

8. **Henry David[3] "Harry" Freiermuth** (*Peter[2], David[1]*) was born 17 October 1879 in Watsonville and died there, 6 September 1929.[57] Harry married, in Watsonville, 15 January 1902, **Lou Henrietta Webb**, daughter of William Webb, born November 1883 in Texas, died 14 April 1969 as Lou Lynch.[58]

At the death of his father in 1912, Harry became president and manager of the P. J. Freiermuth Company, the hardware, plumbing and sheetmetal business his father had founded. Under his leadership, the company branched out to include the manufacture of well casings and roofing.[59] Following Harry's death, the business passed to his younger brother George.

Henry and Lou Freiermuth had four children:[60]

i. Peter[4] Freiermuth, b. 21 Mar. 1904, d. 5 Sep. 1981, Santa Cruz Co.; m. Lillian Marie Blanc, b. 13 Oct. 1898 in Missouri, d. in Santa Cruz Co., 23 Mar. 1997. Both were buried in Valley Church Cemetery.[61] No ch.

13 ii. Arthur George Freiermuth, b. 6 Aug. 1906, m. Gertrude Alice Skillicorn.

iii. Ruth Cecilia Freiermuth, b. 4 Feb. 1910 in Watsonville, d. 22 July 1977; m. Tom Rowan. No ch.

14 iv. Elizabeth Freiermuth, b. 11 Feb. 1917, m. George Wagner.

---

married Lorena Roberts. See William H. Weisgerber household, 1930 Census, Hennepin Co., Minn., Minneapolis, ward 13, E.D. 27-242, sh. 4A, dwelling 60, family 75, p. 252.

53. Birth from Red Wing records, cited by Julia Sjöberg; death from CDA.
54. Marriage information from Julia Sjöberg. Pearl Flanigan's death certificate abstract states her maiden name was Schroeder and that she was born in Minnesota in the correct year.
55. Pearl K. Flanigan household, 1930 Census, San Diego Co., Calif., city of San Diego, E.D. 37-137, sh. 2A, dwelling 21, family 49, p. 197. In 1920 they were in Boligee Twp., Greene Co., Alabama. Pearl listed herself in 1930 as a widow.
56. Birth and death from CDA.
57. Birth from World War I draft registration card at Ancestry.com; death from California Death Index, 1905-1929, at www.vitalsearch-ca.com; tombstone and monument at Watsonville Catholic Cemetery.
58. Lou's full name is from Harry's World War I draft registration card. Their marriage date was published in Watkins, *History of Monterey and Santa Cruz Counties,* 212. Her birth and death are from her tombstone at Watsonville Catholic Cemetery, where she was buried beside her husband Harry. No other death record was found.
59. Mimeographed history of the P. J. Freiermuth Co., written by George Freiermuth in the early 1930s, from the files of the Pajaro Valley Historical Association, Watsonville.
60. Births and deaths from CDA.
61. D. D. Fletcher, *A Tombstone and Vital Record Survey to the Historic Valley Church Cemetery* (Bonny Doon, Calif.: Bonny Doon Publ., 2002).

Loretta Freiermuth as a child
From Ted Judge archives

9. **Loretta Julia**[3] **Freiermuth** (*Peter*[2], *David*[1]) was born 6 November 1881 in Watsonville and died in San Jose, Santa Clara County, 25 October 1932.[62] Loretta married **Philip G. Sheehy**, son of John Sheehy and Ellen Bowen, born in May 1872 in or near Watsonville, died in San Jose, 2 January 1941. They had five children, as related in the Sheehy chapter.

10. **George Peter**[3] **Freiermuth** (*Peter*[2], *David*[1]) was born 19 August 1894 in Watsonville and died in Santa Cruz County, 17 March 1961; he was buried in San Bruno, San Mateo County. George married **Adele R. Laporte**, born 6 January 1893, died in Watsonville, 7 December 1995.[63]

62. Loretta's date of birth from family information is consistent with the 1900 census, Philip Sheehy household, Santa Clara Co., Calif., Santa Clara Twp., E.D. 75, sh. 6B, dwelling 132, family 132. Her daughter Ellen's 1906 birth certificate states that Loretta was twenty-five at the time; her death is from the California Death Index, 1930-39, www.vitalsearch-ca.com.

63. Birth and death of both George and Adele from CDA; marriage information from Fr. Harry Freiermuth.

George became the president of the P. J. Freiermuth Company following the death of his brother Harry and eventually, in 1945, sold the business and retired.[64] He and Adele had one child:

15 i. GEORGE J.[4] FREIERMUTH, b. 31 July 1920, m. AILEEN CONNELL.[65]

11. KATHERINE L.[3] WEBER (*Katherine*[2], *David*[1] *Freiermuth*) was born in San Francisco, 20 December 1887, and likely was the Katherine C. Henrich who died in Los Angeles County, 7 October 1971.[66] Katie married about 1918, **JOHN MARTIN HENRICH**, born 22 July 1881 in Germany, died in San Mateo County, 20 July 1952.[67]

Following the death of her mother in 1942, Katherine was appointed guardian to manage the affairs of her sister Frances Mary Weber, who had been a patient at Napa State Hospital for a number of years.[68]

Katherine and John Henrich had two children:[69]

i. JOHN EDWARD[4] HENRICH, b. 12 Nov. 1919, San Francisco, d. 6 Nov. 1998, Orange Co., Calif.

ii. WILLIAM GEORGE HENRICH, b. 6 Dec. 1921, San Francisco, d. 24 Nov. 2000, Solano Co., Calif.

12. MARY (MARIE) MAGDALEN[3] FREIERMUTH (*Anthone*[2], *David*[1]) was born 10 November 1898 in Minnesota and died there, 20 November 1993, in Spring Park, Hennepin County.[70] She married, 15 June 1926, **BASIL VAN ZANTEN**, born in the Netherlands, 1 October 1898, died in Hennepin County, 2 January 1997.[71]

The children of Mary and Basil Van Zanten included:

i. HAROLD RICHARD BASIL[4] VAN ZANTEN, b. 26 July 1929, Minneapolis, Hennipen Co., Minn., d. 6 Nov. 2002, East Moline, Rock Island Co., Ill; m. JEAN MARILYN MATCHKE.[72]

Generation 4

13. ARTHUR GEORGE[4] FREIERMUTH (*Henry*[3], *Peter*[2], *David*[1]) was born 6 August 1906 in Watsonville and died there, 1 January 1968.[73] He married in St. Patrick's Church, Watsonville, 12 March 1925, **GERTRUDE ALICE SKILLICORN**, daughter of George Edward Skillicorn and Mary Elizabeth Flynn, born 7 December 1908, died in Watsonville, 18 January 2008.[74]

64. Mimeographed history of the P. J. Freiermuth Co., previously cited; Polk's Watsonville city directory, 1939, digitized at Ancestry.com.
65. Births and deaths from CDA; marriage from Fr. Harry Freiermuth.
66. Martin Weber household, 1900 Census, San Francisco, Calif., 41st Assembly District, E.D. 234, sh. 8B, dwelling 172, family 176; CDA. The latter gives the year of birth as 1888.
67. Birth and death from CDA.
68. See San Francisco Superior Court probate files 89957 (Katie B. Weber death, 1942) and 89959 (Frances Mary Weber guardianship, 1942). Frances in 1942 was a patient at Napa State Hospital.
69. California Birth Index at www.vitalsearch-ca.com; deaths from Social Security Death Index (SSDI).
70. Goodhue Co. Return of Births, vol. 3, p. 83 (FHL film # 1,379,164); Minnesota Death Index at Ancestry.com.
71. Marriage information copied from Rootsweb site of Julia Sjöberg, evidently a descendant.
72. Minnesota Birth Index at Ancestry.com; SSDI. He was buried at Rock Island National Cemetery.
73. Birth and death from CDA.
74. Marriage from Fr. Harry Freiermuth; birth and death of Gertrude from SSDI and obituary, *Register Pajaronian,* 29 Jan.

Arthur, in the 1930 census, was an account manager for a hardware store, likely the P. J. Freiermuth Co. in Watsonville.[75] He and Gertrude had two children:

i. HARRY DAVID[5] FREIERMUTH, b. 6 May 1927, Watsonville. Harry is a retired Catholic priest, living now in Watsonville, to whom we are indebted for much of the information in this chapter.

ii. GENE ARTHUR FREIERMUTH, b. 23 Feb. 1930, Watsonville, d. 21 Jan. 2003, Santa Cruz Co.; m. 19 Feb. 1950, MARGARET ANN LASHER, b. 8 Dec. 1931, d. 5 Oct. 1996.

14. **ELIZABETH[4] FREIERMUTH** (*Henry[3], Peter[2], David[1]*) was born 11 February 1917 in Watsonville, died at Pebble Beach, Monterey County, 9 February 2005; m. **GEORGE WAGNER.**[76]

15. **GEORGE J.[4] FREIERMUTH** (*George[3], Peter[2], David[1]*) was born 31 July 1920 in Watsonville and died in Santa Cruz County, 9 June 1986.[77] George married **AILEEN CONNELL**, born about 1925 in Kansas, died in Hollister, San Benito County, 19 May 2004.[78]

2008, e-edition.

75. Arthur Friermuth household, 1930 Census, Santa Cruz Co., Calif., city of Watsonville, E.D. 44-25, sh. 19B, dwelling 16A, family 18A.

76. Birth and death information for Elizabeth from the SSDI; marriage from Fr. Harry Freiermuth.

77. Birth and death from CDA.

78. SSDI; marriage from Fr. Harry Freiermuth.

Book Three

Ted Judge's Stepfather: Albert Sylvan Taylor

Ancestors of Albert Sylvan Taylor,

Stepfather of Theodore Timothy Judge

Theodore Timothy Judge
b. 1 Apr. 1921, Westwood, Lassen Co., Calif.
d. 11 June 2008, The Forum, Cupertino, Calif.

Albert Sylvan Taylor
b. 16 Aug. 1899, San Francisco, Calif.
d. 9 Sep. 1995, Saratoga, Santa Clara, Co., Calif.
m. 11 May. 1929, Oakland, Calif.

Hazel Agnes Russell
b. 5 Jan. 1900, Karlo, Lassen Co., Calif.
d. 12 Dec. 1988, Santa Clara, Calif.

Andrew Oscar Taylor
b. 17 Mar. 1871, Missouri
d. 23 Aug. 1942, Oakland, Calif.
m. 17 July 1898, San Francisco, Calif.

Emma Josephine Farneman
b. 11 Nov. 1875, Calif.
d. 31 Jul. 1966, San Francisco, Calif.

Albert Taylor
b. 18 Oct. 1840, Jefferson Co., Ohio
d, 23 Jan. 1909, Red Bluff, Calif.
m. 20 Feb. 1862, Guernsey Co., Ohio

Mary H. Coleman
b. 14 Mar. 1841, Scott Co., Iowa
d. 4 Nov. 1917, Red Bluff, Calif.

John Farneman
b. abt. 1827, Montgomery Co., Ohio
d. 14 Nov. 1892, Atlanta, Idaho
m. 17 Apr. 1870, Jordan Valley, Ore.
div. abt. Jun. 1879, Alturas Co., Idaho

Mary E. Moore
b. 24 June 1837, Moniteau Co., Missouri
d. 4 Jan. 1904, San Jose, Calif.

Joseph Taylor
b. 1792 - 1796, Maryland
d. 19 Dec. 1870, Guernsey Co., Ohio
m. 7 Aug. 1823, Jefferson Co., Ohio

Margaret Meek
b. abt. 1802, Jefferson Co., Ohio
d. aft. 1880

Charles Coleman
b. 5 Oct. 1818, Jefferson Co., Ohio
d. Mar. 1853, Guernsey Co., Ohio
m. 7 Aug. 1823

Martha Robinson
b. 1820, Penn.
d. aft. 1870, prob. Ohio

John Farneman
b. 15 Nov. 1791, Frankstown, Penn.
d. 10 Feb.1870, Delphi, Carroll Co., Ind.
m. 17 May 1818, Montgomery Co., Ohio

Polly Kuns
b. abt. 1800, Frankstown, Penn.
d. 1866, Carroll Co., Ind.

Vincent Moore
b. abt. 1788, Pittsylvania, Va.
d. aft. 1860, prob. Calif.
m. 12 Jan. 1812, Pittsylvania, Va.

Nancy Hatchett
b. abt. 1797, Chatham, Pittsylvania, Va.
d. 12 April 1865, Tehama Co., Calif.

Overview

Ted Judge saw little of his biological father after his parents divorced when he was a toddler. His mother married again, Albert Sylvan Taylor, her friend of many years, who then adopted Ted in all but name. While Ted's biological paternal ancestors immigrated from Ireland to California, his stepfather's ancestors can be traced back to the earliest days of our nation. Their descendants followed a classic migration pattern, settling for a while in Ohio, Missouri, and Iowa before reaching California. While they may have come to try their hand at mining, they moved on to pursue other occupations all across the state. They worked as turkey farmers, cattlemen, stage drivers, railroad inspectors, trolley car men and teachers. Some of the small towns where they lived are now ghost towns—places that soared with dreams of gold and silver then faded away—Owyhee, Idaho; Unionville, Nevada; and Bodie, California.

This section of the book, originally intended to be minimal because it does not ascend from Ted's biological father, soon evolved into a colorful panorama typical of the "Wild West." The ancestral lines of Albert Sylvan Taylor's mother, those of Farneman, Moore, and Hatchett, are not merely colorful; they are both exciting and tragic. This section consists of a traditional genealogical descendancy along the Taylor line over three generations and a narrative encompassing three generations along Albert Sylvan Taylor's maternal line.

Ancestors in the Taylor paternal line—the Taylors, Meeks and Colemans—crossed the Ohio River from Maryland, Virginia and Pennsylvania in the early 1800s before Ohio became a state. The next generation migrated west as new lands opened up and better opportunities presented themselves. That story starts with Joseph Taylor, who reached Ohio when land first became available. His son Albert married the family's young housemaid and then left to fight in the Civil War. Returning after three hard years, he and his young wife went to Missouri, where they raised a small family and then left for California, finally reaching Tehama County in the 1880s. Their son Andrew Oscar Taylor, one of only three of seven children to reach adulthood, married another survivor, Emma Josephine Farneman, the third in a line of strong pioneer women, each with a story worth telling.

Emma's ancestral story starts with her grandmother Nancy, who endured a long marriage to an adventurous man who could not stay out of trouble. She followed him first to Iowa and then to Yuba and Butte counties, California, where her life ended at the hands of local Indians. Nancy's daughter Mary (Emma's mother) was married with four small children when the tragedy occurred. She and her husband, perhaps understandably, left the area soon afterwards for the silver mining region of southwestern Idaho, where she soon took up with a much older, successful farmer who had been raised in a Dunkard family, John Farneman. This ill-matched marriage soon ended in a scandalous, public divorce, after which Mary, with a new lover, headed for yet another mining boomtown, Bodie. It is within this dysfunctional family situation that Emma Farneman grew up. Emma seems to have emerged from her traumatic childhood with a determined need for order. Her father's only daughter, she used her inheritance to purchase a house for her widowed mother to live in and became a school teacher, stern in demeanor and reclusive in her later years.

Andrew Oscar Taylor and Emma Josephine Farneman, so different in many ways, but alike in that each endured a stressful, disruptive childhood, became the parents of Albert Sylvan Taylor, the hard-working, adored stepfather of Ted Judge.

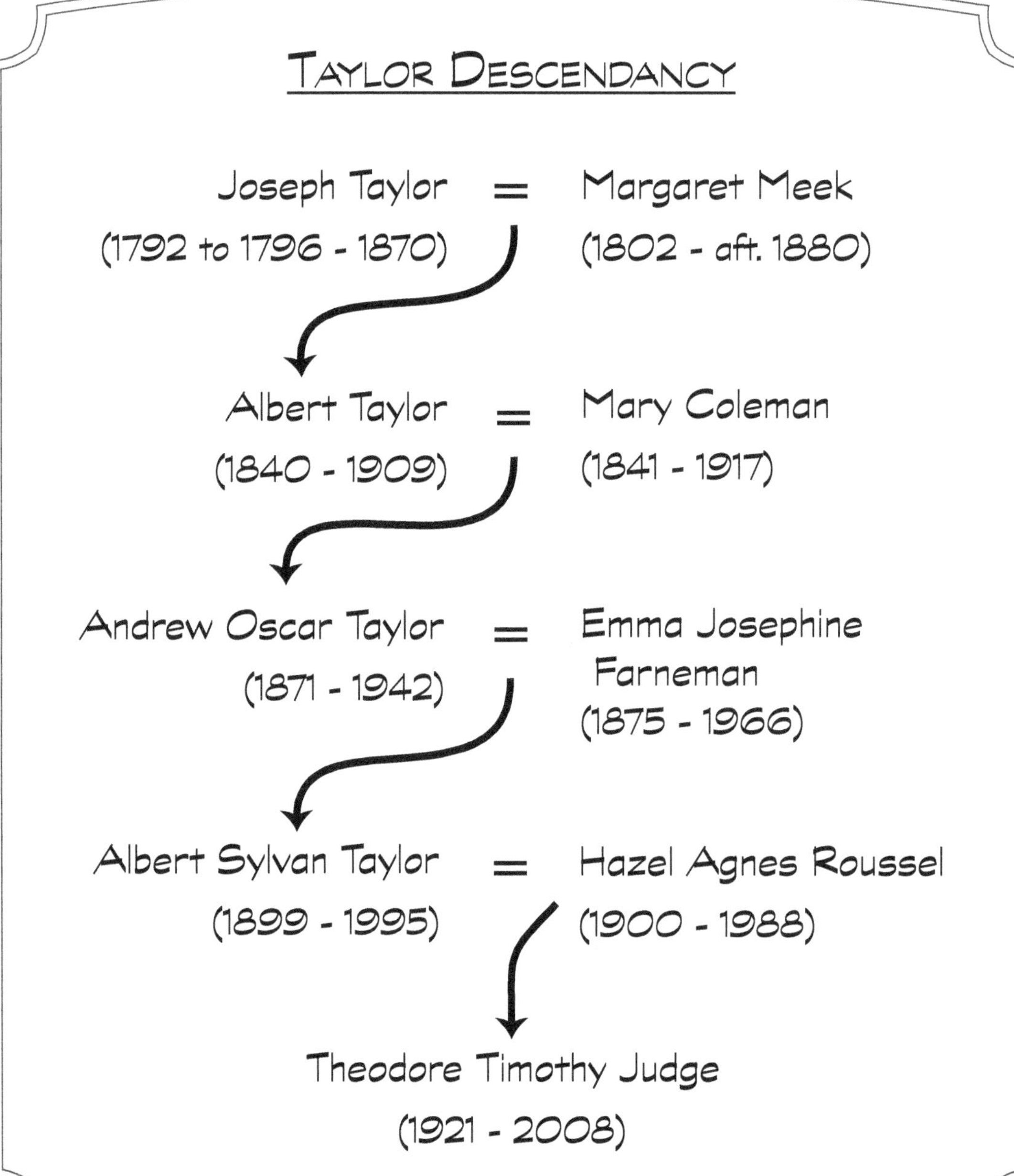

Taylor descendancy from Joseph Taylor to Ted Judge

❧ The Paternal Ancestry of Albert Sylvan Taylor

Albert Sylvan Taylor was the man whom Ted Judge called Dad throughout his life. Albert's ancestry was of interest to Ted in his later years, but he knew little about it. This brief history is offered as a beginning for others to build upon. It begins with Joseph and Margaret (Meek) Taylor, Albert's great-grandparents. While Ted's biological ancestors on his father's side were largely recent immigrants from Ireland who joined the California gold rush, his stepfather's ancestors arrived on the continent much earlier. They were involved in the major early conflicts of our nation and pushed west with the earliest pioneers. While the Meek family has been traced back to early Virginia and Maryland, the Taylor side has been less thoroughly researched.[1]

The Meek family moved across the river from Brooke County in what is now West Virginia, to the newly formed Jefferson County, Ohio Territory, between 1798 and 1801. The Taylors may have come early also, but just when is difficult to determine. There were a number of pioneer Taylor families along the eastern border of what became the state of Ohio in 1803; it has not been possible at this point to sort out their records.

Joseph Taylor, according to later census enumerations, was born in Maryland 1792-96. He first appears in records with any measure of certainty in 1823, when he married Margaret Meek in Smithfield Township, Jefferson County. His presence in the 1820 census is uncertain. In 1820, a Joseph Taylor, Sr., and a Joseph Taylor, Jr., were enumerated side by side in Smithfield, but Joseph Jr., age 19-25, if the man we are looking for, appears to have had a young wife. If the correct Joseph Taylor, Margaret may have been his second wife or the female in 1820 may have been his sister.[2] Isaac Meek, written to have been Margaret's father, was enumerated in the same township.[3] The Joseph Taylor enumerated in Smithfield in 1830, age 30-39, had no young daughters as would have been expected, but that may have been an enumeration error. In 1840 he appears to be there with the expected assortment of children.[4]

1. James R. Meek, *Genealogical Record of the Meek Family 1660-1934* (Bellaire, Ohio: Progressive Print Co., 1934), 16; limited availability, electronic copy courtesy of Joe Logan. All Meek information, unless otherwise noted, comes from this small publication.
2. Joseph Taylor household, 1820 U.S. census, Jefferson Co., Ohio, Smithfield Twp., p. 212 (top): Joseph Taylor Sr. was enumerated adjacent to Joseph Taylor Jr., the latter heading a household consisting of only one male age 19-25 and one female 16-25. In 1830, only the younger Joseph (age 30-39) was there.
3. Isaac Meek Sr. household, 1820 Census, Jefferson Co., Ohio, Smithfield Twp., p. 217 (bottom), (indexed by Ancestry.com as "Meck"). The household consisted of only one female of an age (16-25) who could have been Margaret, but who more likely was her sister Jemima. Jemima, according to the *Meek Family* genealogy, did not marry until 1824.
4. Joseph Taylor household, 1830 census, Jefferson Co., Ohio, Smithfield Twp., p. 136.

393.

Certificate No. 2905

The United States of America,

To all to whom these presents shall come, Greeting:

Whereas, Joseph Taylor Junr of Jefferson County, Ohio has deposited in the General Land Office of the United States, a certificate of the Register of the Land Office at Zanesville whereby it appears that full payment has been made by the said Joseph Taylor, Junr according to the provisions of the act of Congress of the 24th of April, 1820, entitled "An act making further provision for the sale of the Public Lands," for the West half of the South East quarter of section four in Township four of Range two, of the unappropriated lands in the Military District subject to sale at Zanesville, Ohio containing seventy three acres and twenty four hundredths of an acre according to the official plat of the survey of the said Lands, returned to the General Land Office by the Surveyor General, which said tract has been purchased by the said Joseph Taylor

NOW KNOW YE, That the **UNITED STATES OF AMERICA,** in consideration of the premises, and in conformity with the several acts of Congress, in such case made and provided, have given and granted, and, by these presents, do give and grant, unto the said Joseph Taylor and to his heirs, the said tract above described: To Have and to Hold the same, together with all the rights, privileges, immunities and appurtenances, of whatsoever nature thereunto belonging, unto the said Joseph Taylor and to his heirs and assigns forever.

In testimony whereof, I, Andrew Jackson **PRESIDENT OF THE UNITED STATES OF AMERICA,** have caused these Letters to be made Patent, and the Seal of the General Land Office to be hereunto affixed.

Given under my hand, at the City of Washington, the first day of July in the year of our Lord, one thousand eight hundred and thirty one and of the Independence of the United States the fifty fifth signed April 17 1833

By the President, Andrew Jackson

By A. J. Donelson Secy

Commissioner of the General Land Office.

Joseph Taylor land patent
From Bureau of Land Management

A man clearly the correct Joseph was farming in Guernsey County in 1850, where he remained until his death.[5] This land may have been purchased long before the family relocated. In 1820 a Joseph Taylor, whether senior or junior, paid taxes on 150 acres near Zane's Trace and the National Road in Sections 2 and 9 in Oxford, Wheeling Township, Guernsey County.[6] In 1830, a Joseph Taylor, Jr., of Jefferson County purchased land in the Ohio River Survey and United States Military Survey in Guernsey County.[7] This land was offered for sale to veterans of the War of 1812, which suggests that if he's the correct Joseph Taylor, he was born in or before 1796. A map published by the Library of Congress in 1855 shows two large pieces of farmland marked as owned by Joseph Taylor.[8]

Joseph is said to be buried on his farm near Millinersville. His son William and son-in-law, Alexander Cessna, co-administered his estate.[9] His widow Margaret in 1880 was living with their youngest son, Jacob.[10] Her death and final resting place are unknown.

Genealogical Descendancy

1. **Joseph[1] Taylor** was born in Maryland probably between 1792 and 1796 to undetermined parents. He died on his farm in Wheeling Township, Guernsey County, Ohio, 19 December 1870.[11] Joseph married, 7 August 1823, **Margaret Meek**, born about 1802 on Short Creek near Mt. Pleasant, Jefferson County, Ohio, the daughter of Isaac Meek and his second wife Rachel Hedges.[12]

While Joseph's ancestry remains undetermined, Margaret is written to have descended from Guy Meek, from Shrewsbury, England, of Welsh ancestry, who in 1661 received a land grant in Anne Arundel County, Maryland.[13] Her descent is through his son Isaac and grandson Isaac, who was born in 1746 near Annapolis and died in Short Creek Township, in what was then Jefferson County, now Harrison County, Ohio. Statehood was around the corner, and Isaac Meek became a member of the first Legislature of Ohio in 1802.

A Joseph Taylor, not the "Col. Joseph Taylor" of Cambridge described elsewhere but likely this Joseph, receives brief treatment in Wolfe's *Stories of Guernsey County* as follows:

> *Joseph Taylor, from Pennsylvania, located on what afterward became the William McClelland farm, in 1817. Taylor was a Dunkard and preached occasionally.*[14]

5. Joseph Taylor households, all in Guernsey Co., Ohio: 1870 (as Tailor), Wheeling Twp., dwelling 40, family 39, p. 5 (634 left); 1860 Wheeling Twp., dwelling 39, family 39, p. 6; 1850 Wheeling Twp., dwelling 991, family 1001, p. 455 (left).
6. William G. Wolfe, *Stories of Guernsey County, Ohio: History of an Average Ohio County* (Evansville, Ind.: Unigraphic, 1978), 1049.
7. Bureau of Land Management database, located at www.glorecords.blm.gov/PatentSearch. This purchase consisted of 73+ acres in Range 2, Twp. 4, Sec. 4 in the W ½ of the SE ¼.
8. Library of Congress geography and map division, *Guernsey County, Ohio, Land Ownership Map, 1855*, Family History Library (hereafter, FHL) fiche #6079866.
9. Joseph Taylor estate administration, 19 January 1871, in Guernsey Co. Administrator's record, bk. 2, p. 158 (FHL film #894,960).
10. Jacob Taylor household, 1880 census, Guernsey Co., Ohio, Wheeling Twp., E.D. 81, sh. 9A, dwelling 85, family 91.
11. "Death Records, 1867-1908" prepared by Guernsey Co. Probate Judge (FHL film # 894945).
12. Meek, *Genealogical Record of the Meek Family*, 16. The death of a Margaret Taylor (along with that of a Joseph on p. 34) is noted in Guernsey County Deaths, bk. 1, p. 60, but this was not examined.
13. This and much of the following information is from the Meek Family genealogy, cited above. Family lore of Laurice Johnson of Menifee, Calif., granddaughter of Isaac Meek and Rachel Hedges, is consistent with the information published in the book.
14. Wolfe, *Stories of Guernsey County*, 988.

Dunkards are a conservative Old German Baptist sect, similar to the Amish in that they are pacifists and lead a comparatively non-conforming life. They originally settled in Pennsylvania, but today remain more concentrated in rural Ohio and Indiana.

The Meek family history notes fifteen children were born to Joseph and Margaret but only eleven have been confirmed from census enumerations and other sources:[15]

i NANCY[2] TAYLOR, b. Ohio, 23 May 1823, d. Red Bluff, Tehama Co., Calif., 7 July 1899.[16] Nancy m. in Ohio, 29 July 1849, ALEXANDER F. CESSNA, b. 21 Dec. 1821 in Pa., d. in Red Bluff, 3 Mar. 1890.[17] Their son, James C. Cessna, b. in 1850 in Pa., died 11 Jan. 1920 in Red Bluff. Nancy appears to have been the only family member besides Albert who went to California.

ii. RACHEL TAYLOR, b. _?_; m. 31 Dec. 1844, LEMUEL DALLAS.

iii. CATHERINE TAYLOR, b. _?_; m. 21 Nov. 1852, ANDREW LEDLIE.

iv. MARY TAYLOR, b. Ohio about 1825; m. __?__ TAYLOR.

v. EMILY TAYLOR, b. Ohio abt. 1827; m. 31 Aug. 1851, WILLIAM GRIMES.

vi. WILLIAM TAYLOR, b. Ohio about 1830.

vii. JOHN TAYLOR, b. Ohio abt. 1832.

viii. SALATHIEL TAYLOR, b. Ohio abt. 1836; m. MARGARET HURSEY.

ix. OLIVER TAYLOR, b. Ohio abt. 1838.

2 x. ALBERT TAYLOR, b. 18 Oct. 1840; m. MARY H. COLEMAN.

xi. JACOB MEEK TAYLOR, b. 10 March 1843; m. AMANDA SERVISON.

Generation 2

2. **ALBERT[2] TAYLOR** (*Joseph*[1]), the son of Joseph Taylor and Margaret Meek, was born in Jefferson County, Ohio, 18 October 1840, and died in Red Bluff, Tehama County, California, 23 January 1909.[18] Albert married in Guernsey County, Ohio, 20 February 1862, **MARY H. COLEMAN.**[19] Mary, the daughter of Charles Coleman and Martha Robinson, was born in Scott County, Iowa, 14 March 1841, and died at her daughter Grace's home in Red Bluff, 4 November 1917.[20]

While Albert came from a comparatively settled family of comfortable circumstances, Mary endured a stressful childhood. Her lineage extends back to before the Revolution, covered

15. Information, unless otherwise noted, is from the Meek genealogy, from census enumerations previously cited and from *Guernsey County, Ohio, Marriage Records*, 4 vols. (Cambridge, Ohio: Ohio Geneal. Soc., 1987), vol. D, covering 1844-1861.
16. Keith Lingenfelter Collection, Special Collections, Meriam Library, California State University, Chico, Calif.; marriage extracts are found at www.csuchico.edu/lbib/spc/lingenfelter.
17. Lingenfelter Collection, cited above.
18. For birth, see Meek, *Genealogical Record of the Meek Family*, 16; death from California Death Index, 1905-1929, at www.vitalsearch-ca.com (hereafter CDI). Corp'l Albert Taylor's tombstone in Oak Hill Cemetery notes his Civil War regiment and company but only the years of his birth and death (www.findagrave.com).
19. *Guernsey County Marriage Records*, vol. D.
20. The marriage of Charles Coleman to Martha Robinson 15 Oct. 1837 is recorded in *Guernsey Co. Marriage Records*, entry no. 2533. Mary's birth and death are from CDI and Oak Hill Cem. transcriptions at http://www.calarchives4u.com/cemeteries/tehama/oakhill-tz.txt. Additional information on the Coleman family is archived at CGS.

in detail in a diary kept by her uncle, the Rev. Andrew Coleman.[21] Mary Coleman was the younger of two daughters, born a few years after the family moved from Guernsey County, Ohio, to Scott County, Iowa, along with Mary's paternal grandfather and most of her father's siblings and their families. When Mary was eight, her grandfather and an aunt to whom she was quite close died. Her father evidently was already ill with heart trouble, and when other family members decided to move on to other states, Mary's parents and sister returned to Guernsey County. Her father died there within a few years at thirty-nine.[22] Mary's mother was left destitute and went to work as a washerwoman.[23] Within a few years Mary's older sister Anna married James W. Wilson, and Mary went to work as a housemaid.[24] In the 1860 census, Mary was enumerated as a housemaid in the Taylor household, and at age nineteen, she married one of the younger Taylor sons.

Albert Taylor, son of a successful farmer, and Mary H. Coleman, housemaid in the Taylor home, were married less than eight months before Albert marched off to join the Union Army. He enlisted early, 22 August 1862, a month before Lincoln issued his preliminary Emancipation Proclamation.[25] Albert served in Company B of the 122nd Ohio Infantry, organized at Camp Zanesville in October 1862.[26] Having said goodbye to his pregnant wife, he did not return for three years.

The Civil War took Albert far from farm life. Company B engaged in continual skirmishes in Virginia and Maryland, guarded stores in Baltimore and did duty in New York City during the draft riots of March 1863.[27] Albert was listed as a prisoner of war in Winchester, Virginia 15 June 1863.[28] After his release, he returned to battle. His regiment, consisting of 1065 men, lost seven officers, eighty-six enlisted men in battle, and one hundred and thirty-seven from disease. Company B was at Appomattox during Lee's surrender. Albert was promoted to corporal 13 May 1865 and mustered out at Washington D.C. a month later. The treasured fork Albert Taylor carried during three years of combat was passed down through the family over at least three generations.[29]

Their first child died shortly after Albert returned from war. After the birth of their second child in 1866, the family removed to Missouri where one child was buried and two more children were born, including Andrew, the step-grandfather of Ted Judge. In the 1870 census in

21. Information on the composition and migration of this family was originally communicated by descendant Richard Worthy of Westfield, Ind., who obtained a transcript of the diary of Andrew Coleman, the oldest brother of Charles Coleman, Mary's father.
22. His sad obituary is transcribed into the Coleman diary. What little land they had had to be sold in order to pay his debts; see Guernsey Co., Ohio, Administrators, executor's docket, vol. C, 1846-1857 (FHL film #894,959), Charles Coleman estate.
23. Martha Coleman household, 1860 census, Guernsey Co., Ohio, New Birmingham Twp., post office Milnersville, dwelling 377, household 342, p. 143. Mary was doubly enumerated in both her mother's household and in the Joseph Taylor household: Guernsey Co., Wheeling Twp., dwelling 39, family 39, p. 199 (left).
24. Coleman-Wilson marriage from *Guernsey County Marriage Records*, vol. D.
25. Sons of Union Veterans, National Graves Registration Project, collected and reviewed submissions for burials. Those approved by the National Graves Registration Officer have been placed in an ongoing database available at www.suvcwdb.org/home.
26. Soldier data for Albert Taylor (Union) from the American Civil War Research Database, a subscription database by Historical Data Systems, Inc. accessed at www.civilwardata.com.
27. Frederick H. Dyer, *A Compendium of the War of the Rebellion [Ohio] : Compiled and Arranged from Official Records of the Federal and Confederate Armies, Reports of the Adjutant Generals of the Several States, the Army Registers and Other Reliable Documents and Sources* (Cedar Rapids, Iowa: Torch Press, 1908). A transcription can be found at www.ohiocivilwar.com/cw122.html.
28. Gilbert E. Sabre, *Nineteen Months a Prisoner of War,* (New York: American News Co., 1865), 204.
29. A letter accompanying the fork, sent by Ted Judge to Maryemma Juve, found in the Ted Judge archives at CGS.

Speedwell Township, St. Clair County, Albert was recorded as "farmer."[30] Albert and Mary with sons Joseph and Andrew, then pushed west again, this time all the way to California. The family was enumerated on the 1880 census in West Grafton, Yolo County, where again Albert was farming.[31]

On 1 October 1883 Albert was awarded a homestead land entry of 158.49 acres consisting of two lots in section 2, twp. 27-N, range 4-W in Tehama County.[32] The last Taylor child, Grace, was born the following year; one month later two of the older children died of scarlet fever. They, along with members of the family of Albert's sister Nancy Cessna, are buried in the Taylor/Cessna family plot at Oak Hill Cemetery in Red Bluff.[33]

Albert Taylor tombstone, Oak Hill Cemetery, Red Bluff, California

By 1900 Albert owned a house in Red Bluff free of mortgage and was working as a school janitor.[34] Then sixty, he may have found farming no longer physically possible. In 1891, he filed for and was awarded an invalid pension based upon his Civil War service.[35]

Seven children were born to Albert and Mary Taylor, only three of whom reached adulthood:

i. CHARLIE[3] CESSNA TAYLOR, b. Guernsey Co., Ohio, 1 Mar. 1863, d. there, 7 Mar. 1866.

ii. MARGARET FRANCES TAYLOR, b. Ohio, 6 Apr. 1866, d. 5 Oct. 1871, Missouri.

iii. JOSEPH THURLOW TAYLOR, b. Missouri, 28 Oct. 1867; m. MINNIE _?_.

3 iv. ANDREW OSCAR TAYLOR, b. 17 Mar. 1871; m. EMMA JOSEPHINE FARNEMAN.

v. LEOLA IRENE TAYLOR, b. Calif., 8 Oct. 1876, d. of scarlet fever, Red Bluff, Tehama Co., 11 Oct. 1884, interred in the Taylor/Cessna family plot, Oak Hill Cem., Red Bluff.

vi. CLIFFORD COLEMAN TAYLOR, b. Calif., 28 July 1878, d. Red Bluff, also of scarlet fever, 17 Oct. 1884, interred in the Taylor/Cessna family plot.

vii. GRACE TAYLOR, b. Calif., 9 Sept. 1884; m. (1) ABRAM LINCOLN ZELNER and (2) JOSEPH ISADORE CASALE.

Generation 3

3. ANDREW OSCAR[3] TAYLOR (*Albert[2], Joseph[1]*) was born 17 March 1871 in Missouri, the son of Albert Taylor and Mary H. Coleman. He died in Oakland, Alameda County, California, 23 August 1942. His ashes were inurned, along with those of his wife, at the Chapel of the

30. Albert Taylor household, 1870 census, St. Clair Co., Missouri, Speedwell Twp., dwelling 56, family 56, p. 476.
31. Albert Taylor household, 1880 census, Yolo Co., Calif., West Grafton twp., E.D. 163, sh. 16, dwelling 113, fam. 116.
32. His land entry description is from the Bureau of Land Management database, located at www.glorecords.blm.gov/PatentSearch.
33. Oak Hill Cem. records.
34. Albert Taylor household, 1900 census, Tehama Co., Calif., Red Bluff Twp., E.D. 184, sh. 24A, dwelling 537, family 539, p. 318.
35. This file, application 1045.197 (certificate 847.540) is indexed at www.footnote.com but was not pursued. Albert's Civil War service and burial site were validated by the Sons of Union Veterans, National Graves Registration Project, and a brief service record placed in the database at www.suvcwdb.org.

Chimes in Oakland.[36] On 17 July 1898, in San Francisco, Andrew married **Emma Josephine Farneman**.[37] Emma, born in California, 10 November 1875, the daughter of John Farneman and Mary E. Moore, died in San Francisco, 31 July 1966.[38]

Andrew Taylor and Emma Farneman each experienced childhoods filled with the upheavals of many pioneer moves and the deaths of siblings. Andrew was born to a father who spent three years fighting in the Civil War, then moved his family successively further west from Ohio, farming and burying children in Missouri and then California. Emma was the only child of her mother's second marriage, born into a complex family of multiple marriages and raised in the chaotic mining town of Bodie. Her ancestry and early life are covered in detail in the following chapter.

Emma was educated to become a teacher at what was then San Jose Normal School.[39] While she was teaching school in the Sierra, Andrew was exploring the world. He sailed as a cabin boy on a ship from San Francisco to Honolulu on 20 March 1896 and returned 5 May.[40] Somewhere they met and then married in 1898 in San Francisco.[41] Their marriage was announced in the *Evening News*: "Miss Emma Farneman of San Jose and Andrew Taylor of Red Bluff were married in San Francisco on July 17th."

Andrew worked for a year as a railway conductor in San Francisco and then headed for the Sierra Nevada and a job with the Southern Pacific Railroad.[42] Following the birth of their son Albert in August 1899, mother and son joined him, and they lived with his brother Joseph. Both men worked for the railroad, Andrew as a car inspector and Joseph as a car repairman.[43] Emma was enumerated twice in the 1900 census, in both Washoe County, Nevada, and in San Jose, where she was living with her mother, Mary E. (Moore) (Dikeman) (Farneman) Baker in the house Emma purchased with money inherited from her father.[44]

For several years, Emma and Andrew split their time between the mountains and the Bay Area. In 1903 they moved to San Jose, where Emma's mother, Mary, was already ill and where she died a year later. There were legal decisions to be made; Emma was appointed administratrix.[45] In 1904 Andrew received a certificate of service from Southern Pacific in

36. Abstracts of California deaths, 1940-2000, a database at www.vitalsearch-ca.com (hereafter CDA); Social Security Death Index (SSDI); confirmed at Chapel of the Chimes.
37. *San Jose Evening News*, 25 July 1898, p. _?_, (unpaginated clipping in Judge archives at CGS). "Miss Emma Farneman of San Jose and Andrew Taylor of Red Bluff were married in San Francisco on July 17th."
38. CDA; obituary, *San Francisco Chronicle*, 2 Aug 1966, p. 35, col. 8. Emma's obituary identifies both her children, as well as her grandson Ted Judge, then of Minnesota, and grandson Julian Thruston of Tahoe City. "In San Francisco July 31 1966, Emma Taylor beloved wife of the late Andrew O Taylor, beloved mother of Albert S Taylor of Oakland, Mrs Maurice (Maryemma) Juve of Salem Oregon, loving grandmother of Ted Judge of Minnesota and Julian Thruston of Tahoe city; a native of California aged 92 years, a graduate of San Jose State Normal school class of 1894. Private family services were held at Grant Miller Mortuaries."
39. Emma Taylor obituary, cited above.
40. Ted Judge's handwritten notes, now archived at CGS.
41. Ted Judge notes; *San Jose Evening News*, 25 July 1898.
42. Ted Judge notes.
43. Andrew O. Taylor household, 1900 census, Nevada, Washoe Co., Wadsworth Precinct, E.D. 44, sh. 4B, dwelling 89, family 89.
44. Mary E. Baker household, 1900 census, Santa Clara Co., city of San Jose, ward 2, E.D. 67, sh. 7A, dwelling 151, family 161, p. 41.
45. Mary E. Farneman probate, Santa Clara County Superior Court file no. 6124, filed in 1904. This file was reopened in 1906 to account for a successful Indian depredation claim for livestock lost in the late 1880s in the Jordan Valley in Idaho.

San Jose as a car inspector. In 1905 in San Jose he was working as a driver for Kelley Laundry and in 1906, immediately following the earthquake, he was one of the few who were authorized to enter secure areas in the rubble of San Jose.[46]

Albert Taylor ("Dad") with Polaroid, undated
From Ted Judge archives

Daughter Maryemma was born in 1907 in Santa Clara, but by 1910 the family had returned to the mountains. The family lived in Alpine County, where Emma taught and worked as an enumerator in the 1910 census, then later moved to Nevada. In the 1910 census of Markleeville, Alpine County, and in the 1920 and 1930 censuses of Mottsville and Centerville, Douglas County, Nevada, Andrew's occupation was recorded as "farmer."[47] In 1929, in Nevada, their son Albert married Hazel Agnes (Roussel) Judge, a divorcee with a young son, Ted Judge, and their daughter Maryemma married the district attorney of Lincoln County, Nevada, Julian Thruston. Andrew and Emma saw Maryemma bury her firstborn child in 1936 and bear a second in 1937, after which the Taylors returned to the Bay Area, where Andrew died in 1942.

Albert and Emma Taylor had two children:

4 i. Albert Sylvan[4] Taylor, b. 16 Aug. 1899; m. Hazel Agnes Roussel.

ii. Maryemma Taylor, b. 15 April 1907, Santa Clara Co., Calif., d. in Salem, Marion Co., Ore., Feb. 1998.[48] Maryemma m. first, 29 June 1934, Julian Regan Thruston, from whom she was divorced in 1942.[49] She m. second, Maurice Norman Juve, b. 14 July 1905, d. 10 July 1980, Salem.[50]

Generation 4

4. **Albert Sylvan[4] Taylor** (*Andrew[3], Albert[2], Joseph[1]*) was born 16 August 1899 in San Francisco, and died 9 September 1995 in Saratoga, Santa Clara County. He married in Oakland, at the Chinese Methodist Church, 11 May 1929, as her second husband, his close friend of a number of years, **Hazel Agnes Roussel.**[51] Agnes was born 5 January 1900 in Karlo, Lassen

46. San Jose city directory, 1905.
47. Andrew O. Taylor households: 1910 Alpine Co., Calif., Twp. 1, dwelling 12, family 12; 1920 Douglas Co., Nev., Mottsville Pct., E.D. 5, sh. 10A, dwelling 210, family 210; 1930 Douglas Co., Nev., Centerville Pct., E.D. 2-1, sh. 3B, dwelling 54, family 54.
48. Birth from California Birth Index, death from SSDI.
49. Marriage announcement in *Reno Evening Gazette;* their divorce was reported in the same paper, 19 Dec. 1942 (www.newspaperarchive.com, no page numbers provided).
50. Marriage from *Wallowa County Chieftan,* 17 July 1980; his birth and death from SSDI.
51. Birth and death from CDA and funeral card, Ted Judge Archives, CGS. Souvenir marriage record, archives of CGS.

County, and died 12 December 1988 in Santa Clara County.[52] Her ancestry and life before her second marriage are covered in the chapter titled "Descendants of Eleanora (Bush) Harman Foley Woods Holmes."

Albert registered for the World War I draft from Nevada. His registration card describes him as a tall, slender man with blue eyes and dark brown hair.[53] According to the 1930 census, however, he was never called to serve.[54] A staunch union man, he was a longtime conductor for the East Bay Transit Company and was granted lifetime privileges by his local union after paying his dues for fifty years. Albert and Agnes and her son Ted lived for many years in the Montclair District of Oakland. While they did not have any children together, Albert was the father that Ted acknowledged throughout life.

Photo of Albert Taylor ("Dad") with Ted (by car), undated
From Ted Judge archives

Albert's parents, Andrew and Emma, lived near the family for a number of years preceding Andrew's death in 1942, after which Emma moved to San Francisco. Emma, at that point quite reclusive, still allowed Agnes, a nurse by training and a tiny, fiercely private woman, to look in on her.

Albert Taylor (far right), street car conductor, Oakland
From Ted Judge archives

In their final years after his retirement, Al and Agnes lived in Sunnyvale, Santa Clara County. Albert was known as a kind man and extraordinary gardener. "His gladiolas stood right up."[55] Agnes's son Ted, who spent his own retirement years as a private investor, evidently shared these skills with his stepfather, for on Albert's 1995 death certificate under employment is entered, "private investor."[56]

52. State of California death certificate, Hazel Agnes Taylor. Agnes died in a convalescent hospital in Sunnyvale following a stroke.
53. World War I draft registration cards, digitized at Ancestry.com.
54. Albert S. Taylor household, 1930 census, Alameda Co., Calif., city of Oakland, E.D. 1-33, sh. 11B, dwelling 168A, family 213.
55. Interview with his cousin, Bette Baughman Webb.
56. Death certificate, Albert Taylor, CGS archives.

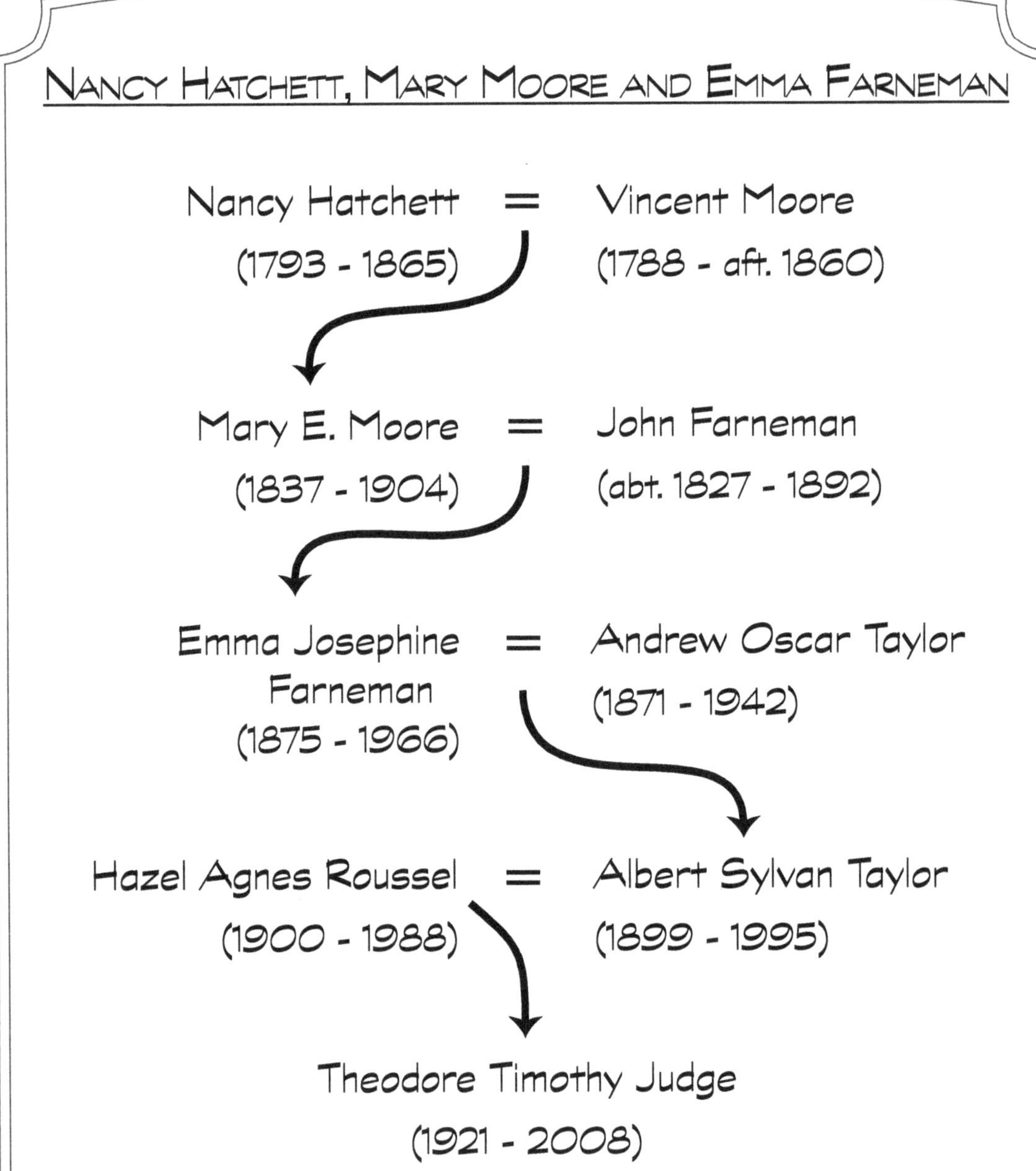

Descendancy along Taylor maternal lines

❧ The Matrilineal Ancestry of Albert Sylvan Taylor: Three Generations of Adversity and Adventure in the Early Far West

Just as Albert Sylvan Taylor was "Dad" to Ted Judge, Albert's mother Emma was the only "Grandma" Ted came to know. As described in the previous chapter, Emma was a very organized woman, a school teacher for many years in both urban and rural California; relatives discovered upon her death that she had been an avid collector of stamps. It is Emma's maternal ancestry that unfolded a colorful and at times tragic story of pioneer women that encompassed three generations of adversity and adventure in small towns we no longer hear much about.

The lineage of this matrilineal trail is shown graphically on the facing page. The story begins with Nancy Hatchett, who began life as the daughter of a slave-owning Virginia family in the late 1700s, married a man who seemed unable to stay out of trouble and ended her life tragically as a widowed grandmother on a turkey farm in Butte County, California, killed by Indians. Her daughter, Mary Moore, lived a wild existence in various mining towns that are no more. Finally, Mary's daughter Emma, perhaps shaped by her unsettled childhood, became a stern, orderly school teacher. This story is worth telling here, just as it may have been told to Ted.

The Tragic Life of Nancy Hatchett

Nancy Hatchett was the daughter of Edward Hatchett and Mary Newsteys Blagrove, born about 1797 near Chatham, Pittsylvania County, Virginia, a part of Virginia that later became the state of West Virginia. Little is known of her childhood until, when about fifteen years old, she married Vincent Moore of the same county, son of slave owner Thomas Moore and his wife, Nancy Ann Whaley. The first actual record we have of Nancy and Vincent is the marriage bond paid by Edward Hatchett, 12 January 1812.[1] Moore family researchers say Vincent and Nancy had their first two sons in Pittsylvania County, William Moore in 1816 and Thomas Jefferson Moore, 12 August 1817. William must have died in infancy because Vincent had no children when on 23 May 1816 his father, Thomas Moore, signed his will.[2] "My son Vincent to hold and enjoy the place where he now lives and to include 100 acres,

1. Joel Ricks, comp., *Pittsylvania County, Virginia, Marriage Bonds, 1767-1864* (Salt Lake City: Genealogical Society of Utah, 1937), 176. Vincent appears to have been born about 1788.
2. No records have been found for this William, and the name is used again for their fifth child, suggesting their first son died young. Additional information on the Moore family is archived at CGS.

to have my negro Nelson. Should Vincent die without issue, the property to revert to the family." [3]

Vincent Moore's father died 27 August 1816, naming in his will his wife and his eleven children, among whom he divided land, livestock, personal effects and twelve slaves: Lucy, Cate, Nance of Ephraim, Patty, Juno, Kason, Peter, Nelson, Simon, Gabriel, French, and Anthony. Vincent received Nelson.[4]

Shortly afterwards, Vincent and Nancy removed to Pike County, Missouri, where in 1818, Vincent bought 160 acres of land.[5] The 1820 U.S. Census for Missouri Territory no longer exists, but in 1830 a string of Moore families lived close together, Vincent among them, enumerated with a wife, five children and one slave.[6] On 1 April 1838 Vincent Moore "of Ralls County" purchased at the Palmyra land office two 40-acre parcels in Sections 17 and 23, Twp. 51N, Range 6W, both near the West Fork of the Cuivre River, an area now in Audrain County, Missouri.[7]

Many members of the Moore family were Baptists. Vincent's sister Penelope married a Baptist minister, the Rev. Willis Hopwood. His brother Merrimon Moore became a minister, and in 1834 his brother James Moore set aside an acre of his land in Pike County for the erection of the Siloam Baptist church. James and another brother, Levi Moore (who had married sisters Elizabeth and Nancy Shellhorse, respectively) were active members in Siloam until a schism within the congregation led to their shifting in 1851 to the new Indian Creek Baptist Church.[8] No records were found pertaining to Vincent's church membership, if he had any.

Vincent appears to have been the proverbial black sheep in his family. From 1838 through 1840, four complaints were filed in Audrain County Circuit Court involving Vincent Moore and his family. In November of 1838 Vincent was arrested and charged with betting at "three up," an illegal game of some type. Other men charged with him were ordered to pay $100 each to the court or give evidence against him, which they did. The case was continued to 1839, during which Vincent spent part of the time in jail. Also in 1838 Vincent was charged with stealing a heifer from Greenberry Johnson.[9] In March of 1840 Vincent was charged with grand larceny for stealing a cow. The case was continued for more than a year, and the trial was eventually assigned to Boone County after Vincent's lawyer argued, and the court agreed, that Vincent could not get a fair trial in Audrain County. The sheriff took Vincent from the Audrain County jail to Boone County, where a jury was unable to agree on the charges and they were dismissed.

---

3. Lela C. Adams, comp., *Abstracts of Pittsylvania County, Virginia Wills, 1767-1820* (Easley, S.C.: Southern Historical Press, 1986), 198-199.
4. Adams, *Abstracts of Pittsylvania County, Virginia Wills,* 198. Much information has been collected on the Moore family and many of their descendants and is available from CGS.
5. Larry Thomas, *Biographical Sketch of the Thomas Moore and Nancy Whaley Family,* from Whaley-L Archives, posted at www.rootsweb.com.
6. Vincent Moore household, 1830 census, Pike Co., Missouri, p. 248.
7. Patent information at www.glorecords.blm.gov; Gregory A. Boyd, *Family Maps of Audrain County, Missouri: with Homesteads, Roads, Waterways, Towns, Cemeteries, Railroads, and More* (Norman, Okla.: Arphas Pub. Co., 2006), 20.
8. Pike Co. Chapter, Daughters of the American Revolution, comp., *Cemetery Inscriptions, Pike County, Missouri,* 9 vols. (Louisiana, Missouri: Pike Co. Chapter, Daughters of the American Revolution, 1986), 4: 21-2, 72.
9. This and all of Vincent's court troubles can be found in the Audrain County, Missouri, Circuit Court Records, 1837-1868, Family History Library (hereafter, FHL) film #974,693: State v. Vincent Moore on pp. 42, 58, 69, 109, 117, 130, 156, 163, 171, 173 and 174.

At some point during this legal wrangling, men may have come to Vincent Moore's farm and assaulted his wife, Nancy. It is also possible that he was unconscionably litigious. He filed suit against William Still, Andrew Still, Spencer Daviss, John Daviss and Francis Wisdom, for $1,000 in damages for assault and battery of Mrs. Nancy Moore and larceny of plaintiff's property. Vincent lost the case and had to pay costs. Thomas J. Moore, presumably Vincent's eldest son, also filed suit in 1840 against William Still, but for trespass. He, too, lost and had to pay court costs.

In 1840 the Vincent Moore household was enumerated in Cuivre Township, Audrain County; their seventh child, Mary, who will be of primary interest here, was then about two or possibly three.[10] By 1844 the family was on the move. Vincent and Nancy sold forty acres to Thomas Jefferson Moore for $60 and moved on to Iowa. By 1850, Vincent was gone, while Nancy and four of their children were in Muscatine Township, Muscatine County, Iowa.[11]

According to family stories, Vincent had left his wife and four children about 1849 and gone "round the Horn" to California. However, evidence suggests he may not have gone "round the Horn" but traveled overland, perhaps with former Pike County neighbor Walter Crow, instead. Walter went to California from Missouri in 1849 and, seeing the need for livestock to "feed the miners," returned to form a cattle drive, in which a number of Moore family members participated.[12] Vincent Moore's oldest son Thomas, like his father, left a wife and children in Iowa to go to California. He arrived in Grass Valley in October of 1849, spent time in Nevada City and "Rabbit Creek" (now LaPorte) and mined with his brother Edward. Thomas then returned to Iowa in 1850 to collect his family, but was back in Butte County by 1856, when his second to youngest son was born. Vincent's son William also went west in 1849, perhaps with Vincent. When William died in 1921, his obituary, published in the *San Jose Mercury News,* 20 May 1921, reads, "...born in Missouri, March 8, 1826. He crossed the plains...arriving in California in 1849..." and then goes on to recount some events he shared with his father along the way.

Vincent may have returned to Iowa to collect his wife and younger children, or they may have traveled west with others to join him, probably in 1851-52. Whenever they came, Nancy and the rest of their children were settled in California by 1860, near Marysville in Yuba County.[13]

Leaving the Midwest was likely a good idea for Vincent. He had been in and out of trouble there and perhaps saw California as a place to reinvent himself. Moore researchers report that Vincent died in the early 1850s, but this evidently was not the case. He was enumerated on the 1860 census near Marysville with Nancy and their youngest son, Napoleon, and close to their son William and daughter Nancy Cavin. Vincent was listed as a farmer with $1,000 personal property.[14] Vincent and Nancy's daughter Mary, at this point married only a few years, was living in Lassen Township, Tehama County, with her first husband, Joseph Dike-

10. Vincent Moore household, 1840 Census, Audrain Co., Missouri, Cuivre Twp, page 9.
11. Nancy Moore household, 1850 Census, Muscatine Township, Muscatine County, Iowa, dwelling 281, family 981, p. 356B. Nancy, then 53, headed a household reportedly consisting of Vincent 19, Nancy 10, Mary 11 and Napoleon 7.
12. The Moore story is almost entirely taken from "The Story of Thomas Jefferson Moore Sr.: His Ancestors and Descendants" (by John Shirley Moore, publ. in the Paradise Genealogical Soc. publication, *Genealogical Goldmine,* vol. 25, issue 2, pp. 99-104 and issue 3, pp. 19-23, 1992).
13. Vincent Moore household. 1860 Census, California, Yuba Co., Marysville, dwelling 1180, family 1753, p. 976.
14. *Ibid.*

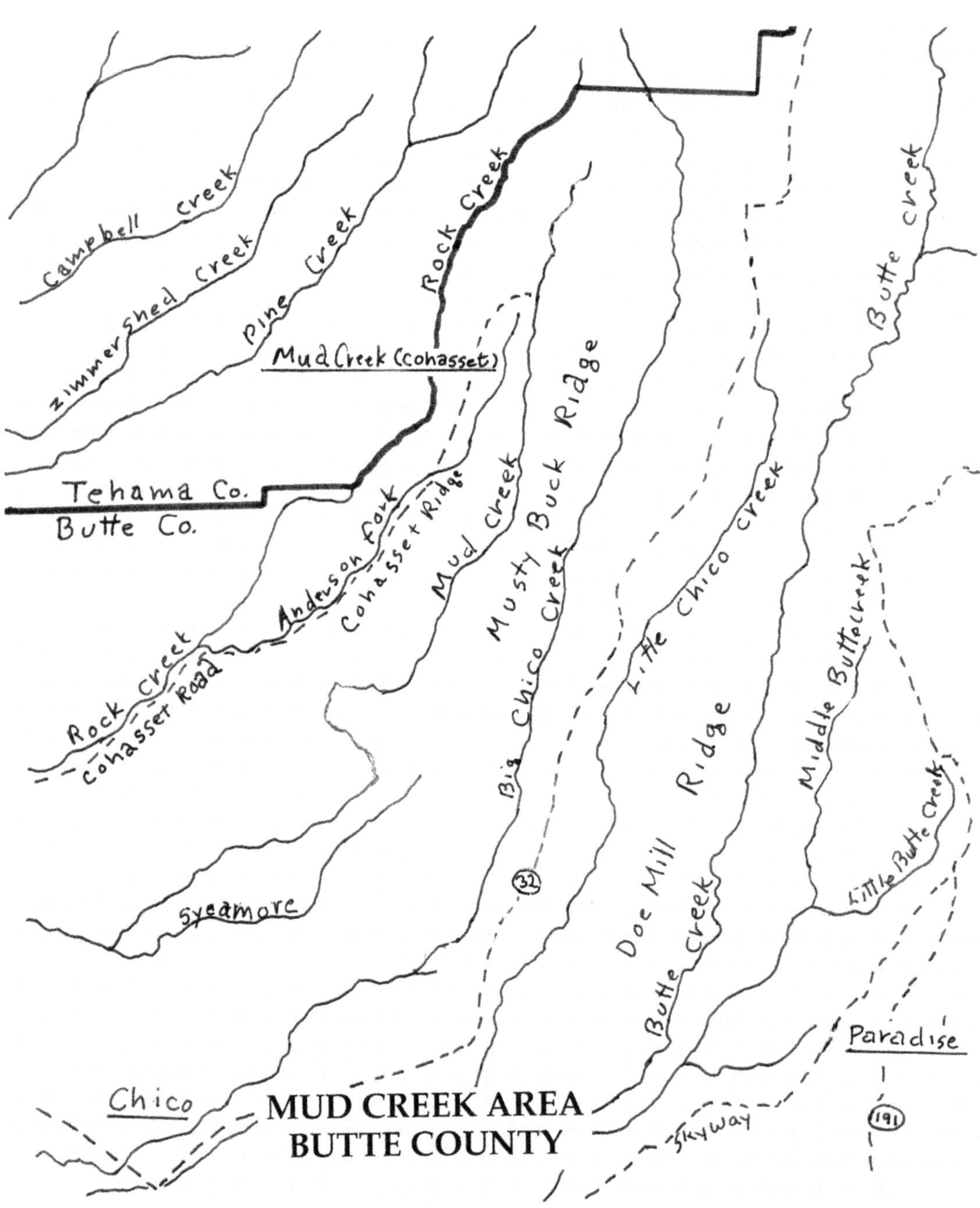

Map of Mud Creek/Cohasset area of Butte County
Drawn by Bill O'Neil

man.[15] Vincent must have died between 1860 and 1865, but no death or burial record has been found.

Eighteen sixty-five proved a fateful year for the surviving Moore family. The widowed Nancy and son William were living on a farm on Mud Creek, not far north of Chico, where they raised turkeys. Periodic depredations by the Mill Creek Indians were common and often ended tragically. One day in April, William rode out to buy a load of shake bolts to build turkey crates. When he returned later that day, he reportedly discovered his mother's body near the empty turkey pens. There are two versions of her death, the first perhaps considerably more embellished than the second:

> *...His trip was uneventful and he returned as soon as he procured his load of shake bolts. A short distance from home, he heard the report of a gun. Since he was unarmed, he left his team tied to a sapling and cautiously crept forward to investigate. He heard the shouts of Indians as they proceeded up the canyon, away from the cabin. He unhitched one of the horses from his heavily laden wagon, and rode it to a neighboring farm house for help. They were so frightened by his story they refused to return with him, stating that if the men left, there would be no protection for their womenfolk, which was true.*
>
> *So he went back to his home alone. He entered the cabin and called for his mother, but there was no answer. As he left the cabin, he looked up the small hill toward the turkey pens, which were somewhat concealed by low bushes. Imagine his shock, when he saw the body of his mother on the ground near the bushes. A hasty investigation disclosed that she had been shot through the back. He carried her into the cabin and placed her on the bed, then he brought the team and wagon to the barn. The wagon had to be unloaded before he could use it to transport her body for burial.*
>
> *He drove the wagon to Joseph and Mary E. (Vannoy) [sic] Dikeman's place which was on the old stage road. These people were distant relatives; Mary E. (Vannoy)[sic] Dikeman was the sister of Frances Matilda (Vannoy) Moore, and Frances Matilda was the wife of Thomas Jefferson Moore Sr.* [16] *They washed his mother, dressed her and prepared her body for burial as best they could. That night, the Indians returned to the Moore's ranch, stole the turkeys and burned down all the buildings.*
>
> *The next day the family drove to the ranch of Nancy's son, Thomas Jefferson Moore Sr., near Nord (but nearer to the Plez Quinn place). From there an undertaker by the name of Breece from Chico was summoned and he took charge of the arrangements. She was buried in the Chico Cemetery under the spreading branches of a large oak tree. A few years earlier, its branches threw shadows across the newly dug graves of the three Hickock children who were also massacred by roving Indians. At present (1979) the location of her grave is unknown. Earlier, May Belle (Moore) Rice stated that she had seen a wooden grave-marker at one time marking Nancy's grave, but that it was rotting away. She also stated that the grave was near Dan Bidwell's plot on the southwest corner of the cemetery.*[17]

15. William Dikeman household, 1860 Census, Tehama Co., Calif., Lassen Twp., dwelling 147, family 147, p. 876.
16. Articles written by John Shirley Moore and May Belle Moore for the Paradise Genealogical Society in the 1980s incorrectly accord Mary the maiden name Vannoy. They were incorrect; the passage should read Mary E. (Moore) Dikeman (previously cited). Extensive information on both the Vannoy and Dikeman families is archived at CGS.
17. Transcription of the "Story of Nancy Hatchett Moore" from "The Story of Thomas Jefferson Moore, Sr." in *Genealogical Goldmine,* 1992, prev. cited.

A second version, considerably shorter, written near the time of the event by an early Californian named Sim Moak states:

> *On the thirteenth of April, 1865, a band of this same tribe descended on the Moore home on Mud Creek, which they robbed of over a thousand dollars, after having killed old Grandma Moore. Before leaving they set the house on fire and burned the body of Mrs. Moore up in her own home.*[18]

William's obituary in 1921 affirms the story: "His mother was killed by the Indians near Chico, Butte County, in the early fifties."[19]

The Many-Husbanded Life of Mary Moore Dikeman Farneman Baker

Mary E. Moore, daughter of Vincent and Nancy Hatchett Moore, was the fifth of nine children. Born in Boonesborough, Moniteau County, Missouri, 24 June 1837, she died as Mary Baker in San Jose, Santa Clara County, California, 4 January 1904, following a tumultuous life that could be fodder for a television series.[20]

Still young when her father left Missouri for California, Mary remained behind in Iowa with her mother, Nancy, and younger siblings before coming west. In Butte County, California, 20 May 1856, Mary married Joseph Dikeman, a carpenter, born in Pennsylvania about 1828.[21] Over the next eight years they had four children: Benjamin Franklin in 1857, William O. in 1859, George Washington about 1862 and Minnie about 1864.[22]

Joseph Dikeman, like the Moores, settled along Mud Creek on the northern portion of Cohasset Ridge, straddling the Butte-Tehama County border.[23] In February 1865, some ten years later when the land first became available for purchase from the government, Joseph Dikeman made a cash entry.[24] Raids by local Indians posed an ongoing problem, however, and two months later, in April 1865, Mary's mother Nancy was murdered. About this time, the wagon road from Chico to the silver mining area in western Idaho Territory was completed as far as the Jordan Valley, which stretches along the Jordan River in today's Malheur County, Oregon, into Owyhee County, Idaho.[25] Many families headed east, either to mine

18. Quotation from account of Sim Moak, "The Last of the Mill Creeks (1862-1870)," pp. 60-72 in *Ishi, the Last Yahi: A Documentary History* by Robert F. Heizer and Theodora Kroeber (Berkeley, Calif.: Univ. of California Press, 1979), 72.
19. *San Jose Mercury News,* 20 May 1921, p. 4.
20. Santa Clara County Recorder, "Record of Deaths, City of San Jose," vol. C, 1889-1995 (FHL film #1,302,030).
21. Butte County Marriage Licenses and Certificates, 1851-1879, Bk. A, p. 13 (FHL film #1,299,184). Additional information on the ancestry of Joseph Dikeman is available from CGS.
22. Joseph Dikeman household, 1860 Census, Tehama Co., Calif., Lassen Twp., dwelling 147, family 147, p. 876. Only Minnie was in the Farneman household in 1870 (Owyhee, Idaho Terr., Wagon Town Distr., dwelling 33, family 33, p. 196). The other children were in California at the time, as evidenced in a short note in the *Owyhee Avalanche* newspaper, 13 August 1870, that she "had left for California for the purpose of bringing her sons to Idaho." Benjamin died 19 May 1872 in Unionville, Pershing Co., Nev. (monthly compilation of deaths recorded in the magazine *Overland Monthly,* vol. 9 (issue 1), pp. 102-104. William was alive at the time of the 1880 census, but not at the time of his mother's death; George d. 17 Dec. 1937 in Plumas Co., Calif.; Minnie m. Richard Ford in 1883 and in 1897, Isaac Benjamin.
23. Joseph Dikeman previously owned 320 acres of squatters' land on Mud Creek, which he sold to Thomas Moore in 1857; John Shirley Moore, "The Story of Thomas Jefferson Moore," previously cited. New land in Tehama County did not open up for patents until 1865.
24. For patent information, see www.glorecords.blm.gov.
25. Richard Burrill, *Stolen by the Mill Creek Indians: Survival Stories of Butte and Plumas Counties* (Chester, Calif.: The

Kuns cabin, Delphi, Carroll Co., Indiana, built c. 1828.
Kuns family descendants in their everyday, traditional Dunkard dress.
Courtesy of the Carroll County Historical Society

or to provide supplies to the miners. Following the murder of her mother, Mary's fears for the safety of her own family can only be imagined. She was twenty-eight and had four children under age eight; the Dikemans, or at least Mary, evidently joined the exodus.

Several of Mary (Moore) Dikeman's siblings moved away in the years following their mother's murder. By 1868 her brother William was running a cattle business and a stage stop in Oriana, Humboldt (now Pershing) County, Nevada.[26] Humboldt County also became the new home of her brother Napoleon and her sister Nancy (Moore) Cavin, who had lived near their mother in 1860.[27] Vincent Moore, Jr., who registered to vote in Butte County, California in 1868, is noted in the Butte Great Register of Voters as having "left the state."[28] Joseph Dikeman appears to have become part of Mary's trail of former husbands soon afterwards; the circumstances are not clear. In 1870, Mary was in the Jordan Valley with a new husband, John Farneman.[29] Joseph Dikeman was not found living in the Jordan Valley, although a John Dikeman is mentioned in Mary's depredation claim (see following).

John Farneman, Mary's second husband, spent at least ten years in the gold fields of California before going to Idaho. He mined in 1850 in Trinity County and in 1860 in LaPorte, Sierra County.[30] Born about 1827 in Ohio, he was the son of Dunkards, a pacifist sect whose members lived simply, spoke German and farmed diligently.[31] No records have been found,

---

Anthro Co., 2003), 57. Idaho retained its territorial status until 1890, when it became a state.

26. Indian depredation affidavit. See below.
27. H. G. Cavin household, 1860 census, Humboldt Co., Nev., Unionville post office, Buena Vista Twp., dwelling 69, family 29, p. 104; N. A. Moore lived in the adjacent dwelling.
28. Paradise Genealogical Society, "Butte County, California, Great Register: 1867-1908" (FHL film #1,831,809, item 3).
29. Jno. Farneman household, 1870 Census, prev. cited.
30. J. Farman (Farneman), 1850 Census, Trinity Co., Calif., dwelling 96, family 96, p. 73; John Ferneman (Farneman), 1860 Census, Sierra Co., Calif., La Porte Twp., dwelling 286, family 259?, p. 788.
31. John was the son of John and Polly Kuns Farneman, formerly Vaneman, who married 17 May 1818, in Montgomery Co., Ohio, and later moved from there to Carroll Co., Ind., where they purchased land from the federal government.

however, to show that he continued in this faith. He left the Sierras for Idaho Territory with the first rush toward the new mines there, not to mine but to farm, at which, judging from numerous newspaper articles in the *Owyhee Avalanche*, he was quite successful.

Even in Idaho, harassment by local Indian tribes continued. In 1903, Mary submitted a depredation claim to the government to recover $8,200 for losses incurred of hay and livestock stolen by the Paiute Indians in November of 1866, March of 1867 and September of 1868. Only the 1868 claim was honored because the U.S. government had not yet completed a treaty with the tribe during the first two years. Mary had to settle for $3,075.[32] Her deposition provides insight into the harsh conditions the settlers endured. It remains unclear whether Joseph Dikeman may have been the John Dikeman mentioned in the claim or whether he ever made it to the Jordan Valley.

> *Mary E. Farneman (June 13, 1903). Age, 60 years. I reside in San Jose, California. In September, 1868, I was living in Jordan Valley, Owyhee County, Idaho. I am the claimant. I owned horses and cattle while living there: 25 head of horses and 24 head of work oxen. The Piute Indians made a raid through Jordan Valley, drove off the cattle and horses, and shot the cattle with poisoned arrows. The people residing there at the time were there, but the Indians stole the cattle and horses at night. I saw the Indians driving them off. They took all of the 25 horses and 24 head of oxen. The settlers tried to prevent the Indians from taking the stock, but they were overpowered by the Indians. I was acquainted with the value of horses and cattle in that locality at that time; these horses were worth $100 each, and the oxen $50 a head. These horses and cattle belonged to myself and my husband, and were community property.*
>
> *I was born in the State of Missouri and never lived outside the United States. I was married in 1856. My husband is dead; he died in 1892. I was living with my husband in 1868. He was engaged in hauling supplies for the Government. The testimony offered now is in support of the loss of 1868 only.*
>
> *My husband was hauling hay and grain for the Government and used these horses and cattle for this purpose. He bought the horses at different places; some in California and some in Idaho. There was no one associated with my husband in this hauling, and he had no partner. My husband was born at Delphi, Indiana, and he never resided outside the United States. John Brady and James Batchelor lost property at the same time my husband lost his. Brady is dead, and Batchelor lives in Jordan Valley. Batchelor lost horses and cattle. They burned up a blacksmith shop for Brady. A man by the name of John Dikeman lost 10 yoke of cattle. He is dead. Bill Beachy lost all he had; he ran a stage. The Indians drove the horses off to their reservations, and the cattle they killed with poisoned arrows. My husband did not recover any of his horses, nor did he receive any indemnity for his loss. I know the date of this loss because every year when the Indians would make a raid—1866, 1867, 1868—I wrote it down. I had money of my own invested in these horses and cattle apart from my husband's property and money. My husband paid differ-*

More information on both the Kuns and Farneman (or Vaneman) families is available from CGS. That these families were Dunkards is evidenced in Thomas B. Helm, *History of Carroll County, Indiana* (Chicago: Kingman Bros., 1882), 327.

32. Copy of claim no. 9950 submitted by Mary E. Farneman, settled 13 March 1906, obtained at the National Archives in Washington, D.C., in January 2010 by Holly Cutting Baker. See Appendix for selected pages.

Mr. & Mrs. Baker in Bodie
Courtesy of Kent Stoddard, Mono County Historical Society

> *ent prices for these horses; some from $75 to $100; most of them $100. He did all the buying of the horses and also of the cattle. He paid $50 a head for the cattle. I was present when these horses and cattle were taken, and I saw the Indians take them. They drove them in a northwest direction. Fifteen hundred dollars of my money was invested in this stock. I claim the right of indemnity to the entire loss of 1868 by reason of being the widow of John Farneman, and his only heir, and also in my own behalf.*

Depositions submitted by other witnesses in support of this claim included those from her brother William, then of Evergreen, Santa Clara County, California, and also Amos Springer, the former sheriff of Owyhee County, who deposed that John Farneman had a sizeable ranch, was running a stage(coach) station and hotel on the route along the Jordan Valley between Silver City and Three Forks Camp and also had a dairy business.

While Mary claimed and her deponents attested that John Farneman was her husband at the time, it seems she did not marry him until 17 April 1870.[33] Mary did not have all four Dikeman children with her in 1870, only Minnie. Inasmuch as the Farneman marriage was announced in Sacramento, it seems likely that at least two, and possibly three of her children had been left behind near Chico with relatives. Indeed, on 15 August 1870, the *Owyhee Avalanche* newspaper ran: "Mr. & Mrs. Farnaman were in town last Sunday. Mrs. Farnaman left for California for the purpose of bringing her sons to Idaho." It is not clear if her eldest child, Benjamin Franklin Moore, ever came to Idaho. He made his way to where his Moore uncles and aunt lived in Unionville, Humboldt (now Pershing) County, Nevada, where he died 19 May 1872 at age fifteen.[34]

John Farneman apparently also maintained a residence in San Francisco, where he may have spent the winter months. The *Owyhee Avalanche* issue of 4 October 1875 implies as much: "H.S. Chasbro and John Farneman of San Francisco are in town." John and Mary Farneman's only child, Emma, was born in California, in November of 1875, but the family was back in Idaho again several months later. We learn then that John's interests extended beyond farming to mining. The 12 February 1876 issue of the *Owyhee Avalanche* named John Farneman an investor in the "War Eagle Mining Company, Location principal place of business, San Francisco, California. Location of the Works, Owyhee County, Idaho Territory…."

Despite John's worldly success, his marriage to Mary deteriorated amid very public accusations. John didn't just file for divorce, he took out a summons for divorce in large print in the 22 March 1879 *Idaho Statesman* newspaper, accusing Mary of having committed adultery with Joseph Baker and citing numerous specific times and places—February through July of 1878 in Atlanta Hill, Alturas, Idaho; July 1879 at Kelton, Utah, "and since that time living in adulterous intercourse with said Joseph Baker."[35] Mary responded, also in the *Statesman*: "The statement of John Farneman, published in the Statesman, that I lived in adultery with Joseph Baker is a falsehood or a lie. I was granted a divorce two months before his summons appeared in the paper. Mary Farneman."[36] The divorce was heard 6 June 1879 in Rocky Bar, Alturas County, Idaho; perhaps there was an earlier divorce in Utah, perhaps

33. Their marriage was reported in the evening edition of the *Sacramento Bee*, 2 May 1870, when it was announced: "Marriages: in Jordan Valley, I.T., April 17, John Farneman to Mrs. M. E. Dikeman of Chico."
34. *Overland Monthly* death announcement, vol. 9, issue 1, 1872.
35. *Idaho Statesman,* "Special Notices," 22 March 1879.
36. *Idaho Statesman,* "Special Notices," issues of April 23 and 29, 1879.

not.[37] A month later John married his second wife, Mary Dunster of Oakland, California, a marriage that ended with her death in 1890, and took yet a third wife shortly before he died.[38] A marriage record for Mary and Joseph Baker was not found, although Mary used the name Baker for the better part of the rest of her life, with the exception of the depredation claim filed in 1903.

At the very time Mary's marriage to John Farneman dissolved, a new mining town, Bodie, California, boomed. The government established a land office there in January 1879. By July the newspapers were bragging that Bodie had seven barbershops and an opera house. Hopeful miners streamed into Bodie by wagon, stage, on horseback or on foot, among them, Joseph and Mary E. Baker. By the first week in May, Mary and Joseph Baker were already selling property they had previously purchased.[39] Joseph, Mary, Mary's three Dikeman children and her Farneman daughter, Emma, all using the name Baker, were enumerated in Bodie in June of 1880.[40] They were still there in 1881, when Joseph Baker paid taxes on the land, his house and household goods, but probably left before 1890, when the population had dropped from a high of over 5,000 to only several hundred.[41]

Like all mining towns, Bodie was a wild, dangerous place and hardly a town in which to raise small children. One newspaper in 1881 reported that the town was becoming a resort since there had been no killings in the preceding week. The mines, however, yielded their gold quickly and residents moved on to more promising areas. In 1892 a fire destroyed most of what remained.

About this time, John's Farneman's death was reported in the *Idaho Statesman Mountain Home Bulletin,* 24 Nov 1892:

> *The Bulletin is pained to learn of the death of John Farneman at Atlanta, which occurred on the 14th inst. Dr. Loring of this place was called to Atlanta a few hours after his arrival there on Monday. Mr. Farneman was an old resident of Atlanta and was highly esteemed by all. He leaves a widow—having been married only a few weeks ago to Mrs. Perry—and a daughter in California.*

Nothing more has been learned of Joseph Baker. Mary Baker died 4 January 1904 in San Jose, where she had lived for over ten years in a house purchased by her daughter Emma with money inherited from Emma's father, John Farneman. She was interred in Oak Hill Cemetery in San Jose.[42] Mary's death was reported in a short article appearing in the *San Jose Mercury News*, 6 January 1904:

---

37. District Court, Blaine Co., Idaho, Index to Vol. 1 (FHL film #1,533,527, item 2); it was heard at the June session at Rocky Bar. Blaine Co. was formed from part of Alturas.
38. Marriage from "Alturas County Marriage Abstracts, ref. to bk. 1, p. 29 (FHL film #908,034); Mary's death from *Idaho Genealogical Soc. Quarterly,* vol. 8(4):7. John Farneman's third marriage to Mrs. Eleanor Perry taken from John's obituary and will.
39. Mono County Deeds, Book H, pp. 290-292.
40. Joseph Baker household, 1880 Census, Mono County, Calif., town of Bodie, E.D. 48, sh. 21A, p. 107.
41. Bodie assessment roll, 1881, Mono County Museum, Bridgeport, California; Bodie information and a timeline is posted at the Bodie Foundation website, www.bodie.com/.
42. Santa Clara Co. Recorder, "Record of Deaths, City of San Jose," vol. C, 1889-1995 (FHL film #1,302,030): Jan. 4, 1904; Baker, Mary E.; age 66y 6m 10d; born Missouri; widowed, cause of death cirrhosis of liver.

Mrs. Baker Dies: Mrs. Mary E. Baker died at her home in this city on Monday at the age of 66 years. She was a native of Missouri, and is survived by a number of children who reside in this vicinity.

Her death notice in the other San Jose paper, the *Evening News*, published the same day, provided names of her surviving children: Mrs. A. O. Taylor, Mrs. M. F. Benjamin, and George and William Dikeman.[43]

Emma as a child in Bodie
Courtesy of Kent Stoddard, Mono County Historical Society

Shortly before she died, Mary, under the name of Farneman, filed a depredation claim for some of the losses incurred in Indian raids while living in Idaho, as described above. She died before receiving any remuneration. When the money was received from the government several years later, it was necessary for her daughter Emma, who had been administratrix of her mother's estate, to petition to reopen probate in order to pay taxes on the money received.[44] The original probate file has been lost, and it was only because probate had to be reopened that many of the colorful details of this many-husbanded woman have come to light. The depositions in the claim raise a number of interesting questions. Mary filed the claim under the name of Farneman. Did she never really marry Joseph Baker? The events she filed for took place, moreover, while she was still Mary E. Dikeman. Under oath when asked when she married, she answered 1856, the year of her Dikeman marriage. We are left to wonder.

Emma Farneman Taylor: Coming of Age—from a Chaotic Childhood in Mining Camps to the Orderly Life of a Schoolteacher

Emma Josephine Farneman, daughter of Mary E. Moore Dikeman Farneman and her second husband, John Farneman, was born 10 November 1875, in California, possibly in San Fran-

43. This short death notice led to yet another interesting story regarding her daughter Minnie. Minnie (see earlier) had become the wife of Richard Ford in 1883. As Minnie Ford, she became a fairly well-known performer and actress. In 1897, Minnie Ford announced she was to marry Isaac Benjamin, a circus weight lifter, in an outrageous ceremony planned to take place in the lions' cage at the Chutes, an entertainment park in San Francisco. The Justice of the Peace who had been engaged did not show up at the last minute, perhaps understandably; they were married by another Justice of the Peace a day later (*San Francisco Chronicle*, 29 Nov. 1897, p. 7, col. 5, and *San Francisco Call*, 30 Nov. 1897, p. 5, col. 4). Ike Benjamin (actor, b. New Jersey 1864) was incarcerated in Oakland City Prison at the time of the 1900 census (Alameda Co., Oakland ward 5, E.D. 366, sh. 6B) and was enumerated in subsequent censuses with other wives. Minnie may or may not have been the Minnie Benjamin who died in Sonoma Co. at age 46, 31 October 1912.

44. See Santa Clara Co. 1906 probate file for Mary E. Farneman, case #6124, administratrix Emma J. Taylor.

cisco, when her parents were away from their ranch in the Jordan Valley, Owyhee County, Idaho. She died in San Francisco, 31 July 1966.[45]

When Emma was four, her parents underwent a scandalous public divorce, after which her mother ran off with her children and a new man to Bodie. The many chaotic years she spent as a child, mostly in lawless Bodie in what may have been a rather dysfunctional family with a possibly less than stable mother, must have come to play in the type of woman Emma was determined to become and indeed became: focused, strict and orderly. Her father's money allowed her to do this. It seems that John Farneman, still living in Idaho but perhaps moving back and forth between there and his interests in San Francisco, kept in touch with his only child, Emma, as Emma moved from Idaho to boomtown Bodie and then as a young woman to San Jose. In 1892, he left his estate, which must have been sizable, to be divided between Emma and his new wife of only two months, Mrs. Eleanor A. Perry.[46]

Emma at graduation from normal school
Courtesy of Kent Stoddard, Mono County Historical Society

With the money inherited from her father, young Emma Farneman bought her mother a house at 374 East St. John in San Jose, Santa Clara County, California, and lived there as she pursued a teaching credential from the San Jose Normal School.[47] Emma graduated in 1894 and in 1896 was hired to teach school in Bridgeport in Mono County.[48] The local paper, the *Bridgeport Chronicle Union*, on 11 July 1896, reported:

> *Miss Emma Farneman has been engaged to teach the Mono Lake School. Miss Farneman was formerly of Bodie, being better known there by the old timers when a little girl when [sic] Emma Baker she since having taken the name of her stepfather.*

In San Francisco, 17 July 1898, Emma married Andrew O. Taylor, who was described as of Red Bluff at the time of their marriage, but in 1899 was listed in the San Francisco city directory as a conductor on the Market Street Railway.[49]

Andrew continued his work as a railway conductor for a year and then headed for the Sierra Nevada and a job with the Southern Pacific Railroad.[50] Following the birth of their son Albert in 1899, mother and son joined him, and they lived with his brother Joseph; both men

45. Birth and death from abstracts of California deaths, 1940-2000, a database at www.vitalsearch-ca.com, hereafter CDA.
46. Photocopy of will, prepared from records of the Office of the County Clerk of Elmore County, Idaho, and provided by Sampubco, a service available at www.sampubco.com.
47. Interview with Bette Baughman, cousin of Ted Judge; address confirmed in San Jose city directory. San Jose Normal School later became San Jose State University.
48. Obituary, *San Francisco Chronicle*, 2 Aug 1966, p. 35, col. 8.
49. Their marriage was announced in the *San Jose Evening News:* "Miss Emma Farneman of San Jose and Andrew Taylor of Red Bluff were married in San Francisco on July 17th."
50. Ted Judge notes.

Emma (back row, second from left) on Bridgeport schoolhouse steps
Courtesy of Mono Basin Historical Society

worked for the railroad, Andrew as a car inspector and Joseph as a car repairman.[51] Emma, even after marrying, spent time in San Jose with her mother and was doubly counted in the 1900 census—once with her husband in Wadsworth Precinct, Washoe County, Nevada, and once with her mother in San Jose.[52]

In 1903 they moved to San Jose in order to be with Emma's mother, who died in January 1904. Emma served as executrix of her mother's estate, as discussed previously, and they lived there through the 1906 earthquake and a few years afterwards. In 1904 Andrew received a certificate of service from Southern Pacific in San Jose as a railroad car inspector, and in 1905 in San Jose he worked as a driver for Kelley Laundry. Daughter Maryemma was born there in 1907, but by 1910, the family had returned to the mountains. They lived in Alpine County, while Emma taught in schools there, and it was there also that she served as an enumerator in the 1910 census. In 1920 and 1930 in Mottsville and Centerville, respectively, Douglas

51. Andrew O. Taylor household, 1900 Census, Washoe Co., Nevada, Wadsworth Pct., E.D. 44, sh. 4B, dwelling 89, family 89.
52. Mary E. Baker household, 1900 Census, Santa Clara Co., Calif., city of San Jose, ward 2, E.D. 67, sh. 7A, dwelling 151, family 161, p. 41.

County, Nevada, Emma worked off and on as a school teacher. Husband Andrew's occupation in the census was always recorded as "farmer."[53]

Emma's younger relatives recall being terrified of her stern countenance, which perhaps only reflected her fierce determination to succeed in life.[54] Her brief biography, which appeared in a San Jose State Teacher's College history reads:[55]

> *Emma J. Farneman (Mrs. Andrew O. Taylor) … Gardnerville, Nevada; taught in Mono County; married in 1898; lived in San Francisco for a time, then San Jose; has taught in Alpine County since her marriage; removed to Gardnerville, Nevada; has two children.*

Following the marriages of their children, the Taylors returned to the San Francisco Bay Area to be near their son Albert, his wife Agnes and Agnes's son, Ted Judge. Andrew died in Oakland in 1942.[56] Emma became quite reclusive and died in San Francisco in 1966. During these years and perhaps before, Emma amassed a large and valuable stamp collection. Following her death it was appraised at $10,000, yet more evidence of a precise, orderly existence, fashioned by a chaotic childhood little known to those about her.

53. Andrew O. Taylor households: 1910 Census Alpine Co., Calif., Twp. 1, dwelling 12, family 12; 1920 Douglas Co., Nev., Mottsville Pct., E.D. 5, sh. 10A, dwelling 210, family 210; 1930 Census Douglas Co., Nev., Centerville Pct., E.D. 2-1, sh. 3B, dwelling 54, family 54.
54. Information about Emma is from an interview with Albert's cousin, Bette Baughman, September 2009.
55. Sarah Estelle Hammond Greathead, *The Story of an Inspiring Past: Historical Sketch of the San Jose State Teachers College from 1862 to 1928, with an Alphabetical List of Matriculates and Record of Graduates by Classes* (San Jose: San Jose State Teachers College, 1928), 346.
56. CDA.

❧ Appendix

Mary E. Farneman v. The United States and Piute [sic] Indians

In 1893, Mary E. Moore Dikeman Farneman Baker, under the name Mary E. Farneman, filed a depredation claim with the government to recover losses in real estate, personal property and livestock suffered in raids by Paiute Indians in the Jordan Valley, Idaho, over the years 1866-1868. Because the United States did not have a standing treaty with the Paiute Tribe during 1866-67, only the 1868 claim was allowed.

The following pages were selected from that voluminous claim, copied at the National Achives in Washington, D.C., by Holly Baker. Note that Mary presented herself as Mary Farneman, although she may in fact have been Mary Baker at the time of filing and Mary Dikeman at the time of the loss. She died in 1904 before the claim could be ruled upon. Her daughter, Emma J. Farneman Taylor, who was the administratrix of Mary's estate, filed to reopen the claim in 1906.

On 30 June 1906 the estate of Mary E. Farneman received $2,610 in settlement.

This appendix contains copies of four separate documents. It begins with Mary E. Farneman's petition, followed by the depositions of Mary, Nancy Jones and William Moore, then the deposition of Amos C. Springer, the Sheriff of Owyhee Co., Idaho. The findings and conclusion are at the end.

INDIAN DEPREDATION.

No. 9950

IN THE

COURT OF CLAIMS.

Mary E. Farneman

vs.

The United States

AND

Piute **Indians.**

PETITION.

FILED BY

A. L. Hughes

ATTORNEY FOR CLAIMANT

No. 618 F Street, Northwest,

WASHINGTON, D.C.

C. C.

In the Court of Claims of the United States.

December Term, 1893

Mary E. Farneman

vs.

THE UNITED STATES

and

Piute Indians.

INDIAN DEPREDATION.

No. 9950

PETITION.

To the Honorable the Court of Claims:

Your petitioner, Mary E. Farneman by A. L. Hughes, her attorney, would respectfully represent:

1. That she is a citizen of the United States, residing in San Jose, County of Santa Clara, and State of California.

2. That this petition is presented under and in pursuance of the provisions of an act of Congress approved March 3, 1891, entitled "An Act to Provide for the Adjudication and Payment of Claims arising from Indian Depredations."

3. That on or about the dated hereinaftermentioned, A. D., , at or near Jordan Valley, in Owyhee County, in the State of Idaho, a band or party of Indians belonging to a band, tribe, or nation, known as Piute Indians, then in amity with the United States, did then and there, without just cause or provocation on the part of the owner or of the agent in charge, unlawfully take, steal, and carry away or destroy, the following articles of property belonging to said Mary E. Farneman, then a citizen and resident of the United States, each of said articles being of the value set opposite thereto, to-wit:

	Dollars.	Cents.
In or about the month of November, 1866:		
60 tons of hay, worth $50 per ton,	3,000	
In or about the month of March, 1867:		
15 horses worth $100 each,	1,500	
In or about the month of September, 1868:		
25 horses, worth $100 each,	2,500	
24 head of cattle, worth $50 per head,	1,200	
TOTAL, - - -	8,200	

4. That said above-stated items of property so taken by said Indians were reasonably worth the values above set forth; that claimant is entitled to the amount claimed therefor, after allowing all just off-sets and counter-claims; that claimant is the owner of this claim; and that no assignment or transfer of this claim, or of any part thereof, or of any interest therein, has ever been made.

5. That said claim has not been presented for settlement to any official or department of the government.

6. That

8. That no part of said claim has ever been received; nor has any of said property been returned, recovered, or paid for; and that there is now due to claimant thereon, from the United States and from the Piute Indians, the sum of Eight thousand, two hundred dollars.

9. That claimant believe s the facts, as herein stated, to be true.

10. Wherefore, claimant pray s judgment upon the facts and the law, against the United States and the Piute Indians, in the sum of Eight thousand, two hundred dollars; and that her attorney herein shall have judgment therefrom for such lawful fees and expenses as the court may deem proper, and for such other relief as claimant may be entitled to in the premises.

A. L. Hughes
Attorney for Claimant.

By virtue of the power conferred on me by the claimant herein, I hereby constitute and appoint A. L. Hughes as attorney for the prosecution of the foregoing claim, and hereby ratify and confirm all acts of said attorney herein, reserving to myself full and exclusive powers of revocation and substitution in the appointment of such attorney.

John Wedderburn
Attorney in Fact.

District of Columbia,
County of Washington } ss:

Personally before me, a Notary Public within and for the District and County aforesaid, appeared John Wedderburn who, being by me first duly sworn, deposes and says: I am the agent and attorney in fact of the claimant in this case. I have read the above petition, and the facts set forth therein are true, to the best of my knowledge, information and belief.

John Wedderburn

Subscribed and sworn to before me this 22nd day of December, A. D., 1893.

Augustus P. Schell
Notary Public.

IN THE COURT OF CLAIMS OF THE UNITED STATES
december term, 1903.

Mary E. Farneman

vs

The united states

no. 9950.

and

Piute Indians.

The claimant Mary E. Farneman, Mrs. D. E. Jones and William Moor first being duly sworn this June 13 1903, by me at my office, being a notary Public in and for Santa Clara County, State of California, testify as follows, upon interogatories proponded by me J. H. Russell/as claimants Attorney.

John F. Downing of the department of justice at Washington, being present.

Q.
Q. What is your name, what is your age?
A. 60 years
Q. Where do you reside?
A. In San Jose, California.
Q. Where did you reside in Sept. in the year 1868?
A. In Jordan Valley, Owyhee, County Idaho.
Q. Are you the claimant in the xxxx this matter under investigation?
A. Yes.
Q. Did uou own property while you were residing at the last named place?
A. Yes.
Q. What property did you have there?
A. Horses and Cattle?
Q. How many horses and how many cattle?
A. 25 head of horses 24 head of work cattle. Oxen.
Q. What became of these horses and Cattle?
A. They were stolen by the Indians.
Q. Under what circumstances?
A. The Indians were hostile. The Piute Indians made a rade through Jordan Valley drove off the cattle and horses/and shot the cattle with poison arrows, and took away the horses.
Q. What became of the people that were residing there? At the time of the raid?
A. At
A. They were their, but the horses and cattle were stolen at night by the Indians.
Q. How do you know that the Indians took them?
A. I saw the Indians driving them off.
Q. How many of these 25 horses and 24 head of oxen did the ~~Indi-~~ Indians take away?
A. They took the whole band.
Q. Did the white settelers resist the Indianxx and try to prevent the stockx being taken?
A. Yes but they were overpowered by the Indians.
Q. Were you acquainted with the value of horses and cattle at that time and in that locality?
A. Yes.
Q. What were the value of these 25 horses taken as you have stated?
A. $100 each.
Q. What was the value of the oxen taken?
A. $50 Dollars a head.

Mrs. Mary E. Farneman

II.

Q. Who is the owner of these 25 horses and 24 oxen?
A. They belong to my self and husband and were Community Property.

I think that is all.

Questions by Mr. Downing.

Q. Mrs. Farmiman where were you born?
A. I was born in the State of Missouri.
Q. Did you ever live outsede of the United States?
A. I did not.
Q. When were you married?
A. I was married in 1856.
Q. Is your Husband dead?
A. He is.
Q. When did he die?
A. He died in 1892.
Q. Were you living togetherin 1868?
A. Iwas living with my husband.
Q. What business was he engaged in?
A. Halling supplies for the Government.
Q. You have alleged a loss in 1866 another in 1867 and another in 1868, do I understand that the testimony being taken now is in support of the loss of 1868 only?
A. Yes.
Q. What kind of supplies was your husband halling for the Government?
A. Hay and Grain.
Q. Did he use these horses and cattle to hall hay and grain ?
A. Yes.
Q. Where did he get those horses?
A. He baught them.
Q. Where?
A. In different places some in California and some in Idaho.
Q. Was any body associated with your husband in halling hay and grain for the Government.
A. There was not.
Q. He had no partner in hes business did he.
A. No.
Q. State where your husband was born?
A. He was born in Delhi, Indiana.
Q. Did he ever reside out side of the United States?
A. He did not.
Q. Did other parties loose property at the time in '78 your husband lost his horses and cattle?
A. Yes.
Q. Now state how they were and there they live?
A. John Brady is dead. James Batcheler lives in Jordan Valley
Q. What did Batcheler loose?
A. He lost houses and cattle.
Q. Who else lost ?
A. Theu burned up a blacksmith shop for Brady. One man by the name of John Dichman lost 10 yoke of cattle. He is dead.
Hill Beachy lost all he had and he run a stage.
That is all that I can think of.
Q. What did the Indians do with the horses?
A. They drove them off to their reservation
Q. Did your husband recover any of those horses?
A. No.
Q. What did the Indians do with the cattle?
A. They killed them with poison allows.
Q. Did your husband ever recover and indemnity for his loss?
A. He did not.
Q. How do you fix in your mind at this time the date of this loss? Loss?

Mary E. Farneman

III.

A. I have got itwritten down.
Q. Did you write it down yourself?
A. I did.
Q. When?
A. I wrote it down every year when the Indians would make a rade
1866 1867 1868.
Q. Had you money of your own invested in these horses and cattle
apart from your husbands property and money?
A. Yes.
Q. Do you know what price your husband paid for these horses?
A. Different prices. Some from 75 to a 100 dollars most of them
a hundreeddollars.
Q. Your husband did all the buying did he?
A. Yes.
Q. Anf the cattle too?
A. Yes.
Q. Do you know how much he paid for the cattle?
A. He paid $50 a head.
Q. Were you present at the time these horses and cattle were
taken?
A. I was.
Q. Did you see the Indians taking them?
A. I did.
Q. In what direxction did the Indians travel with your stock?
A. Northwest.
Q. What proportion of the money invested in these horss and catte
cattle was your own?
A. $ 1500.
Q. You claim the right of indemnity to the entire loss of 1868
by reason of being the widdow of John Farneman do you?
A. Yes that is correct.
Q. State your present Posr Office address.
A. San Jose , California.
303 East St. John Street.
Q.

Question by Mr. Russell.
Q. Aside from your claim based from the fact that you are a
widow of John Farneman , do you also claim in behalf of your
self personally by reason of the $1500 of your own money
invested in this stock?
A. I claim it, he being his only heir.
And also in my own behalf.
Mrs. Nancy A. Jones testifies asAfollows: Mary E. Farneman
Q. Please give your age, name and residense?
A. Mrs. Nancy A. Jones? I was born in 1843. San Francisco.
~~Q. Where did you live in~~
Q. Where did you live in Sept. 1868?
A. inin Oreana , Humboldt Co., Nevada.

Q. Were you acquainted with Mary E. Farneman and her husband
at that time?
A. Yes.
Q. Did you know of depredations by Indians about that time in
Jordan Valley in Owyhee Co. State of Idaho?
A. Yes.
Q. From whom of this did you learn of this?
A. By John Farneman husband of claimant
Mr. Downing this heresay testimony is objectional.
Q. What did John Farneman tell you at that time?
A. He told me that he had lost horses and cattle and other
property, by the Indians.
Q. Where was John Farneman living at that time?
A. At Jordon Valley Owhee Co.
Q. Did John Farneman state how many cattle and horses he lost?
A. She says that he lost 25 head at that one raid. And 24 head
of cattle at the last raid.
Q. When did John farneman tell you this?
A. Very shorthy after the depredation was commited. N. A. Jones

IV.

That is all Mr Downing.

Questions by Mr. Downing.

Q. Mrs. Jones, what business was the claimants engaged in in Sept. 1868?
A. He was farming and kept a hotel.
Q. Is that all?
A. Government station , there was soldierw ther ar about there.
Q. Do you know how many head of horses ME. Farneman had? In Sept 1868?
A. Well I dont know how namy he had, he had a great many horses
Q. Do you know how namy cattle he had at that time?
A. No I do not know how many he had I know that he had a good many at that time.
Q. You know nothing of any ~~law~~ of claimants cattle of horses in Sept. 1868, except what others have told you do you?
A. No I dont know anything only what thay and others have told me.
Q. What relation are you to Mrs. Farneman?
A. I am her sister.
Q. Have you any interest in this claim?
A. Nothing at all.
Q. In Sept. 1868 how far did you reside from Mrs. Farneman?
A. I dont know exactly hoe far I lived on the sme stage road that she lived on.
Q. Do you know of your own knowledge of anyany depredation domitted by yhe Piute Indians in Sept. 1868?
A. Only as I was told by the parties interested. There was depredations going on all over the state at that time.

That is all. N. A. Jones

Quwstions by Mr. Russell.
Q. What is your mane residents and age?
A. My name is William Moore, my age is going on 78 residents is Evergreen, California.
Q. Where did you live in sept. 1868?
A. I liveed in Oreana , Humboldt Co.
Q. Did you know the claimant at that time Mrs. Fqrmenam?
A. Yes I have known her ever since she was born she is a sister of mine.
Q. Did you anything about a rade by the Piute Indians?
A. Oh yes they were commiting depredations all the time there in 1868.
Q. Where?
A. On the Owyhee and Jordan Valley.
~~xxxxxxxxxxxxxxxxxxxxxxxxxxxxxxxxxxxxxxx~~
Q. Do you know about John Farneman the husband of the claimant loosing any property at that time by depredation of Indians?
A. Yes he lost horses and cattle both that year.
Q. Do you know how many?
A. I dont know exactly how many 30 or 40 head.
Q. What was the value at that time at Jordan Valley of horses of the grade of those owned andlost by John Farneman?
A. I think the horses were $100 a piece or a little more.
Q. How much were the cattle worth?
A. $60 or 70 dollars each.

That is all.

Witness to signature J. H. Russell

Questions By Mr. Downing. William his + mark Moore

N. A. Jones

V.

Q. Mr. Moore in Sept. 1868 how far did you reside from Mr. Farnemaн.
A. We were both keepin stage stations and were both on the same rout.
Q. About how far , was it 5 miles or 20?
A. On the same rout on the same road. 50 or 60 miles apart.
Q. What business were you engaged in?
A. Taking care of stage stock and keepong station.
Q. What business was Me. Farnekan engated in in Sept. 1868?
A. In taking care of stage stock to.
Q. Ddd he have stage stock of hes own to take care of or was it stocj owned by some body else?
A. He said that they were his stock.
Q. He had no partner interested in hes stock ?
A. I dont know if he had he was silent.
Q. Do you know of your own personal knowledge of his lossing any of his cattle or horses by the Indians in 1868.
A. When we were fighting the indians through there we saw them driving them off.
Q. Whose stock did you see the Indians drive off?
A. Well Farneman Well I saw them drive Farnemans stock off?
Q. What year?
A. 1868.
Q. Cold weather or warm weather?
A. Well it was getting pretty cool out there in Sept.
Q. How many of Mr. Farnemans horses did you see tje Indians have in Sept?
A. I dont know.
Q. How many cattle?
A. I dont know we had no time to stop and count.
Q. Why?
A. Well we had to br on the lookout for ourselves?
Q. Do you know how many horses Mr. Farneman owned in Sept. 1868?
A. I do not.
Q. Do you know how many cattle he had in 1868?
A. Well I dont know exactly he claimed that he had a 100 head of cattle I dont know.
Q. In what direction did the Indians travel with those houses?
A. South.
Q. How far south ?
AI dont know .
Q. Did anyone follow the Indians after theu took the horses?
A. I couldnt tell , I dont know.
Q. Were any of Mr. Farnemans horses ever recovered?
A. Not that I know of.
Q. Did the Indians take the horses along with the cattle
A. I think they did.
Q. About how far did the Indians take those cattle?
A. I couldnt tell you how far they took them I dont know.
Q. Did you see these cattle in the possession of the Indians?
A. I saw that the Indians had possession of the catile.
Q. How far had the Indians taken those dattle at the time you saw them.
A. 10 or fifteen miles.
Q. Were the dattle taken in the day time or at might?
A. In day lightwhen I saw them.
Q. And did they take the horses in the daytime?
A. Yes when I saw them they had them in day time.
Q. How far were those horses from Mr. Farmemans home at the time the Indians took them.
A They were on what we called the range it mightof been 2 or 4 miles or 3 or 4 .
Q. Where were the cattle?
A. On the ravgr too.
Q. What kind of cattle were they? Milk cows, calves , or what?
A. Most of them were milk cows.

William his + mark Moore

Witness to signature

vi.

Q. Any calves?
A. Well I couldnt tell you now if thee was they were very few.
Q. Was Mr. Farneman running a dairh business in connection with his farming anf caring for the stage station?
A Yes i thimk he was running the whole thing together.
Q. Were you in the habit of seeing Mr. Farnemans cattle so as to unable you to pick out his cattle from cattle belonging to other people?
A. No I was not every man picks out his own cattle.
Q. How long was it after the Indians took those cattlw Before you saw them in the possess ion of the Indians?
A. They might of got 8 or 10 miles off from where thwy took them from.
Q. Whar time of the day did you sfirst see the cattle?
A. It eas in the afternoon sometime I couldnt tell now.
Q. Were any of those cattle that were taken work oxen?
A. No I dont think so.
Q. What was the age of those horsee?
A. I dont know I dont know how old they were
Q. They were they old enough to br bromen to work?
A. I think that they were all work horses pretty much.
Q. Do you know whee Mr Farneman got those horses?
A. No I dont.
Q. Did he buy those cows or raise them?
A. Well I coulcnt tell you that either
Q. Did you buy and sell horsee and cattle at that time?
A. Yes thousands of head. I sold one man $ 10500 worth of cattle
Q. What is your Post Office address?
A. San Jose, tulley road No. 5.
That is all.

William his + mark Moore

Witness to Signature
N. A. Jones

IN THE COURT OF CLAIMS OF THE UNITED STATES

MARY E. FARNEMAN

vs. No. 9950

THE UNITED STATES

AND

PIUTE INDIANS.

DEPOSITION OF AMOS C. SPRINGER

as a witness in the above entitled cause, taken before George Pattison, a Notary Public in and for the City and County of San Francisco, State of California, at the office of Charles A. Shurtleff, No. 120 Sutter Street, in said City and County of San Francisco, the 8th day of February, 1904; claimant being represented by Charles A. Shurtleff, her attorney, and the defendants by W. G. Palmer, U. S. Special Attorney.

Amos C. Springer, being duly sworn as a witness, testifies as follows:-

DIRECT EXAMINATION BY CHARLES. A. SHURTLEFF.

Q. State your name, age, residence and present occupation?

A. Amos C. Springer, 64 years of age, Boise City, Idaho, mining.

Q. ~~Bixxxxx~~ Where were you residing in the year 1868?

A. Owyhee, Idaho Territory.

Q. Were you acquainted with Mary E. Farneman and her husband John Farneman, at that time?

A. I was.

Q. How long had you been acquainted with them at that time?

A. I had been acquainted with Mr. Farneman since 1864, and with Mrs. Farneman since the latter part or '67.

Q. How near did you reside to them in the year 1868?

A. Twenty miles.

Q. What was your occupation in the year 1868?

A. I was Sheriff of Owyhee County.

Q. In what business was Mr. and Mrs. Farneman engaged in at that time?

A. They were ranching, and kept an eating station on the road between Silver City and the Government Fort of Camp Three Forks, Owyhee County. He also hauled a great deal of stuff to the Fort, particularly hay; he was one of the most thrifty farmers there, and used to sell the Fort from 100 to 125 tons of hay a year, and I have bought as high as 125 and 130 tons a year from him.

Q. Were you at his ranch during any time in the year 1868?

A. I was, frequently.

Q. What, if anything, do you know as to whether claimants had any horses or cattle on their ranch in 1868?

A. They did. They had a large amount of stock, cattle he had about three or four hundred head, I mean in 1868; all told, brute and mares, anywhere from 75 to 100 head.

Q. What, if anything, do you know of claimants losing any of their horses or cattle in the year 1868?

A. The Indians raided him in '68 and took both horses and cattle.

Q. Do you know the month of 1868 that this occurred?

A. In the Fall, I don't know exactly the month, but I know it was late in the season because we did not cut hay in that County until about July, and didn't get it stacked until August, and at the time of the raid a hay stack was burned up. It was about the first of October.

Q. Do you know how many horses he lost?

A. I don't know the number, but I know that he lost a pretty good bunch, for I had a talk with him and he said: (defendant objects to witness stating this conversation, as hearsay Defendant excepts) "They hit me pretty hard this time.

Q. Do you know how many head of cattle he lost this time?
A. I don't know just how many, they drove ~~all~~ them off in a band.
Q. Did you have any conversation with Mr. Farneman touching the number of cattle they drove off?
(objected to as immaterial, and hearsay - Defendant excepts)
A. I did.
Q. What was that conversation?
(objected to as immaterial, and hearsay - defendant excepts)
A. We were talking about the Indian raid, and I asked him how many they got away from him at that time; his reply was that he hadn't rounded his cattle up, but they hit him hard. They took quite a band of his horses - some very good ones.
Q. Were you well acquainted with his cattle and horses at that time?
A. I was.
Q. Did you miss any ~~of those~~ cattle or horses, from his possession, after this raid?
A. I missed the horses. I didn't pay any attention to the cattle, as I did not deal with him in cattle, but I dealt largely with ~~horses~~ him in horses. I missed some good work horses that I was there to purchase from him at this time. Of those that were gone, there was four that I wanted. As to what others went I couldn't say, only from what he told me.
Q. Do you know the value of horses and cattle such as were owned by Mr. Farneman at the time and place of this raid?
A. Yes.
Q. Please state those values?
A. He had all classes of stock, from cheap saddle horses to work horses that were worth $200 a piece. He paid me $200 for a black mare that was gone, which I had sold him

just a short time before the raid. Saddle horses were
Q. worth about $80, and his buggy and work horses would range from $125 to $200 per head.

Q. Do you know what his cattle were worth?

A. The work oxen that were taken away from there were worth from $150 to $200 a yoke, and beef cattle about $35 a head.

Q. Do you recollect what price you would have been willing to pay for the four horses whichyou say you intended to purchase of him?

A. They were worth $400 a pair .

Q. How long after this raid was it that you were at Mr. Farneman's ranch?

A. About two weeks.

Q. You were not there at the time of the raid?

A. No, sir.

Q. Do you know what Indians committed this raid?

XX (objected to as incompetent for the reason that it has not been established that the witness had any personal knowledge as to who committed the raid, or as to a raid having been committed - defendant excepts)

A. I am not positive what Indians were, but always considered that it was Winnemucca's band, the Piutes.

Q. When you were there at Mr. Farneman's ranch, what signs, if any, did you see that indicated that there had been a raid?

A. The burning of hay-stacks; three hay-stacks were burned. And the horses being gone, that I was after. There were plenty of bullet holes in the gable end of the house. Plenty of moccasin tracks about the barn and yard xxx where they corralled the stock generally. There had apparently been no stock around there after the raid, and I could see the movcasin tracks in the dust and the manure. I saw old Big-foot's tracks there plainly, and everybody there knew his tracks. He was a Piute and belonged to Winnemucca's band.

Q. How late did xxxxxxxxxxxx the rains begin?

A. Generally the rains don't commence until late in November.

Q. Have you any interest in this claim, or are you related in any way to the claimant?

A. I have not, and am not.

Q. Do you know whether Mr. Farneman was a citizen of the United States?

(objected to as incompetent, and not the best evidence - defendant excepts)

A. He always had the election precinct at his ranch, he was one of the judges, and County Commissioner, always voted, and was one of the solid man of our County.

Q. Did you ever know of Mr. Farneman ever giving any of the Indians in that vicinity or country any provocation which would tend to provoke a raid upon him or his property?

A. None whatever.

Q. Was there an Indian reservation in Owyhee County in 1868?

A. There was not.

CROSS-EXAMINATION BY W. G. PALMER.2

Q. You are not sure but what the time when you went to Mr. Farneman's ranch to buy these horses in the Fall of 1868 was in September, or October, are you?

A. Not exactly positive, but I am satisfied it was about the first of October.

Q. Did you miss any of his work oxen at this time?

A. No. He was hauling hay up to my place that Fall, and to Silver City; he generally sent five teams on a trip, ten oxen to the team, and I know that he was crippled out ax of a team or two at the time of that loss.

Q. You did not have any personal knowledge of this raid at this time, did you?

A. I did not, only what Mr. Farneman and his neighbors told me, but it was a well known fact that this raid was made, though. (Defendant moves to strike out what witness says as to it being a well known fact that this raid was made, as voluntary, not responsive and as a conclusion of law - defendants except)

Q. The first you knew of this raid was what Mr. Farneman told you, was it not?

A. No, I think I heard of it a few days after it was reported in town.

Q/ You did not see this raid made, or see any Indians at this time, did you?

A. I did not.

Q. You spoke about seeing moccasin tracks about Mr. Farneman's premises; it was not unusual to see moccasin tracks any where in that vicinity during the year 1868 even when there was no raid made, was it?

A. It was not unusual.

RE-DIRECT EXAMINATION BY CHARLES A. SHURTLEFF.

Q. Can you state positively whether the time when you were at the ranch of Mr. Farneman, and missed the four horses and other stock from Mr. Farneman's ranch, was before or after you heard of this raid in 1868?

A. Yes, sir, afterwards.

Amos C. Springer

7—666

Court of Claims.

(INDIAN DEPREDATION NO. 9950)

Mary E. Farneman

v.

THE UNITED STATES and the Piute INDIANS.

This case having been heard by the Court of Claims, the court, upon the evidence, makes the following

FINDINGS OF FACT.

I.

At the time of the depredation , hereinafter stated, the claimant was a citizen of the United States.

II.

September, 1868, in Owyhee County, Idaho,

Indians belonging to the Piute tribe of Indians took property of the kind and character described in the petition, the property of claimant , which was reasonably worth the sum of $2610.

Said property was taken, as aforesaid, without just cause or provocation on the part of the owner or the agent in charge, and has never been returned or paid for.

III.

At the time of said depredation the defendant Indians were in amity with the United States.

IV.

At the time of the alleged depredations in 1866 and 1867, the defendant Indians were not in amity with the United States.

V.

CONCLUSION OF LAW.

Upon the foregoing Findings of Fact, the court decides, as a conclusion of law, that the claimant recover judgment against the United States and the Piute Indians in the sum of Twenty-six hundred and ten dollars ($2610.=).

IT IS ORDERED that out of the said judgment the sum of Three hundred and ninety-one dollars ($391.00) be allowed and paid to Simon Lyon , claimant's attorney of record, in full for all services in this case.

The petition as to the depredations set forth in finding IV. is dismissed

Index

www.ingramcontent.com/pod-product-compliance
Lightning Source LLC
Chambersburg PA
CBHW081346280326
41927CB00042B/3150

* 9 7 8 0 9 7 8 5 6 9 4 9 5 *